Sam,
You have made my more ♡ W9-CEU-780
pleasure. Audrey

To Sam McKeel, with lasting thanks
for your loving service to the Bryn
Mawr Presbyterian Church and the
Community Forum.
Wesley D. Avram, pastor
December, 2006

Sam,
It was the greatest of pleasure to work
with you. Andy Musser

With greatest admiration for all
you are, do, think, guide,
inspire, and represent.
Thanks for your leadership —
both for the committee + me!
Donna Barrickman

Sam — you gave us great
leadership. Thanks! John H.

Bravo, Sam for an amazingly well
done job as leader, mentor, prod
+ friend. Keep it up! Rich Allen

Deepening the American Dream

Reflections on the Inner Life and Spirit of Democracy

Mark Nepo, Editor

Foreword by
Rev. Theodore M. Hesburgh, C.S.C.

Introduction by
Robert N. Bellah

SPONSORED BY THE FETZER INSTITUTE

JOSSEY-BASS
A Wiley Imprint
www.josseybass.com

Published by Jossey-Bass
A Wiley Imprint
989 Market Street, San Francisco, CA 94103   www.josseybass.com

Jossey-Bass books and products are available through most bookstores. To contact
Jossey-Bass directly call our Customer Care Department within the United States at
(800) 956-7739, outside the United States at (317) 572-3986, or fax (317) 572-4002.
Jossey-Bass also publishes its books in a variety of electronic formats. Some content that
appears in print may not be available in electronic books.

Credits appear on p. 268.

Library of Congress Cataloging-in-Publication Data
Deepening the American dream : reflections on the inner life and spirit
of democracy / Mark Nepo, editor ; foreword by Theodore M. Hesburgh ;
introduction by Robert N. Bellah.— 1st ed.
    p. cm.
 Includes bibliographical references and index.
 ISBN-13: 978-0-7879-7737-5 (alk. paper)
 ISBN-10: 0-7879-7737-3 (alk. paper)
 1. Christian sociology—United States. 2. Pluralism (Social sciences)—United States.
 3. Democracy—Religious aspects—Christianity. I. Nepo, Mark.
 BR517.D34 2005
 320.473—dc22   2005011501

Printed in the United States of America
FIRST EDITION
HB Printing   10 9 8 7 6 5 4 3 2 1

Contents

PART FOUR
Participating in the World's Soul

Foreword

IT WAS CHARLES DICKENS who put forth his famous injunction, "It was the best of times, it was the worst of times," at the start of his *Tale of Two Cities*. He was talking about the years leading up to the French Revolution, yet his words could apply to almost every time and especially to ours. For we are living in the midst of a tale of two worlds: one headed for greater conflict and collision and one headed for greater community and peace. This dynamic can be seen in divisions that are growing both in the United States and around the world.

So how we proceed is crucial. And whatever we can do to deepen the ways in which we behold each other, listen to each other, and help each other is medicine that can strengthen and heal the spirit of the world. Efforts like the Deepening the American Dream project, sponsored by the Fetzer Institute, are contributing to the more humane of those two worlds we are racing toward. And so I am pleased to support discussions as fundamental as "What does America mean?" "Who are we now?" and "What is it we dream about and aspire to today?"

Over the past six years, the Fetzer Institute has engaged leading thinkers and writers around the country to reflect and write on the deeper course of democracy. Along the way, the Institute has convened public forums to enliven the inner lives of citizens. Whatever you might think of what is written here, whether you agree or disagree, just asking the questions and creating the space for public dialogue strengthens us as a people. By reading these thoughtful essays and reflecting or asking your own questions in the course of your day, you will contribute to bettering the world we leave for our children.

REV. THEODORE M. HESBURGH, C.S.C.
President Emeritus, University of Notre Dame

Introduction

Robert N. Bellah

READING THROUGH THE ESSAYS collected in this book is a feast for the citizen as well as a feast for the soul. Mark Nepo has done an excellent job in weaving together many of the themes in this rich and diverse collection so there is no need for me to try to do that in this Introduction. Rather I want to focus on an issue that comes up repeatedly in a number of the essays: a concern for the shallowness of the ways the American dream is presented these days and an effort to draw on the wisdom traditions to be found in the philosophical and religious traditions of the world in order to "deepen" that dream. I will take it as my task to try to understand one source of the current shallowness and why we have difficulty in this country drawing on these deep resources so readily available in our ever-increasing knowledge of the great traditions.

Erik Erikson, who was my friend for many years, developed a conception of stages of the life cycle, each of which has its attendant virtues and temptations.[1] I want to adapt his scheme somewhat freely to get at certain qualities of American culture and leadership, concentrating on three of his stages: adolescence, adulthood, and old age. According to Erikson, the problem of adolescence is the establishment of identity, and the good outcome is expressed in the virtue of fidelity; the problem of adulthood is attaining the capacity to take responsibility for others as well as for oneself, and the good outcome is expressed in the virtue of care; the problem of old age is to find meaning in the whole of life in the face of one's own imminent death, and the good outcome is expressed in the virtue of wisdom. Of course these problems and virtues are inherent throughout life; they only become relatively prominent at particular points in the life cycle. There are wise children and there are old people who have never established their identity and many who in their whole lives have never learned to take care of others. But there is one particular hang-up that seems to characterize American culture on which I want to focus: we seem to be permanently fixated at the adolescent phase of development.

Adolescence is in many ways a charming phase of life, filled with enthusiasm, excitement, the willingness to take chances, to try new things. For a new country in a new world, constantly exploring new frontiers, it is not surprising that there is a perpetually adolescent quality to American culture. But, as those who have had children, or even who remember their own adolescence know, there is a dark side, a really quite unpleasant side, to adolescence. Erikson characterizes the adolescent task as the establishment of identity, but that task is constantly threatened by identity confusion, by a chaos of feelings that include anxiety and depression and express themselves objectively, to borrow terms from Albert Borgmann, as hyperactivity and sullenness.[2] In the face of the chaos of identity confusion, there is always, according to Erikson, the temptation to ideological closure, to solve the identity problem by identifying with a totalistic external ideological or religious system. And to round out the picture, there is no time in life when the peer group is more important, no time when one so clearly has to prove oneself by showing off, by being tougher, more daring, more glamorous, or whatever, than others. Again sometimes charming, often not so charming. To illustrate my point I would argue that the widely discussed American midlife crisis is nothing but a return of the adolescent identity crisis with all its chaos, self-indulgence, and self-pity in people who have never found out who they are, never solved the adolescent problem. And I would venture that we even have old age crises in America, because many of us never do get over adolescence.

To the rest of the world the charming side of our adolescent culture had been enormously appealing. Vaclav Havel, the former president of the Czech Republic, in his 1995 graduation address at Harvard University, made a telling observation:

> One evening not long ago I was sitting in an outdoor restaurant by the water. My chair was almost identical to the chairs they have in restaurants by the Vltava River in Prague. They were playing the same rock music they play in most Czech restaurants. I saw advertisements I'm familiar with back home. Above all, I was surrounded by young people who were similarly dressed, who drank familiar-looking drinks, and who behaved as casually as their contemporaries in Prague. Only their complexion and their facial features were different—for I was in Singapore.

In one sense, what Havel was talking about is globalization. But if you think about it, where, if not from America, did the rock music, the familiar-looking drinks, the clothes, and even the casual behavior originate? Informality and individuality are American trademarks, but so are consumerism, mass entertainment, and the ideology of the free market. There is almost no major city in the world where a scene such as Havel described could not be found. And although the language spoken in most of those restaurants would not be English, if you entered one, and spoke in English, chances are you would be understood.

And yet the very same people who are charmed by our films, our rock music, our casual manners so much that they want to imitate them are also appalled by our bullying, our claim that we are the best, richest, and strongest nation on earth and that the rest of the world should shape up and be like us or face the consequences—the not at all charming side of our irrepressible adolescence. Because we as a nation are stuck at the stage of adolescence, it is not surprising that so are many of our leaders. Bill Clinton and George W. Bush have each in his own way been more interested in proving how wonderfully charming or strong they are than in caring for the environment or the world. The public tends to vote for the most adolescent leaders. We have a huge deficit when it comes to grown-ups in our society—and thus we have a lack of the virtue of care. The last grown-up president we had was Jimmy Carter. And we have a huge deficit when it comes to wisdom, the virtue of old age, though here again Carter continues to show that some of us can embody this virtue.

The most urgent need for our society today is to develop the culture of care: more than anything else to try to build a global community concerned with global warming, global poverty, and the needs of the billions of people who are left out or who are barely hanging on in the whirlwind of globalization, many of whom are in our own country. There is much to be said about American culture today, particularly our work culture, which makes us "too busy" to be concerned for others, too taken up with anxiety, hyperactivity, and the accompanying sullenness to even remember that others have needs. Neglect is the opposite of care, and our society shows signs of neglect at every level. Our biggest sin of all is neglecting the environment and poverty everywhere on the planet.

But in the Introduction to this volume, where so many of the writers pointed out our need for wisdom, I want to make another point, a kind of detour that is not a detour, and argue that we will not develop a healthy culture of care, we will not even know what really needs caring for, unless we have wisdom, as will be suggested in many of the essays following. We can't wait, in short, to develop an adequate culture of care before turning to the problem of wisdom: we need wisdom now, no matter at what stage of the life cycle we happen to be.

Erik Erikson gives us a preliminary definition of wisdom: "*Wisdom, then, is detached concern with life itself, in the face of death itself.*"[3] A key word here, as we will see, is "detached." The last thing it means is "neglect"; rather it means giving up the hyperactivity, anxiety, and accompanying sullenness, and opening ourselves, quietly and unhurriedly, to what is really there. Only then will we attain a larger perspective, a critical distance, that will allow us to discover what needs to be done and what it is possible to do. I think of a marvelous passage from Cicero's *Somnium Scipionis*, "The Dream of Scipio," where Cicero recounts an experience of Scipio, the great Roman politician and general, as having occurred in a dream. Scipio says that in his dream he met his father and grandfather in the highest heaven where they now dwell:

> When I gazed in every direction from that point, all else appeared wonderfully beautiful. There were stars which we never see from the earth, and they were all larger than we have ever imagined. . . . The starry spheres were much larger than the earth; indeed the earth itself seemed to me so small that I was scornful of our empire, which covers only a single point, as it were, upon its surface.[4]

Scipio's vision shows the insignificance of the Roman empire, for which he bore heavy political and military responsibility. In the dream he asks his father if he might immediately join him in this beautiful heavenly realm, but his father tells him that the only way to get there is to carry out his earthly duties, but to do so with the vision of the heavens in his mind so that he never forgets the relative significance of things. Among the other things Scipio sees, "almost midway in the distance is the Sun, the lord, chief, and ruler of the other lights, the mind and guiding principle of the universe, of such magnitude that he reveals and fills all things with his light." But Scipio does not just see; he hears a "loud and agreeable sound," which, his father assures him, is the music of the spheres.[5]

Cicero's overwhelming emphasis is on the majesty of the eternal and the relative insignificance of the transient, even though he does not lose sight of the relation between moral action on the earth and one's eternal fate. Scipio's subjective reactions are of marginal importance. His sense of the beauty of the heavenly spheres and his scorn for the insignificance of the earth, and even more the empire, are intended to communicate to us the power of the vision, a vision that puts reality in true perspective.

Turning to the opposite end of the ancient world, we might consider the Buddhist wisdom tradition, whose essence is non-clinging, non-attachment; even non-attachment to non-attachment. Perhaps I can best explicate it by a Zen story. The master tells his student to climb a one-hundred foot pole. When the student has reached the top he asks the master, "Now what do I do?" "Climb ten feet higher," says the master. In essence, there is "not one thing" to which one can cling.

To switch radically to a Christian vocabulary, one could say that when one has failed at every effort at self-salvation, one finally recognizes that there is only grace, that only in losing oneself will one find oneself.

For the Stoics, that late flower of Hellenism, that probably exerted more influence on Christianity than any other strand of the classical tradition, we are admonished not to cling to the *pathe*—the irrational motions of the soul, the fears and desires, that dominate so much of our lives. The Stoic ideal is thus *apatheia,* for which apathy is a very misleading translation. For Stoicism did not, any more than the Wisdom traditions of Christianity or Buddhism, teach quietism or escapism. For all of them the only meaning we can find will come through participation in society and the cosmos, not from withdrawal. Let us consider as an example of Stoic *apatheia* the following passage from Book II of the Discourses of Epictetus:

> This Priscus Helvidius too saw, and acted accordingly: For when [the emperor] Vespasian had sent to forbid his going to the senate, he answered, "It is in your power to prevent my continuing as a senator; but while I am one, I must go."—"Well then, at least be silent there."—"Do not ask my opinion, and I will be silent."—"But I must ask it"—"And I must speak what appears to me right."—"But if you do, I will put you to death."—"Did I ever tell you I am immortal? You will do your part, and I mine: It is yours to kill, and mine to die intrepid; yours to banish me, mine to depart untroubled."
>
> What good, then, did Priscus do, who was but a single person? Why what good does the purple do to a garment? What but being a shining character in himself, and setting a good example to others? Another, perhaps, if in such circumstances Caesar had forbidden his going to the senate, would have answered, "I am obliged to you for excusing me." But such a one he would not have forbidden to go, well knowing that he would sit like a statue, or, if he spoke, he would say what he knew was agreeable to Caesar, and would overdo it by adding still more.

The contemplative in action, as the Jesuits put it, was well understood by the Stoics.

The Stoics thought that acting in accord with wisdom was acting in accord with nature, that is, the fundamental order of the natural and human world. This idea is close to the central teaching of another great tradition, namely Confucianism. The Tao, the Way, in a Confucian perspective, is simultaneously the way of heaven and earth and the human way. It includes the primary social relationships—the relation of parent and child, husband and wife, ruler and subject—in ways that resonate with Stoicism. Acting in accordance with Stoic natural law and acting in accordance with the Tao would seem to be remarkably similar. There were certainly Confucians who, like Priscus Helvidius, insisted on remonstrating with the emperor at the peril of their lives.

What these traditions make clear is that the self is not independent from its context, not a deep well into which one must plunge in order to find the truth. The self is extensive, not intensive, defined by its myriad relationships, by its place in a social and natural cosmos, not apart from them. This does not at all imply a conformist self. One's obligation to God or Nature or Heaven or the Tao may entail actions that will place one in stark tension with one's social environment, even at the hazard of one's life. But there is no rejection of society as such, only a criticism of its disorder. One is called to do what one can to bring order into society so that one's social obligations and one's ultimate obligations will be harmonious. What wisdom teaches in all this is a wide view of the whole set of cosmic and social obligations and a proper evaluation of one's own limited place in that whole. One could even say that one gains a sense of immortality from understanding one's participation in a social and natural cosmos that transcends one's finite existence.

From these examples it should be clear that the search for wisdom is not a distraction from the responsibility to care, but a deepening of it, a wider understanding of it. These examples show us that a "detached concern with life itself" is really a deeper concern with life itself than one overwhelmed by anxiety and the pressures of the moment. But I would be remiss if I didn't point out that the quest for wisdom in old age, for "life itself in the face of death itself," has its dark side, just as the search for fidelity in adolescence can end in identity confusion or premature ideological closure and the search for care in adulthood can end in neglect. I am seventy-eight years old so now, if ever, the search for wisdom is on my agenda. But I also know about what Erikson described as the dark temptation that appears in the midst of that search, namely despair, even disgust.

When I look at the world today, when I see how close we are to the edge of the precipice, or that without even knowing it we have perhaps set in motion irreversible changes that are already taking us over the precipice, I am indeed tempted by hopelessness and despair. I was with Jimmy Carter at Camp David in 1979 when he was preparing what came to be called the "moral malaise" speech, the speech that warned us about how serious the energy crisis was and what its long-term results would be, a speech that was derided at the time, but has proven to be all too prophetic today. I cannot but think how different our situation would be now if twenty-five years ago we had taken drastic action to prevent global warming, instead of going on steadily making it worse and worse. I fear not for myself, because these changes though inexorable are not rapid, but for my children and even more for my grandchildren. These days despair and disgust are never far from my doorstep, only growing stronger as I see the heedlessness and denial that control our society.

But, as the Buddhist, Stoic, Confucian, and Christian traditions would tell me, now, just when we fear the worst, we most need wisdom. If we are to have a deeper American dream perhaps it would be an American version of the Dream of Scipio, one in which we would see that our empire is as fleeting as the great powers that have gone before us. There have been many dark times in human history. Now, more than ever, we need people who can face our coming difficulties calmly and with detachment, doing what can be done, faithfully, lovingly, and wisely.

NOTES

1 Erikson discussed his scheme in several books, perhaps the most important of which is Erik H. Erikson, *Insight and Responsibility: Lectures on the Ethical Implications of Psychoanalytic Insight* (New York: Norton, 1964). Useful charts of the stages and their virtues and distortions can be found in Erik H. Erikson, *The Life Cycle Completed: A Review* (New York: Norton, 1982), pp. 32–33 and 56–57.

2 Albert Borgmann, *Crossing the Postmodern Divide* (Chicago: University of Chicago Press, 1992).

3 Erikson, *Insight and Responsibility*, p. 133; italics in the original.

4 Cicero, *"Somnium Scipionis"* (Scipio's Dream), in *De Republica*, VI:16.

5 Ibid., VI:17–18.

DREAM-WALKING
TOWARD AMERICA

THE DEEPENING THE
AMERICAN DREAM PROJECT

Mark Nepo

> *The basis of the American dream is spiritual. It's indestruc-*
> *tible, [though] we may not see it. . . . Believe in who and*
> *what we have chosen, [that] all are created equal. . . .*
> *Believe in them, though they do not believe in themselves.*
> —Florida Yeldell, ninety-year-old
> African American schoolteacher
> from South Carolina

AS A PROGRAM OFFICER for the Fetzer Institute, I have had the privilege
of working with many others around the country on a project called
Deepening the American Dream. It began six years ago, when Rob
Lehman, then president and now chair of the board of the Fetzer Institute, wondered about the inner life of democracy, the way that its citizens
are formed, and the role of spirit in our civic life together. This led us to
gather leading and diverse thinkers together to consider the American
dream in its many incarnations and interpretations, centering on these
fundamental questions: "As Americans, who are we now?" and "What is
it we dream about and aspire to today?"

Their in-depth responses form the essays in this book. Over the past six
years, Fetzer has extended this unfolding dialogue into the public domain
in partnership with Jossey-Bass, an imprint of John Wiley & Sons, by
publishing and circulating these and other essays as free pamphlets. To
date, we have given away close to forty thousand copies to a wide range
of leaders in various fields around the country, including members of Congress through the Faith and Politics Institute, the community of therapists

and spiritual healers through the Shalem Institute, and interfaith communities around the world through the international circles of the United Religions Initiative.

To broaden and enliven the ideas that these writers have explored, Fetzer has also sponsored a number of public forums around the country, primarily at the Library of Congress in Washington, D.C., and at the Presidio in San Francisco. Through the Center for the Study of the Presidency in Washington, D.C., we are gathering young leaders in government with several of the authors to explore the art and soul of leadership. In partnership with the National League for Innovation in Community Colleges and the National Center for Teacher Formation in Community Colleges, community colleges from eleven U.S. cities have hosted community conversations centered on the issues the essays raise. And teachers around the country are using the essays in their classrooms to spark a different kind of conversation about what America is and what it means.

Given the widespread interest and deep conversation across the country that these essays have stirred, Fetzer will continue to publish individual pamphlets in the Deepening the American Dream series. Our conversations about the American dream have also made it clear that it is essential that we deepen our awareness and understanding of how we relate to the world around us. And so, in addition, we have inaugurated a sister series, called Exploring a Global Dream. At the heart of this inquiry are questions such as "Is a global community emerging, and what is our place in it?" "What are the essential qualities of the common man or woman—the global citizen—who seeks to live with the authenticity and grace demanded by our times?" "What does it mean to be a 'global citizen'?" and "What is our spiritual responsibility as citizens of the world and as citizens of this nation?"

The Fetzer Institute's effort in this series and the conversations it has seeded are part of a vital tradition. Pamphleteering has a long and vigorous history in America, tracing back to Thomas Paine's famous pamphlet, *Common Sense,* which in 1776 went through twenty-five editions, selling hundreds of thousands of copies. As the historian Howard Zinn tells us, Paine's pamphlet was not unique: "More than 400 pamphlets appeared in the twenty-five years preceding the Declaration of Independence; discussing questions of disobedience to law, loyalty to authority [and] the rights and obligations of citizens in a society."[1]

Almost a century later, Henry David Thoreau's opposition to the Mexican War and to slavery resulted in his famous lecture turned pamphlet, *Civil Disobedience.*[2] Both of these pamphlets are landmarks in the unfolding of democracy.

In an attempt to reinvigorate public dialogue of this sort, we take our turn in considering essential questions of meaning that relate to the lives we live as Americans, both as citizens and as part of the larger world. These are not just surface concerns, but fundamental questions that have spiritual roots. Scripture from every tradition tells us, in its own way, to love our neighbors. But politics throughout the ages, at its worst, has always drawn and redrawn the line of who's in and who's out, who's worthy of compassion and assistance and who's not.

The future of the world, however, will no longer tolerate dreams of a society in which any are left out. That this is true while so many are left out is the enigma we must solve, if we are to pass the earth on without destroying it or each other.

Into this crucial conversation, we invite you.

Beginning a Conversation

In a phrase, the aim of this book, and the Deepening the American Dream project from which it has grown, is to sow the seeds of a national and international conversation about the inner life of democracy and its citizens, and the relationship of America to the rest of the world.

In inviting key thinkers and writers in our culture and from around the world to explore the nature of the American dream today, we have been (and are still) asking, What is it? What is core to it? What is working? What is missing? What is essential but hidden or dormant? How do we or can we connect the dream of America with the dream of the world? What is the role in our culture for spiritual values like love and forgiveness? And how can humanity best be served by integrating the inner life of mind and spirit with the outer life of action and service in the world?

The heartbreak of September 11, 2001, provided us with a moment that, for Americans, opened deeper ways of being together. This may have been a short-lived opening, a moment that seems to have dimmed. But profoundly, it feels like a soft pause in our culture, a pause that has created some sense of vulnerability in us that has in turn opened a willingness in many of us to hear each other more readily. And despite the seeming hardening of division and animosity evidenced between parties during the 2004 presidential election, the issuing of these pamphlets has demonstrated that there is still a hunger out there for true conversation. More than ever, it is a time for such conversation, a time to clarify who we are as a nation and as a people.

David Abshire, president of the Center for the Study of the Presidency in Washington, D.C., puts it this way:

On September 11, 2001, we were a people united by our common
beliefs. . . . It is a tragedy that those few months of national, moral, and
spiritual unity were so soon lost. Still, we remain bound, whether we
show it or not, by certain principles that are elusive but powerful. . . .
Which, then, is the true America? The America of division or the
America of unity? . . . The America of endless public and partisan warfare or the America of cooperation, civility, and common purpose? The
America of many or the America of one?

After two centuries of freedom, it helps to remember that America is
not a painting that has dried, hanging on some museum wall, but rather a
vibrant river that keeps shifting its course and scouring its banks, widen-
ing its way to the sea. As Vincent Harding, a friend and colleague of Martin Luther King Jr., has said, "Democracy is not a static thing. It does not
stand still. If we don't keep finding ways to expand and deepen democracy, we will see it diminish."[3]

It is interesting that while the Founding Fathers were crafting the magnificent Declaration of Independence, our native fathers were practicing
their own magnificent sense of community. In the Iroquois nation, in particular, there is a custom known as *dream-walking,* in which each person's
individual dreams and sufferings are interpreted to find communal meaning, and those meanings, woven together, are then used to blueprint the
dream for the community. It is no accident that these two sensibilities,
independence and community, flourished at the same time. In our age, it
seems we have a call to marry them further—in fact, an urgency to do so.

In our attempts at the Fetzer Institute to listen to as many voices as possible, we are seeing people from all walks of life, both here and abroad,
enter this process of dream-walking, of interpreting personal dreams and
sufferings as building blocks for a meaningful society and, indeed, a meaningful world. This is one way to think about the deepening of America—
to listen to and interpret each other's dreams and sufferings in order to
build what Martin Luther King Jr. called a beloved community.

There are many things that make the American sensibility resilient, but
perhaps the deepest is our ability to seek, listen, and synthesize the many
into the one, the many into what will serve the common good. The visionary educator and writer Parker Palmer has spoken to this sensibility: "If
we want to live 'in the truth,' we must learn to live in the conversation
rather than in its conclusions of the moment. Truth—which comes from
the same word that gives us *troth*—is found in staying faithful to the fact
that we belong to each other in community."[4]

Two central questions present themselves: Are we willing to listen to and interpret all the voices around us, in ourselves and in the world, and form a chorus of dreaming together? And are we willing to stay faithful to the fact that we belong to each other in community? The essays you will find collected in this book are an attempt to explore the many facets of such questions.

Looking and Listening for America

What do we see through the window of America, and what does the rest of the world see looking back?
—Megan Schopf, artist and facilitator[5]

We are not the first generation to look out onto the world, nor the first generation to be looked at. The French writer Alexis de Tocqueville came to the United Stated during the 1830s to chronicle the character of a new nation. In *Democracy in America,* published in 1835 and 1840, he defined and described the "habits of the heart" that vitalized the experiment called America. He found many contradictory qualities in those early Americans and wrote about them with insight.

In fact, it was de Tocqueville who coined the term *individualism,* and his initial remarks about it are very telling: "Individualism is a calm and considered feeling which disposes each citizen to isolate himself from the mass of his fellows and withdraw into the circle of family and friends; with this little society formed to his taste, he gladly leaves the greater society to look after itself." Such people, he noted, "form the habit of thinking of themselves in isolation and imagine that their whole destiny is in their hands." They cut themselves off from their ancestors and their descendants as well as their contemporaries. "Each man is forever thrown back on himself alone, and there is danger that he may be shut up in the solitude of his own heart."[6] As de Tocqueville foresaw, the habits of our hearts do shape our mental habits.

Part of living the American dream has been an ongoing tension of identity: Are we pragmatic capitalists or expressive individualists? In his landmark study on individualism, called *Habits of the Heart* (1985), named after de Tocqueville's original phrase, the sociologist Robert Bellah traces this ambiguity of identity to two differing sources of American character. The first is Benjamin Franklin's utilitarian individualism, which fosters a stubborn self-reliance that coordinates all things practical ("God helps those who help themselves"). The second is Walt Whitman's expressive individualism, which fosters an undeniable connection between all things ("I celebrate myself; / And what I assume you shall assume; / For every atom belonging to me, as good belongs to you").[7]

Americans have found factions of this split in every generation. The deep question around who we really are has been at the heart of our ever-changing foreign policy: Are we isolationists, focused on tending our own interests, or are we members of a global community who understand that what happens to one happens to all?

We could say that the cost of unbalanced individualism, over two hundred years, has helped create a depth of isolation that cuts us off from our spiritual foundations, our ancestors, our descendants, and even our contemporaries. On March 19, 2003, Senator Robert Byrd addressed these matters on the floor of Congress in a speech called "The Arrogance of Power." He said, "Today, I weep for my country. I have watched the events of recent months with a heavy, heavy heart. No more is the image of America one of a strong yet benevolent peacekeeper. The image of America has changed. Around the globe, our friends mistrust us, our word is disputed, our intentions are questioned. Instead of reasoning with those with whom we disagree, we demand obedience or threaten recrimination."

"Unfortunately," as Carolyn Brown wisely perceives, "if we as a country don't see our shadow side, others—the rest of the world—will see it for us. This accounts for much of the anti-American sentiment and calls us to discover for ourselves the inner life of democracy."[8]

The essays assembled in this volume are part of a call to reexamine both the habits of our hearts and the habits of our minds. In the opening section of the book, philosopher Jacob Needleman leads us, in his essay "Two Dreams of America," squarely into the question "What does America *mean*?" This is a question that he suggests has been gathering strength for decades. So interwoven is the immigrant fabric of our country and so widespread is the increasing diversity of our citizens that it no longer serves to look at ourselves in isolation from the rest of the world and its plethora of traditions. In her essay "Footprints of the Soul: Uniting Spirit with Action in the World," Library of Congress scholar Carolyn Brown speaks deeply about the gifts and frictions that exist between our authentic selves and the society we live in and grow in and how returning to the well of spirit keeps forming who we are in the world.

In looking and listening for America, "we must," as the twentieth-century writer and caricaturist Max Beerbohm is said to have remarked, "stop talking about the American dream and start listening to the dreams of Americans." And we can look and listen anywhere. In my travels as a teacher and facilitator, I have heard many uplifting and heartbreaking stories that reveal the fabric of Americans dreaming. In Maine, I found myself listening quietly to the low voice of a Paspaqua Indian singing "Amazing Grace" in her native tongue to comfort her daughter, suffering with colic. And in Pennsylvania, I found myself pulling up a chair to better hear the story of a sixty-year-old man whose great-great-grandmother's uncle stopped haying in the middle of the day, hooked his scythe in the crook of a tree, and walked off to fight at Gettysburg, never to return. I listened as he told me how no one ever took the scythe down. How the handle of that scythe fell apart, but the heart of the tree grew around the blade. Just as the heart of our nation grew around that devastating battle. How, for a hundred years, it looked as though that tree had a blade growing out of it. Until the sixty-year-old man brought his grandchildren to see it and touch it. And after that, the blade finally crumbled, and the wound in the tree healed over.

In Appalachia, well into the night, I listened to a young man tell the story of a black coal miner's wife who would pick up her baby in the morning and walk to her white neighbor's house and stand in front of the neighbor's broken porch while their husbands were digging together in the earth. She didn't say a word, just stood there rocking her infant, and then shuffled back over the broken path to her home. After several visits like this, the white neighbor began to feel pained by how thin and weary her black neighbor was. She invited her in a few times, but the black mother would not come in or say a word. She just stood there, tired and thin, with her baby in her arms, looking longingly into her neighbor's kitchen. Finally, in some language below all language, the white woman realized that they were starving, and that she was being silently asked to breastfeed the little black baby because the other mother didn't have enough milk in her.

From that moment, they became an odd and holy family: the black and white mothers and the starving infant. And day after day, the black mother brought her baby down the broken path to the white mother's porch and waited outside while her newfound sister rocked the brown baby at her breast as their men wrestled coal from the earth. And day after day, without a word, the black mother carried her sleepy infant home. Neither told a soul. Each day she came, and each day they held the child together in two brief moments, in the giving and the giving back. And the white mother would hush the brown child to sleep, singing, "Here's a bit a honey the bees ain't found." And that baby, all grown up, has taught that lullaby to her children. And it was the grandson of that baby, passed between black and white mothers, who told me the story.

The question returns: Just what will we learn from where we've been and what will we pass on? This brings me back to Robert Bellah, who in describing the aim of his work on individualism, offered two beautiful sincerities: "We want to know what resources Americans have for making sense of their lives" and "We hope this book will help transform the inner moral debate, often shared only with intimates, into public discourse."[9]

We affirm that any authentic effort to be engaged as a citizen will further these two sincerities. It is our hope at the Fetzer Institute that such honest engagement in the American experience will enliven and strengthen who we are as a nation and how we relate to the world we find ourselves in. We hope that such engagements of heart and mind will lift up and make accessible the deep and timeless resources that help us make sense of our lives.

Suffering the American Dream

Then, what of the American dream? Is it a vision or an illusion? Do we need to deepen this dream or awaken from it?
—Jacob Needleman

At first glance, the notion of suffering the American dream may seem harsh. But all dreams and ideas, all ambitions and commitments—whether individual or communal, whether secular or religious—set out an ideal toward which to climb, and being human, it is in suffering the gap between the ideal and the actual living of it that we find out just how loving and compassionate we are. The ideal of the American dream is not exempt from this universal dynamic.

With anything we suffer, it is incumbent on us—as individuals or as a nation—to discern what to do with that suffering. Do we remove what is paining us? Do we remove ourselves? Or do we forge a new relationship between us and what pains us in order to alleviate the suffering? When the great Arthur Miller wrote his landmark play *Death of a Salesman* in 1949, we had no idea what a powerful metaphor he had created. In bringing to life the character of the traveling salesman, Willy Loman, Miller did something that no one in drama had done before. He showed that tragedy can happen to anyone, that suffering the gap between our ideal dream and our attempts to live it is the province of every ordinary person.

In the play, Willy Loman is tortured by his need to succeed and to be liked, and as the story unfolds, we see that the American dream has failed him—or he has failed it. Eventually, Willy commits suicide. He has two sons: the elder son Biff, who at Willy's grave says that his father pursued the wrong dream, and Hap, the younger son, who says, "No, I'm going to do it better, 'cause Willy didn't do it good enough." All along, while Willy is alive and losing his mind, his dead brother, Ben, provokes him with the dream of finding gold in Alaska. The ghost of Ben dangles the ideal of success in front of Willy's sense of failure, like a carrot in front of a donkey. In the end, the tremendous point that Miller makes is that falling in the gap between who we are and what we aspire to can happen to anyone—rich or poor, accomplished or not, well known or anonymous. The final note sounds at Willy's grave when his widow, Linda, cries with heartache into the night that "attention must be paid!"

After two centuries, this speaks directly to the American dream. Attention must be paid. We need to discern: *Are we not pursuing the dream well enough, or is it the wrong dream, or is it a mix of both?* Like Willy's sons, we owe it, to ourselves and our ancestors, to pay attention and participate in helping the nature of the dream evolve further.

We don't have to look far into our history to feel the pain of that gap. Although "all men are created equal," the treatment of Native Americans, the struggle of slavery, and the exclusion of women from the very ideal all point up how we aspire to and suffer from the American dream. Two of our authors have explored these ideas.

In her essay "Created Equal: Exclusion and Inclusion in the American Dream," historian of religion Elaine Pagels provides a compelling exploration of the ways we have interpreted equality as expressed in the Declaration of Independence. More than ever, she says, we need to ask, who is included in the American dream? What do we make of this dream in a waking reality? How shall we take this vision to shape our sense of who we are—as a people, a nation, a community? She calls us to deepen our understanding of the American dream and commit ourselves to extending it to all people worldwide who would share in its promises, blessings, and responsibilities.

We have also suffered the extremes of free enterprise and competition and the drive to win, all of which, in their out-of-balance state, have become addictive. The result has been a self-centered, heartless insistence on the superior claim of our own experience. And this has led to a brutal polarity by which we are slowly killing each other, and others, in the name of patriotism. In his essay "The Grace and Power of Civility: Commitment and Tolerance in the American Experience," David Abshire, the former U.S. ambassador to NATO, addresses these brutal divisions: "Why is our country more polarized than ever and cooperation less and less common? Is it because the very fiber of our society . . . has been lost to partisan, economic, racial, and religious schisms?"

A historian himself, Abshire searches for a common thread that still holds the fabric of democracy together and traces the history of commitment and tolerance at work in governance in an effort to revitalize the respect, listening, and dialogue that constitute civility. He warns that "while commitment without tolerance produces a sort of zealous, destructive fundamentalism, tolerance without commitment entails a moral reserve that can degenerate into moral vacuity or paralysis."

So how do we proceed with such discernments? No one really knows. But encouraging each other to listen to how we dream and suffer this great idea that is America is a good place to begin. As Rob Lehman, the former president of the Fetzer Institute who had the original vision for this whole inquiry, has said:

> In the 1930s, . . . the poet Langston Hughes observed that the origin of a deeper American dream is not to be found in some distant, abstract idea but very near, in the story of our own lives. His insight rings true to this day:
>
> *An ever-living seed,*
> *Its dream*
> *Lies deep in the heart of me.*[10]
>
> The deepening we seek can be found in our own hearts, if only we have the courage to read what is written there.

Perhaps understanding the spiritual foundations of democracy can open the conversation. Jacob Needleman says there is a need "to retell the meaning of America in the light of Spirit."[11] Not only in terms of the religion that sustained the Pilgrims or the sanctity of life that sustained the Native Americans they met but also in the context of the life force that informs our very human beginnings. If we look more deeply into "life, liberty, and the pursuit of happiness," what antecedents will we find? Will we find wholeness of reality, freedom of spirit, and unconditional love? Are these spiritual elements? Do they make up the water of a common spring from which we all drink?

And perhaps understanding what constitutes our sacred ground as a nation can deepen the conversation. It is revealing to discover that in drafting the famous passage that rests at the core of the Declaration of Independence, "We hold these truths to be self-evident," Jefferson originally wrote, "We hold these truths to be sacred." Franklin and Adams encouraged him to revise it. But something is lost in this revision, something of how freedom grows from the spiritual ground of all life. For when the connection between life and its wholeness is cut, when the connection between liberty and freedom of spirit is lost, when the connection between happiness and unconditional love is denied, a self-interest that is desperate, greedy, and amoral comes to dominate.

And perhaps humility can expand the ways in which we see and listen. As the Old Testament says, "Where there is no vision, the people perish" (Proverbs 29:18). And as Einstein is said to have observed, "You can't solve a problem with the same thinking that created it." Our fate as a community resides somewhere in between, and in our age as in all ages, arrogance blinds us and makes us deaf. In ancient Rome, when a new emperor was chosen, he'd walk into the city, amid all the adulation, with a slave whispering in his ear, "You are mortal, too." Unfortunately, most Americans have lost this sense of humility. Now the rest of the world is whispering in our ear, "You are mortal, too." Will we hear those voices?

Will we hear each other? As Rudolf Steiner observed, "The healthy social life is found / When in the mirror of the human soul / The whole community finds its reflection."[12] This is why we need to understand those who suffer in our society, as well as those who dream, for they reflect back to us where we need to heal and grow in order to be a healthy community. To accomplish this, as diversity trainer Pat Harbour says, "We need to enliven forgiveness for the loss of the dream, which means we need to seek out the history of the distortion of the dream and to honor the suffering perpetrated in the name of the dream."[13] It seems we all need to bear responsibility for both dropping the dream and rebuilding the dream and the courage to "love one another or die," as the poet W. H. Auden says.[14]

After three years of conversation with leading thinkers around the country, Jacob Needleman further offered, in one of our public dialogues, that "perhaps we are not called to deepen the American dream but to deepen the American." This is a simple and profound place to root our conversation. I was thinking about this while on a walking history tour of Kalamazoo, Michigan, where I live. I had gone with a few friends. It was a warm Sunday in September, close to the third anniversary of the terrorist attacks of September 11, 2001. In the park where the town was established by Titus Bronson, a potato farmer who had an appetite for land, we stood near a Native American burial mound in which the city's leaders had placed a time capsule in 1954. It turns out that of all the things that could be left for the future, the capsule contained an edition of the 1954 *Kalamazoo Gazette* and an array of coins. What is someone hundreds of years from now supposed to surmise from such selections? Perhaps, sadly and rightly, that we value commerce and current events— money and our own story—more than anything else.

It was then that I learned that Lincoln had spoken in this very park in 1856. He had come to support others who were running for office. And by all accounts, he was thought, at the time, to be too hesitant in speaking out against slavery. Even great leaders have an evolution of heart and mind and courage, like everyone else.

As we listened to our tour guide telling these stories, I noticed a man nearby who appeared to be homeless. He was sitting on a bench and had a tattered bundle next to him. I could tell he was listening to our guide chronicle Lincoln's early hesitation about abolishing slavery. He listened as we learned how the white landowners sent the Potawatomi tribe west by train, how they made them give up their land and relocate to a reservation in Illinois.

Watching the homeless man take this all in made me realize that our guide was just citing facts. But the sad, agitated, tattered stranger, all by himself, was of the lineage of the displaced. I could tell that he heard these facts differently. As we moved on, I kept looking back, wondering what his experience of freedom was. What was his American dream? And what kept me from asking him?

I tell this story here because part of the intent behind this book, behind all the dialogues that inform these essays, is the desire to imagine America beyond the dispassionate facts and to leave something meaningful and useful for the future—something beyond our love of money and our infatuation with our own story.

I can't help but wondering what Lincoln would say to the homeless man sitting near the old Indian burial mound. How have Americans evolved after nine generations? What is the evolution of our dreams and sufferings after 229 years? Through the difficult work of love and forgiveness, how do we listen to "the huddled masses yearning to be free"—those coming here and those already here? How do we strengthen America by including them? How do we reinvigorate a democracy that enters the world "with malice toward none and charity toward all"?

Deepening the American Dream

Democracy is an unfinished experiment.
—Walt Whitman

According to Carolyn Brown, "'Deepening' means expending the effort to see the world anew and risk whatever may follow—the discomfort, disorientation, and anger or fear that might greet us if we venture into the unfamiliar. We need to see the world with eyes unspoiled by habit, to hurl ourselves outside our unthinking frames of reference."[15]

Transpersonal psychologist Frances Vaughan, too, has remarked, "We find ourselves both inspired and sobered by a renewed appreciation of the lofty ideals on which our country was founded and challenged by the stark recognition of our human failings."[16] How we bridge that gap between our ideals and our failings depends on our willingness to expand our preconceived sense of life and society. Most often, to deepen, we need to see clearly. We need to return to what the Eastern traditions call a "beginner's mind," meaning a complete and fresh openness, as though we know nothing at all about what we wish to understand. To do that, we need to break our own patterns, the habits of our minds. The essays in this section of the book center on this challenge.

It is this breaking of habit that the scholar and teacher Robert Inchausti explores in his essay, "Breaking the Cultural Trance: Insight and Vision in America." He takes a convincing look at how we see and, just as important, how living in the current culture of America has impaired our deepest seeing. This sort of deepening calls us to look beneath nationalities to the common humanity we are all rooted in. Huston Smith, a renowned scholar, professor of world religions, and best-selling author, asks if we can deepen the American dream until it becomes a global dream, not imposing America on the world but enlivening and feeding the common roots that all nations share.[17] In "From Cruelty to Compassion: The Crucible of Personal Transformation," the psychiatrist and writer Gerald May takes us on a compelling journey to the perennial bottom of who we are, at our best and our worst, and explores how to use that knowledge to live together from a place of spirit and compassion, regardless of what country or tradition we call home.

All of this speaks to the need to be both independent and connected, resilient and compassionate in an ever-changing world. In an article on the philosophical roots of al-Qaeda, the scholar Paul Berman challenges the stubbornness of our America-first trance: "The terrorists speak insanely of deep things. The antiterrorists had better speak sanely of equally deep things. Presidents will not do this. Presidents will dispatch armies, or decline to dispatch armies, for better and for worse. But who will speak of the sacred and the secular, of the physical world and the spiritual world?"[18]

We have a democratic, mystical tradition that can answer this. In looking more closely at Walt Whitman, Robert Bellah notes that "for Whitman, the ultimate use of the American's independence was to cultivate and express the self in order to explore its vast social and cosmic identities."[19]

It is this mystical sense of our common humanity that begs returning to. As Episcopal priest and writer Cynthia Bourgeault observes: "If the post-modern universe so often seems random and meaningless; if the great American dream seems sometimes to have shrunk to a bizarre caricature of itself—perhaps the problem is not that our vision has grown too small, but that we are using too little of ourselves to see."[20]

As Whitman and Bourgeault confirm, we need to recover a larger sense of self to see with. In breaking our cultural trance, we are invited to return to a cosmic sense of self that opens the undeniable connection between all living things. Perhaps we as Americans are on the verge of rediscovering the common seed from which both our national and our global citizenship sprouts, along with the belief that both our independence and our interdependence will be strengthened by knowing and honoring these common roots.

We are clearly at a crossroads in how we see ourselves, in how we participate or not in the global community, in how we imagine and live out the American dream. We can no longer, in de Tocqueville's words, leave the greater society to look after itself or risk being shut up in the solitude of our own hearts. As Robert Bellah tellingly reports, "de Tocqueville saw the isolation to which Americans are prone as ominous for the future of our freedom."[21] In the span of 170 years, these social premonitions have all come true. We are often isolated, shut up in our own solitudes, cut off from our ancestors, descendants, and contemporaries. But Whitman's song still calls. None of this is irreversible. Even in the nineteenth century, de Tocqueville noted the compassionate impulse that was also American: "Citizens . . . are bound to . . . turn from their private interests and . . . look at something other than themselves."[22]

What is it we look at when we turn from ourselves? What vast social and cosmic identity awaits that joins us together? What are the common roots of all nations? How do we nourish them? What stands in our way? Many have started to dialogue around these questions, and more than lobbying for any one outcome or any one political agenda, it is our hope at Fetzer and in this volume to simply and deeply irrigate the conversation, for we believe that democracy, fully engaged, will rediscover and re-imagine itself. Through all our work, we are asking in all quarters, from the country of one's soul to the soul of many countries, if leadership and community can be understood and embraced in a different way.

In truth, transformational change often occurs when we choose or are forced to turn to something larger than ourselves. Whether it takes place or not often depends on two connected dynamics: one is that the greater the human experience of separateness, the greater the level of fear and violence, and the other is that the greater the awareness and experience of wholeness and interconnection, the greater the human capacity to love and forgive. These insights came from a yearlong conversation among the circle of trustees of the Fetzer Institute. Thus we come to the question, How do these spiritual laws of cause and effect—between separateness and interconnection, fear and love, violence and forgiveness—affect our lives, our relationships, our communities, our nation, and the world? To pursue this question in honest kinship—by listening to and interpreting each other's dreams and sufferings—is one way to practice democracy. Probing what can shift a consciousness of separation to a consciousness of connection, on all these levels, is crucial to deepening the American dream.

Participating in the World's Soul

We are caught in an inescapable network of mutuality, tied in a single garment of destiny. Whatever affects one directly affects all.

—Martin Luther King Jr.,
Letter from Birmingham City Jail

The same barriers of fear, preconception, isolationism, and trance that block us from knitting the fabric of our own American society into a whole also exist between us and the world. Our constant challenge, then, is to remove these barriers, both in America and in the world. How do we dream toward the future and preserve the best of our history? How do we participate in the world's soul, the universal ground of being that is common and perennial to all human life? Traditions from around the world have many names for this, but all stem from a humble acknowledgment that we are all innately connected in a human citizenship that precedes all national claims. So how do we honor this basic connection and evolve in sharing our time on earth? These concerns are not a just a luxury of holistic thinking but point to an acceptance of the ever-growing fact that like it or not, we all need each other.

The essays in this culminating section probe these very barriers, revealing our common humanity and our common struggles as Americans. In "Opening the Dream: Beyond the Limits of Otherness," Rev. Canon Charles Gibbs, executive director of the United Religions Initiative, explores America's relationship with the rest of the world. He proposes that "the future of America cannot be separated from the future of the rest of the world. There are no longer chasms deep enough or walls high enough to protect us from others or to protect others from us. So what do we do? We might begin by seeing ourselves as citizens of Earth and children of the abiding Mystery at the heart of all that is." And in "The Politics of the Brokenhearted: On Holding the Tensions of Democracy," Parker Palmer speaks to the conflicts and contradictions of twenty-first-century life that are breaking the American heart and threatening to compromise our democratic values.

One severe barrier that impinges on our lives has been described in conversation by Huston Smith as a by-product of progress: "Modernity inflicts us with a tunnel vision of the nature of reality that has shut out huge and ancient resources that have helped humanity for centuries to love and care for each other and the earth."[23]

So breaking through our self-made barriers is one of our most pressing tasks, if we are to find a way live together. This brings to mind a perennial paradox about the nature of experience that applies to nations as well. It centers on the mystery that no one can live your life for you, and yet we need each other to be whole and complete. We often cycle through this struggle; fighting off the influence of others to discover and be who we truly are, and then fighting off the loneliness of that discovery in order to feel the sweetness of belonging.

It is interesting that as America individuates as a nation, we can sense that we are maturing with regard to this paradox. The farther we journey and the older we get, the more we realize that we need others to be whole and complete. In the nineteenth century, we were captivated as a nation with our independence and our "manifest destiny" to expand our borders to their continental limits. By the second half of the twentieth century, we were beginning to coexist with each other as we explored what Stephen Covey termed our interdependence.[24]

Today, we often find ourselves leaning more and more into relationships while remaining confused about whether we are better off as self-reliant and independent. In light of all this, Jacob Needleman pointedly asks, "Is America necessary?"[25] It is a shocking question. He goes on to say that without the search for meaning and community that arises from our inner lives, America is not relevant. But even more pointedly, if, as intended, America is kept vital as an ongoing experiment "to protect and guard the inner search for truth and conscience" then "America is necessary to the world." But Needleman states plainly that without the search for meaning and community that arises from our inner lives, America would lose its relevance and be no different than any other form of government.

To keep the experiment alive in our own time, we are being asked to deepen where we look for meaning, to expand the circle in which we share that meaning, and to realize that we are more together than alone. We, at Fetzer, believe that the critical issues facing the world today require that we go below political, social, and economic strategies to the psychological and spiritual roots of those issues. In entering these realms, we are being forced to search for meaning and community beyond our own borders. Finally, we are being asked to consider what the Buddhist monk and writer Thich Nhat Hanh has termed our "interbeing." For this time, as both Thich Nhat Hanh and the Dali Lama have said, the Buddha will come as a community, not an individual. So now, with the press of one interrelated world and the limits of any one way of seeing, we are being asked to imagine, "How can we go there together?"

Yet despite our promise and place of power in the world, America has its own internal war of values: to cherish things or people, to consume or preserve, to be self-reliant or interdependent, to isolate or bridge, to lead or listen, to live in fear of the future or to stay in love with the present. Most of all, America has become the pinnacle of a timeless conflict that eventually finds all civilizations: a conflict between supremacy and humility. The question waits inside every human decision: Do we have dominion over the earth, or are we simply part of something larger?

In many ways, America has become an efficient, contradictory culture whose overambitious citizens often aspire to be God-like but whose devotions often manifest as addictions to the material world. All this to say that we have inadvertently built a complex civilization that faces the ocean, though we often live with our backs to the sea. And yet it is a land more free than anyone has ever imagined. In this, America gives rise and refuge to every kind of response to life.

At times America reminds me of a jungle. There, everything alive is allowed to grow according to nature's laws. Lush and unruly, the environment gives rise to every kind of flower and weed. There is life at every level: snakes along the jungle floor, monkeys in the thick lower branches that twine into one another, and large birds in the singular reaches that form the tops of trees. And after centuries, the taller trees have formed a canopy. By sheer growth, they have secured the right to drink from the sun's light first, leaving the smaller vines and plants to twist and slink in odd directions to grab their sliver of light. Some of the smaller plants are choked from any light and simply die. Still, the land is so lush and brilliant that all forms of life want to migrate there. At times, it seems that America and its people, with the best of intentions, have grown in this way. For freedom is a different experience for those twisting for their sliver of light than for those privileged trees that form the canopy. Still, accepting how precious a thing freedom is, the question before us, as before the Founding Fathers, remains: What is freedom for? What does one do with complete freedom? Produce and consume? Or root and care for each other?

So here we are. Dream-walking on the precipice of everyone's dreams and sufferings, looking for ways to spin the golden threads and bloodied cords into the tapestry of a beloved community. And like it or not, we are becoming the world and the world is becoming us. The borders of the world are strongly and quickly blurring. For example, there are 180 different languages being spoken and published in greater Los Angeles today. Even as I write this, the world is not just being mirrored in the streets of America but spilling into the streets of America. So the question becomes, as the civil rights historian Vincent Harding puts it, "How do we prepare ourselves inwardly to participate in the oneness of humanity?"[26]

Still, you might ask, why is all this necessary? Let me share an analogy raised by a dear friend and mentor, the physician and painter Joel Elkes. In the wake of September 11, 2001, Joel asked me and others to consider the world as one universal body, and, if this is so, then, he went on, the terrorists and those consumed with self-interest are like cancer cells, destroying the whole for the sake of the part. Moreover, he said, we, in our call to find each other and heal each other, are, in every question asked and every suffering heard, cells in the immune system of humanity. By simply gathering and holding space for "the better angels of our nature," as Lincoln termed it, we preserve the world. It seems an overwhelming task, but to paraphrase Martin Luther King Jr., "I believe what the self-centered have torn down, the other-centered can build up."

And every effort, no matter how small, becomes a healthy cell that matters. And we can start anywhere. Even here.

NOTES

1   Howard Zinn, *Artists in Times of War* (New York: Seven Stories Press, 2003), p. 96.

2   Ibid., p. 102.

3   Vincent Harding, as part of an authors' dialogue held at the Fetzer Institute, June 6–9, 2004.

4   Parker J. Palmer, *A Hidden Wholeness: The Journey Toward an Undivided Life* (San Francisco: Jossey-Bass, 2004), p. 127.

5   Megan Schopf, as part of an authors' dialogue held at the Fetzer Institute, June 22–24, 2002.

6 Alexis de Tocqueville, *Democracy in America,* ed. J. P. Mayer, trans. George Lawrence (New York: Doubleday/Anchor, 1969; originally published 1835 and 1840), pp. 506, 508.

7 Robert N. Bellah, *Habits of the Heart* (Berkeley: University of California Press, 1985), p. vii. The Franklin quote is from *Poor Richard's Almanac* (1757). The Whitman lines are from "Song of Myself" (1855).

8 Carolyn Brown, as part of an authors' dialogue held at the Fetzer Institute, June 22–24, 2002.

9 Bellah, *Habits of the Heart,* p. x.

10 Langston Hughes, "Let America Be America Again" (1936). From *The Collected Poems of Langston Hughes,* copyright © 1994 by The Estate of Langston Hughes. Used by permission of Alfred A. Knopf, a division of Random House, Inc.

11 Jacob Needleman, as part of an authors' dialogue held at the Fetzer Institute, June 22–24, 2002.

12 Rudolf Steiner, "Motto of the Social Ethic" (1920).

13 Patricia Moore Harbour, as part of an authors' dialogue held at the Fetzer Institute, June 22–24, 2002.

14 W. H. Auden, "September 1, 1939" (1939).

15 Carolyn Brown, as part of an authors' dialogue held at the Fetzer Institute, June 22–24, 2002.

16 Frances Vaughan, as part of an authors' dialogue held at the Fetzer Institute, June 22–24, 2002.

17 Huston Smith, as part of an authors' dialogue held at the Fetzer Institute, June 22–24, 2002.

18 Paul Berman, "The Story of Sayyid Qutb," *New York Times Magazine,* Mar. 23, 2003, p. 20.

19 Bellah, *Habits of the Heart,* p. 35.

20 Cynthia Bourgeault, as part of an authors' dialogue held at the Fetzer Institute, June 22–24, 2002.

21 Bellah, *Habits of the Heart,* p. 37.

22 de Tocqueville, *Democracy in America,* p. 510.

23 Huston Smith, as part of an authors' dialogue held at the Fetzer Institute, June 22–24, 2002.

24 Stephen R. Covey, *The Seven Habits of Highly Effective People: Restoring the Character Ethic* (New York: Simon & Schuster, 1989).

25 Jacob Needleman, address at the Library of Congress, Jan. 29, 2003.

26 Vincent Harding, as part of an authors' dialogue held at the Fetzer
    Institute, June 6–9, 2004.

PART ONE

LOOKING AND LISTENING FOR AMERICA

TWO DREAMS OF AMERICA

Jacob Needleman

1. Statement of the Question

BOTH IN ITS EVERYDAY usage and in its etymology, the word *dream* includes two radically opposed meanings and points in two radically opposed directions of human life. A dream is a vision of truth, of what can be and ought to be; it shapes our fundamental intention and purpose; it calls us to the life we are meant to live and the good we are meant to serve. Such is Jacob's dream (Genesis 28) in which he is given to see the entire cosmic order with God above commanding and promising him the fullness of a sacred life on earth.

And a dream is a deception, a night creature of mere seeming; or a daylight phantom that draws us away from the reality of the present moment, idling the engines of our psyche and spirit in imagined pleasures or terrors. Worse yet, a dream is an illusion masquerading as a vision, as when we say of someone that his or her goals are "only a dream." Not only individuals, but groups and collectivities, including nations and even whole civilizations, may come under the sway of such dreams. History offers many examples—too many. We need only look at the bloody tracks of our era's dreams of national, racial, or religious superiority; or its sometimes hypnotic submission to economic and scientific ideologies—all fueled by the suggestibility of the crowd. And if we turn further back in history or look toward other cultures throughout the world, we will be astonished at the spectacle of the fantastic dreams that have dominated the minds of the peoples of the earth, dreams that lie at the root of the universal plague of war.

Then, what of the American dream? Is it a vision or an illusion? Do we need to deepen this dream or awaken from it?

Can anyone doubt the importance of this question? In one form or another, it is a question that has been gathering strength for decades, and it now stands squarely in the path not only of every American, but, such is the planetary influence of America, of every man and woman in the world. What really *is* America? What does America *mean*?

To think well and truly about this question, we need to relate it to the deepest inner questions that mankind can ask. Because, in our bones, we know this is no longer—if, in fact, it ever was—only an external issue, unrelated to our inmost yearning to understand the sense and purpose of human life itself, the sense and purpose of our own life and death. In our bones, we know that we do not wish to feed on illusions either of a "patriotism" that sets us against or above the rest of the human race, or a "realism" that denies the ideals of America, ideals which in their essence reflect something of what can be called the universal, eternal vision of what it means to be *fully human*.

Deep within ourselves we know we do not wish to dream our life away; we wish for truth, not "truth"; we wish for freedom, not "freedom"; we wish for an independence that enables us to serve and obey what is greater than ourselves, not an "independence" that is little more than an adolescent fantasy of power or a nightmarish cosmic isolation. Truth, freedom, independence: yes, these are among our most treasured American values, but America did not invent them. Their source lies far back in time, deep within the heart and spirit of mankind's great spiritual traditions. It is America, however, that once brought hope to the world by injecting these values into the lifeblood of modern society.

Even to begin to put our question in these terms, undefined as they yet may be, is to be thrown a lifeline. Can we take hold of it? Can we ponder what it really means that the values we associate with America originally reflected aspects of an ancient, timeless wisdom?—that it is in this context that we may rediscover the American dream considered as a vision of truth? And yet, at the same time, can we recognize that at any moment the place of these values may be invaded by counterfeits bearing the same names and wearing the same colors? How to understand that in order to deepen the American dream, it is first of all necessary to awaken from the American dream?

In order to remember the vision of America, we need to free ourselves from the illusion of America. This will require of us at least an honest, first-hand approach to the inner, *metaphysical* dimension of our American values—for it is in this dimension that the vision is rooted. And it is this dimension that it is necessary to recover and hold onto. Without it, the vision inevitably decays into illusion: ideas and words that were once life-giving and full of hope inevitably become fantasies that mask our ignorance of ourselves and of the kind of work that is actually required of us.

At the same time, it will be necessary to keep our feet on the ground and try to bear in mind what nations really are, including America, and in what rough-and-tumble world they are obliged to act. Without including this element in our inquiry, we run the risk of falling prey to another kind of illusion: a misplaced spirituality that regards nations as though they were persons, and which holds the American nation to standards of behavior that we ourselves, as individuals, do not and—as we are—cannot live up to. Or, what is equally fantastic, which regards America as a holy community obliged to act selflessly and meekly in the jungle of the world it lives in—like a community of saints or spiritual aspirants. At the same time, in order to face this whole issue squarely, we will have to consider that a genuine spiritual community cannot exist in the world as we know it apart from a larger environment of favorable political and social conditions. And, considering this, we may come to the conclusion that one of the great purposes of the American nation is to shelter and guard the rights of all men and women to seek the conditions and the companions necessary for the inner search.

2. The Two Dreams of America

It is tempting to take the next step of our inquiry by making a sharp and sharply judgmental distinction between the materialist and the idealist goals of the American people. The "American dream" in its familiar, cliché-ridden forms could then safely be relegated to the realm of illusion or, at least, superficiality. We all know the words associated with this version of the dream: wealth, success, unlimited social and entrepreneurial mobility, material comfort—even to the point of specifying some of the exact economic parameters: a house of one's own, maybe two nice cars, two nice, well-educated children, and so on. One would certainly wish to deepen this version of the dream by turning to the ideals of brotherhood, equality, and the Bill of Rights. But, in the last analysis, so a critic might suggest, these ideals themselves have now become largely instrumental—so many means for securing material gain and for lubricating the machinery of American capitalism. What were once moral principles, considered as ultimate ends, for which material security was but a means, have been turned around to become tools of the American illusion of materialist happiness.

There is an obvious truth in this view, and in a sense it is one of the most fundamental criticisms that can be made of the American dream. But we must proceed with caution. To distinguish between the two dreams of America, the illusion and the vision, may not be so simple a matter as to label the one materialistic and the other spiritual or ethical. Certainly, the great wisdom teachings of the world invite us to think more carefully about this distinction than many of us are prone to do.

To illustrate the need for a more careful examination of this distinction, and by way of introducing into our discussion some necessary aspects of the world's wisdom traditions, I would like to call upon two immigrants to America, both men of exceptional education and acumen. The first, Dr. Carlo Brumat, is Italian by birth, trained in science and business management, a man of phenomenal cultural breadth and academic expertise cutting across science, mathematics, the humanities, and the social sciences. I had come to know him when he was the visionary dean of an innovative school of business leadership in Monterrey, Mexico. The second is Ghulam Taymuree, formerly professor of technological engineering at Kabul University. He and his family left Afghanistan for America just after the Soviet invasion in 1981 and now, with his brothers, he runs a successful automobile repair business in Oakland, California.

Dr. Brumat is a tall, powerfully built man in his sixties, a modern Renaissance man if ever there was one. Educated in physics and mathematics at UCLA, he lived for many years in America and speaks and—if one may say it—thinks and feels almost like an American. Except when he is speaking his native Italian, when his Americanness is completely absorbed into the being of a pure northern Italian; or when he is speaking flawless Spanish, French, German, when he becomes a uniquely cosmopolitan and gracious Mexican, Parisian, or German. His voice is strong and warm, but it can hardly keep up with the speed of his mental associations and the vigor of his physical gestures.

In almost every respect, Ghulam Taymuree seems the exact opposite of Carlo Brumat, not only physically and in his personality, but in his relationship to the American dream. Slightly built and soft-spoken, he stays contained in his own atmosphere, and he gestures not with his arms or hands, but only with his clear, dark eyes.

Taken together, these two men, both of whom love America (although Dr. Brumat might resist this characterization), articulate and even incarnate what it is necessary for us to understand about the American dream as both vision and illusion.

Carlo Brumat

On Saturday, March 20, 2001, in Monterrey, Mexico, Dr. Brumat and I were seated in front of a large-screen television waiting for the inauguration of George W. Bush. We were good-naturedly arguing about America, as we often did, but now more intensely than usual as the noon hour in Washington approached.

After the inaugural speech was finished and as Dr. Brumat and I sat down to lunch, I remarked to him how both our attitudes had changed midway through the speech. We had both been laughing at this or that, anticipating some of the President's notorious gaffes or malapropisms when, at a certain moment, we both sat up a little straighter and began to pay serious attention.

"What was it that suddenly interested you?" I asked. "We were both surprised by the speech; it was much better than either of us expected, wasn't it?"

"Yes," he said, "I thought the speech was effective—except, of course, for those parts that seemed to imply that freedom and liberty are an American monopoly. That irritated me, because it is actually wrong and stupid, historically and anthropologically."

He went on:

"Americans don't seem to know their own history. If you go back to Jefferson, for example, you can clearly see the sources from which he received his ideas. These aspirations—freedom, liberty—are aspirations of the human animal; they are universal, or nearly so. So why do Americans believe they have invented them?

"But, what I liked about the speech was that he tried to convey a more balanced ethos, bringing in the community and the ideal of compassion, and not hitting so hard on the individualistic ethos, which is said to be one of the characteristics of the American—I mean, Americans are supposed to be individuals who think for themselves. By the way, I would say that is a great illusion. I find Americans, on the average, the least politicized and hence the most easily manipulated individuals that I have ever met—certainly, more so than any European that I can think of."

He paused for a moment, scanning my face, and then continued:

"On the other hand, I think the individual American, if you abstract from his naïveté, is, well generally, *nicer* than the average European. As a neighbor, it's probably better to have an American neighbor; he will come over when you arrive there—that was my experience, and I know many others who have experienced the same thing. They would come and say, is there anything I can do to help you; and they would actually mean it. This I ascribe partly to the experience of the frontier. From the very beginning, the vast openness of the frontier has deeply shaped the American character. You went where few people were, and you had to rely on each other and help each other. So, I would say that, as individuals, Americans tend to be nicer. Not as deep, sometimes, but what stands out is the *good will* of the average American.

"It's America as a corporate entity that constitutes the problem. To a large extent, it's the frontier mentality again, but on a corporate scale, where it eventually becomes destructive. Almost from the very beginning, the need and the possibility of constant expansion defined America economically, socially, and politically—as well as psychologically on an individual basis.

"Frederick Jackson Turner saw this very clearly.[1] He showed that America was a society needing constant expansion. And now this constant expansion can only be gained by intruding into the lives of other people—into their countries, sometimes in a purely territorial sense, but also economically through the American form of capitalism, and into the minds of other peoples, through the media . . ."

There followed a discussion of other forms of capitalism, such as the so-called "Rhine model" in Germany, that, according to Brumat, are more socially stable and contained. The American version, however, is now dominating the world. Germany, for example, is being forced by the conditions created by America to abandon its more moderated form of corporate capitalism.

"This is one of the main features of what is called globalization. America is imposing the rules and other countries, in order to stay competitive, have to play by these rules, which ultimately means surrendering aspects of their culture that make them less 'efficient' than the workaholic American society." He compared this worldwide phenomenon to how the ancient Athenians for a short while dominated their world, citing Thucydides in the famous passage from the Melian Dialogue. In the year 421 B.C. sharply militant factions came to power in Athens and initiated an expansionistic, imperialistic policy. An expedition was sent to annex the neutral Dorian island of Melos.

"In that passage, as you know, the inhabitants of the island refuse to join Athens. They want to remain neutral in the war between Athens and Sparta and they say, 'But, we'll fight you if we have to, and we think the gods will be on our side because ours is the just cause.'

"And you know what the Athenian ambassador says to this?" Brumat's shoulders rose and his hands opened upward in the universal Mediterranean gesture of disingenuousness: "The Athenian says: 'Well, it's your privilege to fight of course. But you already know what's going to happen if you do try to fight us. And, as far as we're concerned, we don't think the gods are more likely to be on your side than on our side. Because, from what we know and have observed, the same law rules among the gods as down here.'"

He paused for a moment, his lips curled in a devilish smile:

"'And the law is simple,' the Athenian says: '*the strong exact what they can and the weak yield what they must.*'"

We both laughed, but my laughter was a bit forced. I couldn't let the matter end there. That could not be all there was to Dr. Brumat's attitude toward America. He was too much of an American himself. Also, I knew him well enough to know that however aggressively he made his points, he was always surprisingly open to opposing views. I felt, perhaps foolishly or jingoistically, that the European in him asserted, but the American listened. Over the years, all our arguments about America had led me to the conviction that he was at least as idealistic about America as I was, but that in a certain way, he was personally *hurt* by what he saw as America's crimes and betrayals of its own ideals—almost like a disappointed lover.

"All right," I said, finally, "let me ask you a simple question. What does America *mean* to you? What does it stand for? As an ideal? How do you look at the fact America was once—and for many people still is—the hope of the world, with its ideals of freedom and liberty?"

He replied very quickly, and sharply:

"Well, I think, by actual observation, in actual *fact,* America is the land of the *economic* refugees of the world.

"Certainly, in some cases, but by no means the majority, it has also been the home, the last refuge, the shelter, of the religiously or politically persecuted—like the Jews in Europe or some from Asia and other countries, and, obviously, in its origins, the religiously persecuted from England. But for the legions of Latin Americans, southern Italians and Poles, and so on, who have gone to America, and who keep going to America, I don't think they give a damn about the symbols of freedom and democracy, and so on. They don't even believe that, in terms of these things, America offers them anything more than they could find at home. That doesn't really come into their minds. *But they are sure that in America they can get a better material life.* That's my sense.

"And in all my observations—not a huge sample, maybe a hundred or so immigrants from different countries—I never once heard anyone praising American liberty and democracy or such things. I always heard people saying, 'You know, here in America I have a Lincoln Continental, I have a swimming pool—you think I could have had this sort of thing in Naples? Certainly not!'

"Not once, not even one person ever said anything like 'I have come here because this is the land of freedom.' Not once did I ever hear that. And so, generalizing from this negative result, based on a small sample, I would say simply that most people come to America seeking only a better material life. And it's not just material *things* that they want; it's the whole 'social clarity,' so to say, of the materialism that permeates American culture, where everyone says 'How much is he worth? How much are you worth?' This is not a sentence you would hear in any other language. Americans don't want to hear, 'I'm a virtuous man, I'm self-realized, I'm very much aware of myself, I know myself.' No, they want to hear how many million dollars you have in the bank.

"The American dream? You know, in America the possibility of getting rich is very real, relatively easy. Not that everyone makes it, of course, but the very possibility—and all the new wealth that results from it—constitutes a constant reminder for everyone that they can and should try. So, there is constantly this focus on striving and trying to achieve. In other countries, where the socio-economic stratification has long been more rigid, people come to accept their station in life more easily. . . ."

The conversation led through many qualifications about America and about the values of other nations and cultures. I agreed that many, if not most, immigrants had always come to America for economic reasons, but it seemed to me that, whatever their motives, they bring youth, vitality, difference. They create a flow in and out of our borders that is an essential element in America's feeling of youth and vastness—the openness of its spaces and its economy. And as for American capitalism, it will probably never be tempered by European-style capitalism. I proposed that the economic and physical spaciousness of America is a metaphor for the spiritual and experiential spaciousness that foreigners also encounter in it. We are the land of the misfit; people travel in and out of our borders, and crisscross our enormous nation looking to become themselves. They think they are finding swimming pools, but they are feeding something in our nation, contributing to a renewing flow that we live within. They bring balance—as well as the renewal of American values due to their often strong ethical and family traditions. Even the most materialistic of these immigrants sooner or later may began to sense, maybe not even consciously, something deeper about what America was meant to stand for.

In any case, by the time our discussion ended, we had reached what was for me a remarkable and unexpected opening to the visionary aspect of the American dream. And it came from the lips of Dr. Brumat himself.

But first we need to hear from Ghulam Taymuree.

Ghulam Taymuree

My first serious conversation with Ghulam Taymuree took place at his automobile repair shop some ten days after September 11. Up until then our exchanges were mainly about my car, and only incidentally about his interest in philosophy and spiritual ideas. However, I always came away from him feeling I had been with a man of uncommon depth. And as far as his acquaintance with philosophy is concerned, the range and sophistication of the books that jammed his office and crowded his desk could give points to the personal library of any established scholar in the field.

The San Francisco Bay Area is home to the nation's largest population of Afghan immigrants, and after September 11 there had been stories of mindless attacks on Afghan businesses and storekeepers. My wife and I went to visit him and his brothers at their shop in order to see how they were and to show support for them. We were relieved to see that all was well, and as we were returning to our car, Mr. Taymuree started spontaneously to speak to us about America. We stopped and listened to him for a long time without interrupting, astonished at the depth and quiet power of his feeling for America and what it means. A few weeks later, I returned for the express purpose of listening to him further.

With consummate courtesy he led me up the stairs to his office, an austerely furnished private room from which I was looking down through a large window at the repair shop below, without hearing much of the noise. Once or twice during the conversation we were interrupted by one of his brothers putting to him some question or other in their native Dari, but apart from that, and apart from my being always peripherally aware of the bustling activity below, the room was like a sanctuary.

He began by speaking of his life before emigrating to America. He grew up in a small, "primitive" village seventy miles north of Kabul along the one road that connected Kabul to northern Afghanistan. He spoke of the elders who governed the village, the orchards, the "schoolroom" that was nothing more than a cave or else only a space under a tree—and how, by a stroke of chance, he happened to come in contact with the first American ever to spend a night in an Afghan village. The American—"someone from the embassy"—was passing through on his way to Bamiyan to see the Buddhist statues that were later destroyed by the Taliban.

"The American happened to leave behind a pamphlet—whether accidentally or intentionally I don't know—that had on it the words, 'government of the people, by the people and for the people.' I was fourteen or fifteen years old and I remember staring at those words, sensing that there was something very important in them. But I could not understand it. How could it be? I was a subject—we were all subjects under a king. I could not make out the meaning of those words."

When he was twenty years old, his intellectual abilities brought him a special scholarship enabling him to study in America.

"So I came to America for the first time in 1954. It was in America that I first sensed what it means to be an individual, what it means to be free, what it means to have the possibility of making your own choice. Of course, I did not understand it fully then—the contrast was so great between Afghanistan and America; but I could see that difference in each particular person and in their movement. I mean by movement that you could go anyplace, night or day. Of course, these are things that every American takes for granted. Americans take it all for granted. They just do what they want and go where they want. They don't really feel what it means. But I was astonished. I was deeply astonished."

I asked Mr. Taymuree to explain more about what this freedom of movement means to him. After thinking for a moment, he surprised me by connecting what he called America's "freedom of movement" with the mind, with a certain *energy* of the human psyche. He made this connection by telling me about the first philosophy classes he took in the United States.

"I found the key there that opens the door to humanness, to full humanness. The uncaptured, the *siege* idea."

I looked at him, puzzled. He repeated himself: "The *siege* idea."

"*Seed*?" I asked. I had no idea what he was talking about.

"Siege," he said, "not captured yet. Siege."

"Ah! You mean as in an attack, a siege upon a city or a castle."

"Yes," he answered, "the mind, the thinking, the searching that is not yet captured. When it is captured, it becomes something defined, it becomes science, it becomes this or that, it becomes practical disciplines, technology, whatever."

He leaned forward, as it were, with his eyes.

"But *before* that, it is pure *movement*. . . . You could call it vision . . . a grasping toward the whole scheme of creation . . . the attraction toward Being—that is what I understood from philosophy: what lies inside, deep inside the mind of man—*that's* the thing, that's the sacred essence of the mind of man, that's the movement of freedom."

At that point, without any suggestion of abruptness, he turned the conversation in another direction.

"When I came to this country, I had already read everything I could about the history of my own country, about Islam in all its aspects, and I had read a great deal about Christianity, Judaism—all that. But in America I found what was, to my mind, the quintessential statement about humanness in the sacred document framed by the Founding Fathers of the United States. To my mind, I think they have gone into the depths of history with an unparalleled vision and understanding. There—throughout history—they saw the facts, the strata, of humanness appearing here and there and then disappearing. Like geologists, like anthropologists, the Founding Fathers (certainly drawing also on Locke and others from England)—they had apprehended all this and put it in a frame, under a single proposition . . ." He paused for a moment and said in a passionate whisper: "'Life, liberty and the pursuit of happiness.'"

The quiet way he spoke, the flame in his eyes, his vibrantly still, small body seeming to gather light all around him, made this single phrase—so familiar, so cliché-ridden for most of us—suddenly spring to life. I think I can say I actually *heard* it for the first time. And I began to realize that to deepen the American dream meant to hear it, feel it in a deeper part of oneself! It was not simply a matter of new insights exactly, or of connecting American values with the formulations of the ancient wisdom teachings. Or, rather, yes, it *was* necessary to bring new language and new wisdom into the statement of American ideas, but only for the purpose of allowing them to enter into us more deeply. And, of course, it is this process of offering conditions under which men and women can listen to truth, which lies at the real root of the methods and formulations of the great practical spiritual traditions, and which has been lost in the modern world. True esotericism is nothing if it is not a way of communicating truth that enables it to be heard and freely accepted in the depth of man's heart and mind. This is the compassion of great wisdom, without which it can actually set human beings against each other under the angry light of self-righteousness, no matter how exquisitely articulated it may be. All of which is only to say that deepening the American dream and awakening from the American dream converge beyond the horizon: it means to rescue the idea of America from its "capture" at the surface of our selves, where we are lost in imagination, and to let it enter once again into the truer self that is always calling to us.

Mr. Taymuree continued:

"Life, liberty and the pursuit of happiness—unalienable rights. This is not just the American dream, it's the dream of all human beings. But this *unalienable* right—this right can quickly be taken away, in all of history it has so often been taken away."

Again, he paused, his body perfectly still, his eyes glowing.

"The first one, *life:* not biological life, yes it can be taken away, but it appears again from here and there and there . . . but the second part of the proposition, *liberty:* the whole of our humanness, the whole of what distinguishes us from animals, all our separation from natural life. Liberty, to me, *includes* freedom of choice, political freedom, moral freedom—well, all of that is in its essence, in its reality, when it is real, when it is not just words, when it is deep—it is of the essence of the human mind, the human soul, the uncaptured mind. All *that* is very vulnerable, delicate, fragile, difficult to preserve—like an orchid, it needs certain conditions, a certain ambience, very, very precise conditions, so fragile that if we do *anything,* if we change *any* little bit of it—well, it's like the wing of an eagle: even if you cut even a little part of that wing, you limit the height that the eagle can fly.

"I realized that after the Soviet invasion and before coming to America I had become a kind of zombie. What do I mean by that? I mean that I had become deprived of the freedom of the mind, the freedom of imagination. For someone like myself who comes to America this is a new discovery, this is infinitely precious, this is sacred. I have lived through the history of governments—monarchy, communism; I've witnessed many atrocities; I've been caught in cross fires; I've seen children destroyed; I've seen homes destroyed. I've experienced all of it.

"But what may be the most difficult thing for Americans to understand is that we could not trust ourselves to speak our mind, and finally not even to think. We acquired a robotic nature, we were deprived of what makes us human beings, fully human beings.

"That is what America gives—the possibility of becoming full human beings. That is why I came here; I see that here my grandchildren have the possibility of realizing their humanity."

3. Deepening "the Pursuit of Happiness"

The key to our question is here before us: *to deepen the American dream it is necessary to deepen our understanding of "life, liberty and the pursuit of happiness."* We need to hear it again as though for the first time, not just once, but permanently. We need to become "as little children" in front of such ideas, to become as men and women who have never heard it before, who have lived their lives in subjection to a despotism of the mind and heart, in which freedom as an *inner fact,* and not just as a word or concept, is actually an unknown reality—not political freedom only, but metaphysical freedom, the opening to the uncaptured mind. To experience this reality it is necessary to awaken to a part of the psyche that sees and feels truth directly and sees and feels the good directly—from within our inmost self, the real self that is a particle of the great Self that the Founders sometimes called "the God of Nature and of Man," and which is accessible to us through the activity of what they called *Reason*.

Here let us proceed cautiously. We are trying to approach what may be for us an entirely new understanding of the idea of America, but one which, when we really can hear it, may also strike us as mysteriously familiar, as something we of course knew all along, but have somehow and somewhere mysteriously and tragically forgotten—just as we have mysteriously and tragically forgotten what we really are. We are speaking of *the sleep of America* as an echo of the sleep of man—and of the dreams that visit us in that sleep and which keep us from awakening, as individuals first and then as a society.

We are trying to discover precisely why the pursuit of happiness has decayed; why it has passed from a vision into a phantasm—and even into a nightmare—and what, precisely, is required of us in order to awaken from the fantasy, not just in words, but as a concretely lived fact. We are going to discover that the vision of the Founders may be seen as rooted in an astonishing and timeless truth about man: namely, that *the essence of man is happiness and love* and that this essence is meant to serve the highest reality (call it "God") by serving one's neighbor. In a word, human happiness is literally—*chemically*—inseparable from caring for others. Man is built to serve, he is built to give. Anything pointing away from that truth is, for man, the path to "hell." And anything approaching it is the path to "heaven."

This is an ancient doctrine reaching far, far back into the roots of all wisdom and revelation: the essential self of man in all its uncaptured freedom and energy radiates compassion and devotion and moral power. The fall of man, his "ignorance" or—in Western terms—his "sin," covers over this intrinsic goodness to the point that the human condition seems hopeless. But however hopeless it seems, the truth is that there is, as Jefferson and the greatest philosophers of the Enlightenment saw, an uncorrupted core in the human essence, uncorrupted and uncorruptible—it is "the substance of the divinity" and hence a diamond stronger than any force "under the sun." But it is so covered over, so encrusted with illusion and violent fear, so imprisoned by the resisting forces of the world's egoism ("evil"), that man, to all appearances, and even for all practical purposes, seems no more than (in Emerson's phrase) "a god in ruins" or, perhaps worse, a tortured fruit of animal evolution possessing and possessed by an enormous and dysfunctional brain.

To put it in its simplest terms: the authentic pursuit of happiness is the pursuit neither of physical nor social pleasure, nor of both together. Happiness for man consists in serving the good, which means awakening to that in oneself which can freely obey a higher law and translate it into action for the welfare of others. Such awakening is in itself a joy *beyond the pleasure principle,* compared to which what is usually called happiness is actually a disguised form of anguish, the tortured "happiness" of alternating craving and surfeit that characterizes the uneducated physical body and the unmastered egoism of our illusory sense of self.

⚬◐) (◑⚬

Lest it be objected that we are trying to import alien ideas into the thought of the Founders, we need now to take a passing glance at how Jefferson and the philosophy of the Enlightenment that he drew upon spoke of human happiness. It may be that some of us will find the language of the Enlightenment overfamiliar or perhaps even sterile, due largely to a political and academic "colonization" that has sealed off its potential spiritual resonance. This sense of overfamiliarity of the founding language of America is surely a sign of how far the American dream (vision) of Jefferson and the Founders has decayed into the American dream (illusion) of happiness as sharply characterized by our Dr. Brumat—the new car, the new house, the status, and all that goes with it—the vulgarity, the images of violence we feed our children and ourselves, the endless acceleration of buying and selling that permeates our every day and hour and steals from us the lived reality of time itself. We need to retrieve the life of this language that has shaped so much that is good in America.

We need to liberate the American philosophical language. We are not going to permit the Founders' words to remain static or to be understood simply in the old way that has bred such philosophical and existential decay. We are going to let their words breathe new life and sound new (and deeply ancient) echoes of the great vision of what man is and can become. But to move in this direction, we need, above all, to remember that *we cannot perceive Truth with the false part of ourselves.* This is the great lesson that we must take from our own immigrant heart, our Ghulam Taymuree: it is only from beneath the surface of ourselves that we can see, sense, and feel what lies beneath the surface of the American dream.

"Only the real can perceive the real."

Here, then, is Jefferson articulating the ancient teaching of the convergence of happiness and virtue. Listen first to his characterization of moral sentiment, or conscience, as intrinsic to the structure of human nature:

> The moral sense, or conscience, is as much a part of man as his leg or arm. It is given to all human beings in a stronger or weaker degree, as force of members is given them in a greater or less degree. It may be strengthened by exercise, as may any particular limb of the body. This sense is submitted, indeed, in some degree, to the guidance of reason; but it is small stock which is required for this: even a less one than what we call common sense. State a moral case to a ploughman and a professor. The former will decide it as well, and often better than the latter, because he has not been led astray by artificial rules. In this branch, therefore, read good books, because they will encourage, as well as direct your feelings.[2]

Conscience, then, is not a socially conditioned power, although conditions of the social order can either obstruct or support its action in the individual. Conscience is inborn, but we can and must work to "strengthen" it—that is, to allow it to be heard. Such thoughts cannot but remind us of the age-old teaching that it is obedience to conscience that constitutes true human happiness. But, there is more. It is also obedience to conscience that constitutes true human freedom. Here is Jefferson commenting on the education of children in *Notes on the State of Virginia*:

> The first elements of morality . . . may be instilled in their minds; such as, when further developed as their judgments advance in strength, may teach them how to work out their own greatest happiness, by shewing them that it does not depend on the condition of life in which chance has placed them, but is always the result of a good conscience, good health, occupation, and freedom in all just pursuits.[3]

As Allen Jayne points out in his excellent study of the Declaration of Independence, "by defining freedom as 'freedom in all just pursuits . . . ,' Jefferson was emphasizing that freedom was license to do not anything at all to attain one's 'greatest happiness' but only what was consistent with the moral sense of justice."[4]

In this vein, it is important to note, as Jayne also points out, that the philosophers of the Scottish Enlightenment (Frances Hutcheson and Lord

Kames being chief among them) stressed just this same vision of the convergence of "moral sense" and individual, human happiness. And it was, apparently, just these philosophers who, along with Locke and Bolingbroke, exercised the greatest philosophical influence upon Jefferson as he drafted the Declaration of Independence. Referring, perhaps, to what he had learned from his much admired Scottish mentors and drawing, certainly, on his readings in the literature of antiquity and his own reflections, he writes: "And if the Wise be the happy man, as these sages say, he must be virtuous too; *for, without virtue, happiness cannot be.*"[5]

And further: "We believed . . . that man was a rational animal, endowed by nature with rights and with an innate sense of justice; and that he could be restrained from wrong and protected in right, by moderate powers confided to persons of his own choice, and held to their duties by dependence on their own will."[6]

The sociopolitical implications of this view of the convergent relationship between happiness, virtue and the ultimate authority of innate individual "moral sense," and democracy are, of course, immense. It is the philosophical and anthropological ground upon which America bases its rejection of the imposed political, intellectual, and spiritual authority of monarchs and priests of all kinds. But it is a view that is also fraught with peril. Is it a license for individual subjectivism and, ultimately, relativism in our ethical, mental, and social life? Is it an invitation for the authority of the herd?—the "morality" conditioned mainly by external suggestion (for example, the psychoanalytic "super-ego"), the pseudoconscience manipulated by demagogy, dogma, or media; the mass morality, the mass vulgarity, and, finally, the mass prejudice, fear, and violence that is, of all causal agencies within human nature, surely the chief cause of the horrors of war?

Is all of this what necessarily follows from affirming the primacy of individual conscience in the conduct of life? Certainly not—and to regard it in this way would be to degrade the American vision of the primacy of conscience into a dangerous illusion. It would be to assume that conscience is simply a 24-carat word for whatever we happen to feel is good or bad, which in turn becomes whatever we happen to like or dislike, no matter what the source, inner or outer, of these impulses. And such a view, when rendered more sophisticated by refined philosophical technique or *a priori* political agendas of one kind or another, degrades the idea of conscience into the fundamental human illusion of moral self-righteousness—in Judeo-Christian terms, *pride;* in the language of the East, *ignorance.* And this is to deny the heart of all the great wisdom teachings of the world and also our own moral common sense. But, it should be added, it is also to step onto ground that is close to if not in certain respects identical with much of what is now known as postmodernism or deconstructionism which, without authentic metaphysical *reconstructionism*, leaves us in a wasteland of subjective indeterminism, that is, the intellectual and moral dream (illusion) that freedom equals obeying *no* objective laws. In fact, this condition of "freedom" as absence of submission to objectively higher laws is precisely the chaos that is referred to, among other meanings, in the beginning of the book of Genesis, where the earth is "without form and void." The Hebrew words here are *tohu v'bohu,* which, translated, means also "confused and bewildered."

It is clear that we cannot let the idea that conscience is the source of happiness and freedom stand alone by itself, *unprotected.* Left alone, without carrying it to its natural home among the great ideas of the world's wisdom, it is easy prey for capture and abduction to the land of dreams and illusion. We need to understand that, man being what he is, contact with conscience is as rare and difficult as it is essential to our humanness. Not even the necessary context of great ideas is in itself enough to protect us from dreaming we are obeying the good when in fact we are existentially asleep to the voices that are calling to us from within, the *daimon* of Socrates, the inner *prophetic voice* of the Old and New Testaments and the Koran.

꯭꯭꯭ ꯭꯭꯭

In order to penetrate beneath the surface of the American dream of the pursuit of happiness, we need to look at our origins with new eyes and with a completely open heart, with a spiritual need that is also respectfully aware of the great wisdom traditions that have guided humanity throughout the millennia. With this aim in mind, the aim of simultaneously deepening and awakening from the American dream, we need to look again at the writings and statements not only of Jefferson, but of all the founders of America—including, of necessity, those who serve as the nation's metaphysical founders, regardless of chronology. We are speaking of not only such figures as Washington, Franklin, Adams, and Madison, but of those whose words and spirit have entered into our blood and marrow from a realm and an *origin* above history: Lincoln, Frederick Douglass, Sojourner Truth, the vast entirety of the American Indian culture, including the greatness of its vision of government (for example, the Iroquois constitution) and the pure *being* of the men and women who were its chiefs and counselors—and this is not to mention countless other men and women—some who are already world-historical names, such as Martin Luther King Jr. and others who have been nearly forgotten, whose lives and actions are waiting in the wings of American history, waiting to be summoned as *personae* and icons in the new, awakening story of America.

4. The Hope of the World

If we look in this way at our origins, from this kind of inner wish for our country, our neighbor, and ourselves, we may begin to see with new eyes why America once was the hope of the world and why it may still be the hope of the world. We may understand anew that all of America's physical and economic strength and its inspired form of government and law still offer the world the broad social conditions that allow men and women freely to search for truth within themselves, which means, first and foremost, to struggle for the awakening of conscience and the power to love. This and this alone constitutes the inner essence of the American dream of "life, liberty and the pursuit of happiness." In a word, and to repeat: *the pursuit of happiness does not mean the pursuit of pleasure. It means the pursuit of a life in which one is in touch with that aspect of oneself which alone can bring happiness.*

When we speak of happiness and conscience in this way, we are speaking of the activation in the human presence of entirely new thoughts, feelings, and sensations, carrying an entirely new quality of energy, and connected to the formation within man of an entirely new self or consciousness within the old self—the "new man" or "new birth" of the Christian contemplative tradition; the purification of "trust in God"(*emunah*) in the interior traditions of Judaism; the inner act of submission to Allah at the heart of the practices of Islam (the very definition of which is "submission"); we are speaking of Buddhist compassion (*karuna*); Hindu *ananda* (joy)—the list is long of words and symbols in all the wisdom traditions of the world, pointing to an entirely new state of consciousness that is possible for man, a state characterized by a fusion of objective knowledge, openness to the voice of conscience with the attendant capacity to care for the genuine well-being of one's neighbor and the joy (not "pleasure") of voluntary obedience to a higher reality within and above oneself.

If we honestly consider mankind as it actually is—the state of our world and our own state of being, as it and we actually are—then such an exalted vision of human possibility might well seem desperately remote and itself, if not an illusion, then only an unrealizable goal, however noble. And it is true that throughout history many eloquent expressions of this vision of human possibility have been presented to the world in a fragmentary way, leading people to believe it is a condition of the self that is easily realizable and near to hand. As such, this teaching about man's higher nature has been justly criticized as fantasy—as, for example, Nathaniel Hawthorne bitingly satirized the vision of Emerson and American transcendentalism. It is imperative, therefore, and would be resoundingly "American," if we could discern the practical, experiential evidence for this vision right here and now—in our own lives just as they are and not as we might dream they are or could be.

In fact, the evidence exists right in front of us, in broad daylight, in the form of experiences that are given to almost all of us throughout the course of our lives: the experience of deep wonder, for example, or what we may suffer and directly understand in the confrontation with death, or in the taste of pure joy when we sacrifice what is precious to us for the sake of another. For many of us, we lack only an orientation that would enable us to appreciate the full significance of this evidence. If we but understood all that these experiences tell us about human nature and our own possibilities, it would show not only that every one of us lives most of our life on the surface of ourself, but also that awakening from this dream of life is in fact possible—this life lived on the surface of life, this life of illusion, this life haunted by nightmarish anxieties and hollow daydreams. We would see that not only is awakening possible, but that we have already tasted it—*without knowing it*. We would have before us the experiential basis of metaphysical hope, and the compass point that could direct our search for an inner spiritual struggle within and in the midst of the normal needs, exigencies, and rewards of human life on earth.

In fact, we do have within our own experience the proof that explains why there is no real happiness without real virtue, proof of what America actually offers us and the world insofar as it is a nation that not only allows, but supports and protects freedom of speech, freedom of assembly, freedom of thought, freedom of association, freedom to answer one's authentic physical and social needs, freedom to worship or not worship, freedom, in the metaphysically resonant words of Ghulam Taymuree, to "go anywhere we wish." And, in the end, we must recognize that these political and social freedoms point to the need and possibility to develop within the self the existential capacities that deepen their meaning and transform these freedoms into a concrete force in human life, rather than allowing them to decay into "abducted" concepts that can then be unconsciously manipulated by our egoism, becoming, finally, words that hypnotize us into the manacled dream of "freedom" and the anguished dream of "happiness."

We need to look at these "tastes," these actual experiences we all have had that prove a higher Self exists within us waiting to be allowed into our life. These are glimpses that point us toward the meaning of human life itself and therefore, as a consequence, are essential to the task of deepening our understanding of the vision of America, the idea of America, the hope of America.

We are not necessarily speaking of what are sometimes loosely called "mystical experiences" or of what were once, also loosely, called "peak experiences." We are speaking of the experience of qualities of feeling, sensing, and knowing that could more adequately be termed "impersonal," experiences in which we verify that what the traditions of wisdom tell us is true: I am not my ego—although the ego is part of me; I am not my body—although the body is an essential instrument of the Self; and I am not my thoughts, my logic, my mental associations of information, opinions, and concepts—although all this furniture of the mind is meant to serve (rather than lead) the pursuit of life, liberty, and genuine happiness.

Here are the opening lines of Ralph Waldo Emerson's *The Over-Soul*, the essay rightly regarded as the quintessential expression of his vision of human nature in the universal world:

> There is a difference between one and another hour of life, in their authority and subsequent effect. Our faith comes in moments; our vice is habitual. Yet there is a depth in those brief moments which constrains us to ascribe more reality to them than to all other experiences.

We need to appreciate rightly the *moral* dimension of such moments (it is not for nothing that Emerson speaks of such moments in contrast to "our vice"). In genuinely higher moments we move toward understanding, directly through experience, both our habitual lack of conscience and our potential obedience to conscience. These extraordinary moments are both cognitively and ethically transcendent in that they show us, through experience, that we are in fact beings who can know and see and also *love and will the good.*

If we observe ourselves from this point of view, we will see that all of us have authoritative experiences that can and must be understood as evidence of ourselves as beings in whom knowledge, virtue, and joy are fused—if only a little (a very great "little") and if only for a moment (a very long, even eternal, "moment"). In the experience of deep wonder, for example, looking up sometimes at the night sky or at a leaf or flower, or a detail of the human body, or in the eyes of a loved one, or at the birth of one's child: in such, as it were, common/extraordinary moments, we not only *know* in a new way, we *feel* in a new way. In such moments we are given feeling of a quality that never otherwise enters into our life with all its happy moments of pleasure or satisfaction, with all its triumphs and personal gains, its "fun," its winnings, its prizes, its security and profit, not always even in our satisfaction in providing for our family, and certainly not in the intense "pleasure" of defeating, or imagining the defeat of, our enemy—all, in other words, that constitutes what we may ordinarily call "happiness."

The genuine feeling of wonder is an *impersonal* feeling; it neither affirms nor threatens the ego. It is full of joy that is not "pleasure." But, at the same time, this feeling, this experience, this *state of being* is intensely *moral*. Speaking for myself—and I believe this is true for others as well—I have seen that the state of wonder dissolves all impulses of egoism in a natural way, with no forcing whatever. In this state, for the brief moment that it exists, I see that it is impossible for me to be "offended," to judge another, to hate. In such moments, and in the sense that we are speaking of, I am much closer to being *free*. It is clear that without such experiences and without the work of understanding their significance, our idea of freedom—so central to the values of our society—must inevitably remain truncated and dangerously subject to decay.

But there are other moments which have comparable or even far stronger moral force—also in conjunction with their exceptional cognitive power, offering us knowledge that is inaccessible to us in our state of "habitual vice." In the moment of grief, for example, we are permeated by the depths of sorrow; we are in anguish, we are bereft, we are lost, we are invaded by pain. *But such grief is not negative.* It is not "personal," it is not egoistic. In such moments, even more so, perhaps, than what we have just been speaking of, no one can possibly "hurt our feelings," trouble us, offend us; in such a state it is impossible to hate, it is impossible to seek personal gain. We can even say—and it has been remarked by many—that a man or woman in grief is capable of an astonishing quality of compassion and love. In the midst of such sorrow, one cannot, of course, speak of "joy" in any recognizable way, but one can whisper to oneself, as it were, of a freedom from all imaginary or neurotic suffering and pleasure, an inner emptiness in which the real Self appears and bows its head in sorrow. We have no words for that fusion of knowing and feeling.

In short, in the moment of grief we are one with reality. It is only with the passage of time—sometimes sooner, sometimes later—that the more personal emotions take the place of this impersonal, objective feeling of sorrow and loss. Yes, then, with the passage of time we may feel sometimes unbearable guilt, fear of the future and of loneliness, or the irruption of greed and cunning, or we may feel rage or despair. Such emotions are not easily sectioned off apart from the impersonal feelings that show us another level of selfhood in ourselves. Often such personal emotions are mixed with and fueled by very fine energies and are, in any case, so fundamental that they must be deeply understood and respected (if not "officially approved") as an inescapable element of the human condition. But, speaking in generalities, and in brief, we have before us a human spectrum of emotions, at one end of which are the purely impersonal, nonegoistic feelings that are properties of the Self, while at the other end we see the exclusively egoistic reactions that bring to the world and to our individual lives all its conflict, anxious fear, tension in all its destructive forms, agitation of the mind, envy, suggestibility, and sentimentality.

Again, we are trying to offer recognizable examples of experiences characterized by distinct feelings, thought, and sensations that may be taken as evidence of man's possible inner development. Far more time and space would be needed to "catalog" such experiences and fully to explore what they reveal about the deeper meaning of our values and ideals. These few examples of "inner evidence," by no means the most remarkable, are cited here only to put a little flesh on the idea that the deepening of the American dream cannot take place without deepening both our theoretical understanding, and also our *experience* of ourselves—in a manner that resonates with the spiritual wisdom that is reflected in the original values and ideals brought forth by those who, *throughout our history, even up to the present day,* may rightly be called the Founders of America and of the American dream. And the kind of deepening of the American dream that I am suggesting relates specifically to how we may justifiably extrapolate and expand upon Jefferson's vision of the convergence of virtue and happiness. I am suggesting that there are moments in life when we are given experiences, undeniable experiences, of an entirely new kind and *level* of feeling and knowing (it is always sensed as *new,* no matter how often it may touch us) that shows us, without any doubt whatever, that within ourselves and within each one of us, the Self exists in all its fusion of the capacity to love and the capacity to penetrate into the real world behind the appearances. Acknowledging these moments, reflecting on them, we will come to the conclusion that our first practical need may be ideas and wisdom that can help us in our day-to-day lives to form a truer vision of the structure of the Self, the idea of Man, upon which American democracy and any authentically beneficent social order must be based.

In this context, and again with the aim of illustrating the kind of experience that shows us the contours of the Self behind the "self," I would like to offer one final and especially appealing example brought to me by an adult student in one of my graduate philosophy classes.

The event in question took place in Mexico City just before Christmas. Juan and his five-year-old son were in the living room decorating the

Christmas tree. The doorbell rang and Juan, with his son, went to the door to find a young boy holding his hand out. The boy was about the same age as Juan's son.

In Mexico, as you may know, the general attitude toward begging and beggars is much more accepting than it is here in the United States. People there are not frightened by beggars. Poverty and need are understood as permanent aspects of life and giving to beggars is done every day without any fanfare or artificial sense of righteousness.

Juan told the little boy to wait and returned to the living room. "Give him one of your toys," he said to his son. The boy hesitated and then went to his room while his father patiently waited, all attention. Finally, his young son emerged from the bedroom holding one of his old toys, much the worse for wear. "No," said the father. "Give him your favorite toy."

The young boy stood stock still. After a moment or two, he shook his head no. His father repeated: "Give him your favorite toy." Again his son refused and then began to cry. The father gently, but firmly said again: "Give him your favorite toy."

The little boy very slowly went back to his room and returned holding one of his newest toys. Juan motioned him to go give it to the child waiting at the door. Just as slowly and heavily, the boy walked out of the living room.

A few moments passed. The father had to restrain himself from going to see what was happening at the front door.

Suddenly, Juan's son came bursting into the room, his face radiant. "Papa," he said, "can I do that again?"

I certainly do not wish to gild the lily by overanalyzing this event. I would only point out what seems to me obvious: because of the father's insistence, the child was given the experience of what was for him a completely new kind of feeling—a feeling of personal happiness that was at the same directed solely toward the good of another. He did not feel righteous, he did not feel "altruistic," he did not feel that he would be "repaid" in the long run by God or karma. No, he was simply given the taste of a central aspect of man's essential Self: love.

I am aware that many weightier examples of this inner human capacity could be cited and I do not want to make more of it than it deserves. But neither do I wish to make less of it. Can anyone doubt that this little boy was given a taste of *freedom*? And can anyone deny that the other examples—the experience of genuine wonder, and even, in a deep sense, the moment of grief, as well as the numerous other vertically defined *moments* of our life are also tastes of freedom, not from an outer tyrant, but from an inner tyrant? And who or what is that inner tyrant? What is the struggle and where is the knowledge and what is the nature of the community that can enable a man or woman to work free from that tyranny not for oneself only, but for the sake of one's neighbor? I am saying that the search for this noblest of inner struggles, without which all other ideals of virtue may eventually decay into illusions, requires the protection and support of an outward form of government and social order that is not so common in the tattered and bloody history of the world. I am suggesting that in this direction lies the deep, inner meaning of the hope of America—because it is in this direction that the hope of humanity itself is to be found.

The Guardian at the Door

We are once again with Dr. Carlo Brumat. Our conversation is just now exiting from a long series of indictments of American hypocrisy and arrogance, its foreign policy second to none in self-serving agendas, its economic, military, and cultural imperialism, its coarseness and vulgarity—with sidelong, lingering glances at its technological and scientific creativity, its noble but unrealized ideals, its geographical and world-historical *luck,* its extraordinary capitalistic energy and the simple good will of the politically naïve individual American. We now have nowhere to go but *in*—into philosophy, something we were both waiting for, even if we didn't know it ourselves.

We had come to the question of the nature of virtue itself—which would have seemed a merely academic issue at the beginning of our talk, but which now somehow seemed terribly concrete and practical. I had said something about the whole world seeming now to be more or less losing the sense of the meaning of life itself, partly because of what is called "modernity," of which America was the chief agent. The question of virtue arose from this. "Where is the help?" I said. "Where is the guidance for right living? How do we look at that? Can one seriously believe there is real guidance in the world's religious institutions or in modern science—haven't they become part of the problem, rather than part of the solution? Where can people turn for ideals and direction?" I was not trying to provoke him; I was trying to sum up the place our conversation had come to.

He surprised me by leaning back in his chair and saying, "Well, after all is said about America's failings, I do think that America is a great ideal and more than merely a materialistic ideal. It is the ideal of the pursuit of happiness and that is a very powerful idea. The Europeans may have also had this ideal, but in a personal and implicit sense, not as an articulated creed. This is what the American ideal is telling the world and it is saying that you need certain material conditions that are meant not to be ends in themselves, but the means and the wherewithal to pursue one's happiness."

He paused, and then said, speaking a bit more softly: "The *philosophical* idea of America is the pursuit of happiness. And if you are asking about the real philosophical meaning of that idea, I would certainly say that—at least for me and for many people—it means being in agreement with what the ancient Greeks called your *daimon*—being attuned to your inner voice. For this, of course, you need a certain level of material well-being."

He anticipated my next question by immediately adding, and without his usual gesturing: "But, of course, the inner voice is not there all the time."

"Most of the time . . . ," I started to say.

"It's not there most of the time."

"And so . . ."

"And so . . . ," he continued, "I think the idea is simply to keep searching, because you are not going to find an answer . . . so you just . . ."

"This is really important, isn't it? Is there help for this search? Isn't this what guidance now really could mean? Not moralizing. Not telling us what to do or how to behave or what to think or feel, but helping us understand for ourselves how to search . . .

"To my mind," I continued, sensing that I was beginning to find words to characterize something I deeply felt, but had hitherto been unable to articulate, "this is the new meaning of the art of living. Guidance that is not dogma. Freedom that is not arbitrariness. Principles of living that are not imposed rules. The art of searching . . ."

Brumat interrupted me: "For answers that you are not going to find."

"Maybe you *are* going to find them."

He paused. "Maybe," he said, quietly. "But I haven't."

There was a brief silence, as though we were both looking together at some distant object.

"Is there no such thing as help for the search?" I said.

"Well," he answered, "all the spiritual traditions of the world are out there and maybe they have hit upon the methods—Sufism, for example, which, as you know, I find to be a very agreeable way of thinking."

How far we were from the idea of America! Or were we perhaps only now coming very near to it?

After another pause, I said: "It seems essential to have people with you, companions in the search."

"Yes," he said, "you have to have somebody, not necessarily living now. You can find solace or stimulation, encouragement, by reading past authors."

"But it's not just reading, it's practicing."

"Reading, meditating, practicing, yes . . . and then discussing with other people."

"I think so," I said. "That's part of the search. Now, here is the essential question: are there conditions of social order that allow or even support that search, and others that obstruct it—conditions of tyranny or oppression . . ."

"Like Nazi Germany or Soviet Russia, yes. You need a truly egalitarian society, a condition that allows dialogue."

"Dialogue," I said. "You mean . . . freedom of speech?"

"Freedom of speech . . . and egalitarianism."

"You mean . . . freedom of inquiry? Freedom of thought? Freedom of access to knowledge, not just to become 'smart' and develop new material technologies. Not just to make the trains run on time, but to allow the search for inner truth."

Dr. Brumat was nodding yes.

"But *that* is America!"

"What do you mean?"

"That's near to the original meaning of America. Social order in its metaphysical meaning. It's the deeper meaning of civilization itself."

He was no longer nodding yes. But he was not nodding no either.

"What I'm trying to say is that the American dream, whatever it may have become or will become, is only going to be justified in the long run if it provides conditions that protect this search, that allow men and women to search for their own truth. That's what America is all about, in my opinion, not cars and military power—those things may be necessary as a shield. America as a military and economic power may be necessary as what you could call 'the guardian at the door.' But behind the door, inside the room, something has to be made possible that far transcends the material and physical shield. It's absurd to love the car and the guns and ships, necessary though they may be in the jungle of the world. It's what can go on inside the room that justifies the guardians at the door in the life of nations."

I continued speaking, not really wanting to stop. "At this moment in history, America is the guardian at the door of the spiritual search. Tomorrow, maybe it will be another country, who knows which? Today America is the most powerful country in the world, but it's only going to be allowed to exist if it protects something really precious to mankind and to the earth—which is the search for truth, real truth, not so-called 'truth.' That's what I think."

I waited for Dr. Brumat's response. I was touched when it came:

"I fear, honestly, that most of the leadership of America does not care at all about what you're speaking about."

"Perhaps not, certainly not. But it may not matter, just as it doesn't matter that new immigrants want swimming pools—they still contribute to conditions that make America itself. It's the same with our leaders. Whatever they may believe, they support these same conditions when they support America the powerhouse. The job of our leaders, as leaders of the government, is not to search within, whatever their private life may be. Their job is to protect. Government minds the cup; society fills the cup. What matters is that the cup, and the space inside it, remains.

"All I'm trying to ask is whether there is a way of telling the story of America that reinstates, in new language, its original vision of what it means to search together for our real, essential humanness and what it means for a government to protect that possibility."

"And this search," said Dr. Brumat, "is unlikely ever to come to an end. And, as you also know, it is better to search for the truth than to claim you have found it. This search is something that can keep you going forever, as the main purpose of your life. And, as for happiness, and as for virtue, whatever little progress you feel you have made is enough to fill you with joy . . ."

"Joy and hope . . . ," I said.

"Especially," he said, ". . . especially if you can share it."

". . . and share it . . . ," I repeated the words.

"You see," he then said, "this is fruition without consumption."

We both smiled. "Whereas," he continued, "a great deal of America is about consumption without fruition."

And that was the end of our conversation, apart from my saying, as we got up to leave, "That is beautiful, but this is also the daily bread of Christianity, the truth that you can really share, you can break bread, the loaves and the fishes can be given out—because it's not literally bread they're speaking about, it's truth, it's virtue, it's . . ."

"Love."

"It's love."

NOTES

1 See his groundbreaking essay, "The Significance of the Frontier in American History," in Frederick Jackson Turner, *The Significance of the Frontier in American History* (New York: Ungar, 1963).

2   Jefferson to Peter Carr, 10 August 1787, in Andrew A. Lipscomb and
    Albert Ellery Bergh (eds.), *The Writings of Thomas Jefferson* (Washington,
    D.C.: Thomas Jefferson Memorial Association, 1903), Vol. 6, pp. 257–258.

3   William Peden (ed.), *Notes on the State of Virginia* (New York: Norton,
    1972); cited in Allen Jayne, *Jefferson's Declaration of Independence,*
    (Lexington: University Press of Kentucky, 1998), p. 134.

4   Allen Jayne, *Jefferson's Declaration of Independence* (Lexington:
    University Press of Kentucky, 1998), p. 135.

5   Jefferson to Amos J. Cook, 21 January 1816, in *Writings,* Vol. 14, p. 405,
    emphasis mine.

6   Jefferson to William Johnston, 12 June 1823, in *Writings,* Vol. 15, p. 440.

FOOTPRINTS OF THE SOUL

UNITING SPIRIT WITH ACTION IN THE WORLD

Carolyn T. Brown

MAY YOUR LOVE CONVERT LUCIFER

Even the devil has some good in him.
—St. Anthony

Abba Jacob said: I pray for Lucifer
I rather like him, you know. My moral
theology professor once said God hates Satan.
I said I hope that's not true:
If God hates Satan, God must hate me, too,
because I am a sinner. But God loves me.
If the devil has anything to do with half
the hate and evil that goes on in the world,
as it seems he does, then he is a terrifying being.
On the other hand, his power was broken
by Christ's great gifts of love and life,
and he was created good and beautiful,
and God still loves him.
Why, then, should we hate him?

So I pray for him once in a while,
when I think of it.
I'll bet it makes him
mad as hell.

—Marilyn Nelson[1]

A Quest for the Authentic Life

THE CHALLENGE OF LIVING an authentic life in a dangerous, troubled time is hardly unique to our age. Reflective people through the centuries have struggled to construct a workable interface between the personal and the public and have sought to honor responsibility to family, community, nation, or group while also honoring the inner calling to know and be one's true self. Perhaps in all times, but certainly in our own, the pressure to respond "appropriately" to external imperatives directs us to explicit and clear ends: we know more or less what it means to be a good parent, a good worker, a good citizen, a good consumer, a good whatever. The roles answer and elaborate the physical requirements of sustaining life, creating new life, and organizing in groups to accomplish the first two imperatives. In general, the world cares little about our inner lives as long as we perform our assigned roles reasonably well. And it appears that in a good many cases, we ourselves pay scant attention to our truer selves until something goes visibly awry, until some dissonance of more than accustomed volume insists that we pay attention to an inner life that we scarcely knew we had. We may then go back to religious traditions that we had learned, even if only by rote, to see if some silent, resting wisdom that we had overlooked yet resides there. Or we seek in another's tradition a way of speaking that we can better hear because its language of words and concepts seems fresh to our weary understandings.

Mainstream American culture at the start of the twenty-first century has arrived at such a point of dissonance and unease. The good enemy, the Soviet Union, has been vanquished, and no satisfactory replacement has emerged, terrorism being a bit too shadowy and abstract to fill the void. The gap between rich and poor is growing, at home and abroad, and even the middle is feeling apprehensive about the downward pressure on personal wealth and material aspirations. We are beginning to notice that technology is making us its servants, not the other way around, as we worry about global warming, pollution, insufficient fresh water. The privileged among us contend with the expectations of living in a 24/7 communication nexus, where silence is anathema and doing nothing appears pathological.

There may be other reasons. There may be better reasons. But for whatever reasons, the assertiveness of religious conservatives and the resurgence of interest in ancient wisdom traditions evidence the felt need for new or refurbished road markers that are untainted by current understandings (or misunderstandings). Conservative or traditional versions of familiar religions are on the rise. Words that a few years back would have been unfamiliar to most slip from the tongues of many Americans: mindfulness, Sufi dancing, the desert fathers, the Kabbalah, *vipassana,* sweat lodges, *lectio divina,* and on it goes. Something is afoot.

My own ventures into the terrain of spiritual questing began before it appeared, to me at least, that the country itself might be coming unhinged and instead have been precipitated by small personal disasters that demanded an end to comfortable complacency. Once I began to open my eyes and my spirit, my personal challenges painfully invited me to query the nature of the world I found myself in and my role in creating its realities. Without willing it, by an act of grace uncomfortably imposed, I became a pilgrim.

The surprises along this path have been considerable. Not least among them is that the distinction between inner and outer life now seems an illusion. The emerging view of the planet that we inhabit is that all systems, places, and people are deeply interconnected and that any change to one part reverberates throughout the whole. The earth, that blue marble floating in space, must finally be understood as a single, fragile entity, itself embedded in the system that we call the universe. For purposes of analysis and the power that it yields, it is useful conditionally to see parts as discrete. Nevertheless, the more embracing reality is that within the natural world and the human world all elements are organically related and integral to the whole.

This ecological worldview, as it is often called, is no less true on the smaller scale of our lives as human beings. For each of us, the inner life of the mind and spirit, whether acknowledged or not, is integrally related to our actions in the visible, outer world. There is no escape from this reality. For surely, to quote the title of a wise book by Jon Kabat-Zinn, "wherever you go, there you are," and whoever you are is who you bring into each transaction in the world. Each of our actions bears the footprints of our soul. The two are inextricably fused. Yet clearly this is not self-evident and often does not feel so even to the most introspective of us. It requires examination.

Still, if we understand ourselves to be organic creatures, then no part can be fully disaggregated, for what we do is also who we are, and all elements of the self are interlocked. Perhaps the sense of dissonance and unease arises because we are displeased by the mind and spirit we see ourselves enacting in the world, and when we look at our nation at the start of this new millennium, we are not reassured. Something is amiss. I suspect that we are apprehending a better self waiting to be unburied, some truer, more authentic person than the one we meet in the mirror each morning or see reflected on the television each night. Or perhaps we

recognize that we are multiple selves some one or more of whom is crying for greater presence in the world. We are unsure whether that unheard
voice is devil or angel and have not yet learned or have difficulty remembering that even the devil's message, rightly understood, can hold value
and be transforming.

The seeming gap so many of us experience between who we are and
what we do undoubtedly also testifies to conditions embedded broadly in
the contemporary experience. Even as we struggle to be fully ourselves
and most demandingly to discover who that or they may be, the *zeitgeist*
establishes parameters and limitations. We have available to draw from,
at least in theory, the entire world's intellectual heritage, resources of mind
and spirit beyond what those of other ages could imagine. We would seem
to have less excuse for failure. Still, we are yet creatures of our own time.
Retaining a sense of history should keep us humble even as we recall that
every age, every people, must find a fresh vocabulary for speaking to the
age-old human dilemmas.

The implied "we" may also be a subset of American culture. As I recall,
twenty years ago or so, when deconstruction was becoming the fashion
among mainstream (read "white and male") American literary critics who
were just noticing that cultural presumptions were embedded in the questions they were asking of literature, several African American critics were
bemused and outraged because they had been making the same point,
from the margins of the profession, for years. Only when deconstruction
received a fancy name and became a statement by the mainstream instead
of about the mainstream did it gain currency and, of course, fame and
tenure for its authors. Similarly, then, it may be worth wondering whether
those who speak of the dissonance are speaking for a broad cross section
of Americans or whether "we" are speaking for the experiences of a more
limited group. My guess is that the sense of things out of kilter is widely
felt. I could be mistaken.

In the journey of my own life, the tension between the purported pole
of mind and spirit in contrast to that of service and action, each im-
mensely complex in its own right, has been and remains vexing. I am
a contemplative and closet mystic passing fifty hours a week of my sacred
time on this earth as a "faceless bureaucrat" in a federal agency. Certainly the Library of Congress, where I work, is blessed with a truly noble
mission—to preserve the world's cultural heritage and make it available
now and to future generations—but it is also a structured hierarchy
premised on secular power, and the spiritual, unless well disguised and
in masquerade, must be left at the door. I am hardly unique in struggling
with the tension between the city of man and the city of God in my per-

son and in daily life. Every religious tradition has aimed to provide practical direction for living. Each certainly claims a higher truth, but most likely each arose because living unwisely in a troubled time is a foolishness to avoid at all cost. If you cannot avoid the trouble, you had better find the wisdom.

In my own life, I have found the myths and archetypes of my religious tradition instructive, but also I look to other traditions for sound guidance and insight. If an approach has been tested and found valuable for at least a thousand years—that's my benchmark—then I'm prepared to consider its wisdom. New Age is too new for me. So I measure wisdom against the slow time of the ages, against the myths and archetypes that have continued resonance, against teachings and illuminations that serve as signposts on the journey. Those that have touched me most deeply come out of Christian, early Taoist, and Buddhist conceptual frameworks; from reflections on the hero's journey, so concisely articulated by Joseph Campbell in *The Hero of a Thousand Faces;* from the insights of Carl Jung and the works of the Chinese writer Lu Xun. These have been my lodestones.

My life has been greatly privileged but not without its troubles. The impetus for much that I have learned in this world has come from pain, from my desire to understand its causes and mitigate its impact, from mentors and guides who have loved me with firmness and with gentleness, and from the act of grace that settled in me the desire to know the truth, in the multiple ways that it unfolds, and led me unknowing to the conviction that the truth will set us free—or rather that conditional truths will make us freer than we would have been. And while the particulars of each life are just that, particular to it, the larger meanings sketch a common tale. So what follows tracks this pilgrim's progress so far, the wisdom paid for with pain and reflection and nurtured by love, and some hopes for how greater wholeness might be entered into this conflicted world.

The Hero's Journey: Riches of Mind and Spirit

The biblical story of the fall no doubt derives much of its power from its likeness to the personal loss of childhood experienced by all humans. Born creatures of instinct, as children we experience an undifferentiated world, whether good or bad, where we accept the givens as cosmic norms. Autobiographies in Western literature often depict childhood as a garden peopled by wondrous tokens of the natural world.[2] The most famous depiction of childhood in Chinese culture, the eighteenth-century novel *Dream of the Red Chamber,* similarly employs the garden as the site of childhood. The sense of unchallenged oneness with the world and of time endlessly unfolding without change at some point, gradually or jarringly, becomes an experience of separateness. In contemporary American society, this typically occurs in adolescence with a growing perception that our life extends beyond the family sphere. Emerging sexuality is physical but also a metaphor for the excitement and fearsome nature of discovering our difference.

My own childhood had a garden in it, behind a white colonial house with a white picket fence. I remember billowing clouds in a blue sky, a garden gate that I rode in defiance of the rules, a rose arbor of beauty and scents, an assortment of ants over whom I wielded the power of life and death, and piles upon piles of books to read as I lay in the grass. It was not exactly idyllic, but I was well cared for, well loved, and well protected.

Crossing the Threshold

I remember all too well my own fall. In junior high school I had been "queen" of the class: president of the student government, opening the school day over the public address system. With a buddy I had designed the first installation ceremony for the honor society, an event that we filled with high-minded phrases, candles to represent truth, and such. High school was another matter.

There was, I presume, the generic pain of the age, when one asks, "If I'm more than my parents' child, then who am I?" Certainly for most young people it is a time of high anxiety, a crisis of identity at the moment when the fortunate ones fear that the choice of college will determine success or failure. My particular high school was governed with inexplicable meanness. A friend with a newly broken leg was summarily evicted from the elevator and forced to the steps because he had failed to secure the required elevator pass. The whole atmosphere bore the traces of Simon Legree.

This equal-opportunity persecution was made worse by the confluence of puberty and my discovery that I was black. Of course, I knew that I was black. It was the late 1950s, and I knew quite well that Bull Connor and his dogs and fire hoses represented a particular animosity lying in wait for me should I tread in that direction. But those events happened on television and in a faraway state. So while the disturbing images were engraved in my brain, it was all rather abstract and bore little relationship to my world.

My father had graduated from Cornell University in 1924 and had destined me by birth and his determination to be part of what W.E.B. Du Bois called "the talented tenth," the Negro intellectual elite. I had been the only black student in my junior high school, a high achiever with similarly ambitious friends, most of whom were Jewish. To compensate socially for living in a white neighborhood, my parents had enrolled me in a social club peopled by the children of the Negro elite. But I saw them infrequently and their values, or so it seemed at the time, tended toward the social, not the intellectual.

But my school friends were all comrades in arms; we shared high spirits and untested confidence about our glorious futures. However, when puberty struck, the taboos against interracial dating struck with it, and while my friends from the Jewish 'hood and other members of my peer group from other ethnic backgrounds began to date one another, silent rules forbade my stepping out with them. Unaware of the overwhelming power of cultural taboos, I felt that my friends had abandoned me, and my parents gave me no language with which to name my experience, or perhaps their language could not reach my experience. In any case, having no shield against this experience, I was devastated.

My racking pain, however, apparently was invisible to the naked eye. An old high school classmate astonished me recently with evidence engraved in the yearbook that I had been voted the friendliest girl in the class. "Oh, yes," he assured me, "you always spoke warmly to everyone." My memory was that in my hurt and confusion, I had hardly uttered a conversational word to anyone for nearly three years.

To this day I measure all the pain in my life against that time. I could even say in full truth of the searing pain that later marked a divorce that dashed so many dreams, "but it wasn't as bad as high school." Unredeemed suffering. I had experienced the fall, not into the world of adulthood but, it seemed, straight into hell. Having no larger framework in which to locate my experience, my tender teenage spirit was left vulnerable, unsheltered from the "normal" racial presuppositions of mainstream American culture. I had not yet learned that every misery wisely encountered becomes a source of great learning. Still, learn I did, though I could not have articulated this knowledge at the time. I learned the face and feel of suffering and that it can be survived, or at least that I could survive it. I learned that my color is often a problem to others, or at least a factor to be dealt with. "The Negro problem," as it used to be called, did not belong to me, but others might give me problems because I was a problem to them. I can still be disconcerted when people, white and black, endow my blackness with meanings that it does not have for me and turn me into a walking metaphor for their needs and expectations. I learned the symbiotic nature of celebrity and its fragility. I had been part of the inside circle in junior high school, and suddenly my right to belong there had been withdrawn. Part of surviving was not needing the approbation of untrustworthy colleagues. Those who require admiration will always be at risk. A leader must have followers, and agreeing to follow is a choice. I had come to enjoy respect and inclusion, yet I learned to live without it.

Most usefully, I learned to live on the margins, to be engaged in the world but also to view it simultaneously from a place of alienation, at once an insider and an outsider, the friendliest girl some part of whose real self is nowhere in sight. Marginality is like having second sight. Being African American can be a great advantage because it tends to deposit you neatly on the sidelines. But marginality is an equal-opportunity employer, widely available to anyone who cannot or will not fit. I am naturally a deconstructionist, and seeing from the fringes has served me well. With my tears and loneliness, I had earned the right to see newly, more clearly, to live on both sides of the divide, to understand the belly of the beast while, if necessary, patting his head. It would be many years before I would also understood and accept the moral imperative to love and feel compassion for the beast himself. Wisdom does not come easily to the young.

My suffering had set me on my way to freedom, but I certainly could not recognize it at that point. I did arrive at college, released as if from jail, and entered the halls of the talented tenth at my father's alma mater.

Adventures in Cultural Conflict

My high school had also inadvertently launched me toward the study of Chinese literature. The school assigned its best teachers to its advanced-placement students. Among the best of these were several who were Jewish. With hindsight I suspect that they were survivors, if not literally then psychologically, of the Holocaust. For them European culture represented the high-water mark of civilization, mainstream American culture seemed second in line, and people like me were not within their purview. Scarred by their experiences, perhaps they were trying to find again solid ground after the horrors of World War II. In that environment, somehow I asked what was missing from their definition of what counted in the world. Of course, I discovered gaping lacunae—Latin America, Africa, and the East. My mother, having a strong interest in Asian art, had accented our house with chinoiserie wallpaper, Chinese rugs and vases, books of Asian poetry—a stash of images from the Far East. In response to my alienation and their intellectual neglect of so much of humanity, I "naturally" took up Asian culture, writing my high school senior thesis on "Shintoism and the Emperor of Japan." "My enemies" had ensured that I received an excellent education, a substantial mastery of the then-traditional narrative of Western history, and the tools of reading, writing, and rigorous analysis that made it possible to challenge their presuppositions with my sophomoric strategy. In retrospect I suspect that they were genuinely proud of my intellectual accomplishments and that their pride would not have diminished had they intuited the underside of my motivation for high-level accomplishment: survival and revenge.

At college I began to study East Asia: history, literature, philosophy, art, and the Chinese language. I could now populate my rebellion against European cultural superiority with a historical narrative from a different culture, real facts and dates, and the names and works of individual thinkers.

I was also fascinated by the spectacle of two old and arrogant civilizations, China and the Western powers, each encountering an alien and not fully explicable other with new intensity in the nineteenth century and each trying to shape that charged historical moment through the limitations of their own histories and cultures, through understandings and misperceptions, while locked in a high-stakes game of political power and economic spoils. In that struggle the earlier respect for one another's culture, which had been formed during the centuries of the Jesuits' presence in China prior to the Opium War, had been replaced by the exigencies of economic and military confrontation and activated identities of self firmly grounded in the mutual conviction of the superiority of their races and civilizations.

I can only reconstruct from forty years' distance the fascination this international spectacle of cultural collision must have held for a bruised eighteen-year-old who had to have intuited that the dynamics of cultural encounter that she had experienced with such devastating immediacy in high school had been enacted on the world stage some hundred years before and ten thousand miles away on a grand international scale. The unknowingness on both sides, the weight of history in setting the parameters of the relationship, the consequential misunderstandings, faulty judgments, confusions, the pain and violence that ensued, the full spectacle of cultural conflict—all must have resonated with my still inarticulate understanding of that personal experience of cultural collision in high school. Why else would I, who had never even traveled to Asia and had no East Asian friends, have poured so many hours into the quest to understand this historical moment?

By the conclusion of my freshman year, if not sooner, most of the personal and intellectual themes of my life were evident: a fascination with cultural encounter in multiple arenas and the capacity to be literally or imaginatively in two worlds at once. I have only mentioned two here, the personal world of black and white and the international world of China and the West, but there have been many, many more. In each case I have struggled to see them from a transcendent metalevel, to understand the aspirations and blindness on both sides, to strive for a more inclusive and compassionate understanding of the dynamics. In some sense, I am always striving to be a bridge, across chasms large and small. It is often no fun, but apparently it is the recurring theme of my life's work.

Guides and Mentors, Lu Xun and Carl Jung

In this context of my collegiate studies of China, I met Lu Xun (1881–1936), modern China's greatest writer and intellectual. In his works I found echoes of my own perplexities. I can still recall the visceral impact of reading his short story "The New Year's Sacrifice," whose conclusion evoked in me the physical sensation caused by suddenly screeching chalk scratching across the blackboard, a sound that usually makes people grimace and recoil. As I struggled to embrace and transcend my own pain, he provided spiritual guidance to my own life. Only some twenty years later did I finally understand the basis for this unlikely affinity.

Lu Xun lived on the cusp of China's transformation from an imperial empire to a modern state. Born into an educated family, his early education prepared him to assume high status in the old culture. In his late teens he encountered the "new Western learning" flooding into China at the time and decided to study medicine in Japan. Less than two years into this pursuit, he left medical school following a moment of epiphany. What the Chinese most needed, he concluded, was not someone to cure their bodies but rather someone to heal their spirits. For that literature was the best strategy, he thought, and set out to foment a literary movement.

I must have been touched unaware by the ambition to use an intellectual project to heal wounded spirits, for surely my majoring in Asian studies was a way of addressing my adolescent hurts. Lu Xun's first stories failed, but a decade later he became a writer and within less than twenty years had become modern China's premier thinker, whose ideas dominated the Chinese intellectual scene during the first half of the twentieth century. Known for his uncompromising honesty and biting wit, he was a radical critic of traditional ways and the politics of Republican China. In the late 1920s he became a sympathizer of the emerging Communist movement. After his death Chairman Mao and company distorted the meaning of his life and work and appropriated his reputation. Had he lived into the Communist era, he would most certainly have been reviled and persecuted.

Lu Xun knew his culture well from the inside, having immersed himself in the Chinese classics and in traditional popular literature. Going to Japan gave him a view from the outside, made more dramatic by Japan's far earlier success in modernizing. Many of his cultural blinders, those unconscious presuppositions we all carry, fell away; he became, in modern parlance, a kind of deconstructionist. He was able to see Chinese civilization, in its moment of cataclysmic cultural chaos, simultaneously from the position of insider and outsider, participant and observer. Events in his biography make clear that he was a man who had experienced deep personal suffering and loneliness, about which he refused to speak. But only someone who had known great inner pain could have written as he did of the poor and downtrodden without a trace of condescension, but rather with unrelenting commitment to relieve the suffering.

Although he also studied Buddhism, he rejected the path of release through individual transformation and instead located the source of suffering primarily within the social system, without, however, ignoring the blindness of the human heart. In his fictional world one is either a persecutor or a victim. To be neither is not a possibility. The elite establish the rules and reap the benefits, and the masses have little power and fewer options. The powerful, terrified of losing their position, become callous and small-minded. The subjugated masses either struggle against hopeless odds or accept their fate, their misery, and frequently their death. This structure, based on coercion and driven by fear, is assumed to be inevitable, even moral. The strategy of Lu Xun's short stories was to "name the game." By making visible what had been hidden in plain view, he established the conditions for change.

In my academic work on Lu Xun, I read much by Carl Jung and found his conception of ego and shadow particularly illuminating. The ego, the parts of the self that are valued and acknowledged, happily imagines that it constitutes the whole self. The shadow constitutes that part of the human personality that is rejected, despised, or in some way difficult for the ego to acknowledge. The content of each function may change, but the function remains. Lu Xun's solution to the problem of China's spiritual illness was to give voice to the voiceless, to explore in fictional terms what would happen if one of the masses, or the women, or the otherwise silenced ones, attempted to speak. He worked that problem through in the fictional world to discouraging conclusions. Only within the self and perhaps the family could he imaginatively project spiritual healing. For the rest, he concluded, force would be necessary to change China. Thirteen years after his death, the Chinese Communist Party came to power.[3]

My more studied and mature exploration of Lu Xun's short stories coincided with the second time of great trouble in my life, that of the divorce that "was not as bad as high school." In addition to the pain and fury of this period, it was also a time for contemplation. I was graced with great washes of time during which I read Carl Jung and Joseph Campbell, and I entered psychotherapy in an attempt to understand the part I had played in the dissolution of the marriage. Jung's autobiography, *Memories, Dreams, Reflections,* opened my eyes to the richness of an extraordinary inner life deeply explored, and Campbell, his disciple, named the parts of the universal story of the hero's quest: departure from childlike innocence, which includes the call and crossing the threshold to a more spacious encounter with the world; initiation, the introduction to the ways of the world—the hero's adventures, his securing the boon, perhaps acquiring some ultimate understanding; and the return, when the hero brings the life-transforming wisdom back to renew the entire community.[4] I can remember the moment when it dawned on me with great suddenness that I was a hero in my own quest, that I was in the midst of my own terrifying adventure, and that like any true hero, I had no way of knowing if the demons of the dark would kill and consume me. The reader of heroic stories knows that the hero will survive, but the hero himself cannot share this insight. Even then I understood that despite having spiritual guides and companions who lend critical assistance, as I myself had, the only sure powers the hero can bring to the journey are his own, and the only figure I could hope to control was myself. Some of the monsters lived in the external world, but others lay within me, and figuring out what to do about them was my responsibility, as was my part in the breakup.

The tale is common enough, with its own variations, of course. I had based my life and marriage on a set of suppositions about who I was and the nature of my mate and of the external world. Some of the premises were wrong from the start; others I had outgrown. To maintain the fictional requirements of my worldview and self-identity, I had attempted to kill off portions of myself that were not only not dead but actually creating quite a ruckus. Jung was instructive here. I had a shadow problem whose resolution required, of course, embracing the shadow and incorporating the unloved, unwelcome parts into the whole. What was hidden had to be made known.

But whereas I was living the dynamic in an inauthentic personal life, Lu Xun had probed the shadow problem on behalf of the entire polity and traced its impact with respect to the nation, the community, the family, and the inner self. When he wrote most passionately and with consummate literary skill about what he knew most clearly from his own heart, he also wrote most perceptively about the China of his times.

I had looked in Lu Xun's mirror and seen my own face. Chalk on the blackboard.

Deepening

I had also discovered a unique way of seeing the underlying dynamics of much that passes before my eyes and a mode of analysis that has served me well. Without his tutelage I might not have made the connection between the multiple realms and instead might have directed my eye inward solely to my own life, not outward toward the community and the world. My blackness and fortunate marginality, of course, had primed me to take the insight and run with it and to struggle with the sense of responsibility I might feel to the larger world around me.

My journey into the inner life had certainly deepened my spirit.

"Deepening" as a project, whether applied to the American dream or to something else, requires first having the courage to look hard at reality, to try to step from the center, where the world feels solid and final, to the margins, where the ground shakes a bit and where both trouble and creativity seem to find their home. "Deepening" means expending the effort to be critical and see the world anew and risk whatever may follow—the discomfort, disorientation, and anger or fear that might greet us if we venture into the unfamiliar. We need to see the world with eyes unspoiled by habit, to hurl ourselves outside our unthinking frames of reference. In the evening when I leave my office, I bid good night to the building janitors who are just coming on duty. Every few years when the contract for who cleans the library buildings is changed, a new crew comes on, and I see new faces, new people to greet, and feel a brief concern for old friends who have vanished. In my part of the world, the day crew seems always to be Hispanic; the night crew is black. I do not know the reason for either. But if I ever left the office and encountered an all-white crew, I would be surprised by this strange turn of events. Even I, who should long ago have moved beyond race, have grown accustomed to seeing minorities working at lower-level jobs. Trying to see with eyes unspoiled by habit is no mean feat.

"Deepening," then, is a wonderful metaphor resonant with archetypal imagery, for it draws its power from the implied contrasts to what is shallow. It conveys a sense of danger, as if even in a world of electrical lights and other technological wonders, the old myths of going into the underworld, into the dark, into the unknown and unseen, still hold sway over the human imagination. The underground, in fact, deep-down places in general, are not only fearsome places but also the sites of adventure and mystery, where the unfamiliar or unknown can be encountered, not always to ill effect. Why, after all, have so many heroes of world imagination left the safety of the light for the dangers of the deep or the dark? "Deepening" follows the direction of the Christian myth, which is vertical: the fall. Its analogue in the myth of the hero, enacted on the horizontal plane as a journey across the face of the earth, is darkness, as when in the opening line of Dante's *Inferno,* the hero strays from the path and enters a dark wood. So "deepening" calls forth a full spectrum of Western and other iconographies of light and dark, known and unknown, welcomed and unwelcomed, even good and evil, God and the devil. Jung drew on and reconceived the ancient archetype when he labeled the hidden unknown parts of the self "the shadow."

The key requirement for "deepening" seems to be a willingness to risk death of the self or some precious part of the self in order to secure something of greater value. The hero myth makes literal what is experienced psychologically as metaphor. The hero quakes before slaying the dragon. Our terror in facing inner demons may be no less powerful.

Why would we risk such a journey? According to Jung, few of us do. I have no idea why I chose healing and understanding over anger and bitterness, or love over hatred. Cowardice, perhaps. I dislike anger and fighting. If it was wisdom, then I arrived there through grace, not considered judgment. At the heart of risking must lie, I think, a love that gives us courage to proceed in the face of fear, love placed in us by family, by friends, or through the divine spirit who gives us confidence that surely she will shelter us in her bosom and that at some level quite difficult to articulate, the "I" is safe.

The Hero's Return: A Life of Service and Action

The good news and bad news about myths and archetypes is that the capacity to receive their truths rests, at least in part, on their simplicity and spareness. Real life is messier. In the hero story, the hero usually sets out to secure some object and returns to the community with or without the boon but always with some knowledge or good that has great value for the polity. But typically the stories are more concerned with the journey into darkness and adventure than in how the hero brings the value to the community.

The myths help us distinguish the processes by conceptually separating the deepening of mind and spirit, the acquisition of wisdom, from the act of bringing that wisdom into the world so that society may be deepened as well. But of course the processes more typically happen simultaneously or in rhythmic alternation. The world of action makes one thirsty for water from the well of spirit. But wherever you go, there you are, and the footprints of your soul mark your every action in the world. If your insides are at war, you bring war into the world. If you are at peace, you bring peace. So unless you have met your shadow, invited her in for coffee, listened and absorbed though not necessarily agreed to her message, then when you act in the world, she will be executing her own play in the theater just behind your back. And when the curtain goes down, you may find that your audience has seen a play different from the one you thought you were performing.

If we understand the heroic quest as primarily about the hero's psychological deepening represented as a physical journey, we also observe that the hero's return is a prelude to action and creates good for the entire community. The heroic struggles and triumphs redound to the good of the polity. Embedded in our very concept of "hero" is this public role. The inward journey is the prelude to external action. One of the most ancient of questors, the Babylonian king Gilgamesh, returns after having lost his prize during the journey but nevertheless resumes his royal duties. Other returned heroes contribute other kinds of good. The bodhisattva, among the most pure of returned heroes, rejects nirvana in order to remain in the world to save other souls. After his baptism, which can be viewed as a kind of departure from his previous life, Christ spent forty days in the desert, where he was tempted by the devil in what could be viewed as preparation for taking up the mission of salvation of others to which God had appointed him.

In the case of my "hero," Lu Xun, the phases of deepening are largely invisible. He "did" very little of public note immediately following his nine years abroad. Only after a quiescent decade back in China did he emerge on the public scene as the seminal writer and thinker of modern China. Accounts of his life typically trip lightly over these years. As I came to understand his decade of silence, I also unraveled one of the perplexities of my undergraduate study of Taoism.

Taoism Revisited: Yin and Yang

I encountered the Tao Te Ching in my introductory course in Chinese philosophy. At the time I could make little sense of several of its fundamental concepts. But with full undergraduate naïveté, I believed that if my professors deemed a work a classic, it must be wise. So I tucked these away in my mind as puzzles to be solved in the by-and-by. Thus I encountered the odd notion of *yin* and *yang,* alternating modes of action and inaction that are mutually generating. At the furthest extreme of action, inaction arises; at the furthest extreme of inaction, action arises. Although Taoism falls far from my area of intellectual expertise, this notion articulates much of my lived experience. Out of my periods of greatest inaction, that is, invisible spiritual activity, has emerged highly energetic action in the exterior world. My *yin* decade, lived intensely with Lu Xun, Carl Jung, and other explorers of the inner life, ended with my moving to the Library of Congress to manage, administer, and lead, in very public and visible environments, long days and short vacations. My *yang* decade of public service has placed great pressure on the imperative to remain connected to the contemplative streams. The attempt to do so has required my bridging yet another divide with, as usual, considerable discomfort.

Supporting, even tolerating, stretches of spiritual nondoing seems practically un-American. The blue laws that enforced a noncommercial Christian sabbath have gone the way of the typewriter. We are a culture that values the *yang* spirit. Settling the wilderness, opening frontiers, conquering diseases, warring against poverty, getting ahead, progress and development: these metaphors of our national culture all resound with "doing." One of the most striking and attractive features of the United States is the dynamism of the place. In the digital era, the expression "24/7" is the perfect metaphor for the frenetic pace at which we run and which we are encouraged to embrace as the ideal. Instant news, information, messaging, e-mail, pagers, cell phones—all ensure that any solitude can be broken at any time. I am sometimes nostalgic for the old computer software of WordPerfect 3.0, which from time to time after one had input data too rapidly would flash a white sign on the rich royal blue field that said "Please wait." This gentle request, necessitated by slow computer processors, has been replaced by the advent of multiple windows and simultaneous multitasking. Never a need to pause!

There is nothing wrong with speed and action per se. That is part of the American spirit that has helped make us the prosperous nation that we are. The issue is balance. Where are the regenerative *yin* rhythms, the time to sit in contemplative space, listen to the inner motions of our hearts, and hear the quiet pleadings of the world? When Wayne Muller's book *Sabbath: Restoring the Sacred Rhythm of Rest* was published, I was much taken with the title because I believe each of us needs separation from the din of modern life to reconnect periodically with the dark and hidden *yin* elements in our lives. The meaning of the sabbath extends well beyond the psychological space that I have considered here into the realms of the holy and the sacred. I have glimpsed those dimensions, an entirely different order of existence, but being not yet even a novice in that realm, I will refrain from speaking about what I scarcely know.

Suffice it to say that at this point, American culture is out of balance in its persistent inattention to the complementary demands of spiritual inaction. This appears to be true even in our churches. Friends who are ministers and deeply contemplative themselves have told me that the average American congregation has difficulty tolerating more than three or four minutes of silence. I cannot speak for the multiple practices of multiple traditions. But in my own life I have frequently experienced comfort, sometimes joy, sitting in an empty chapel, only to find that upon returning for a service, I literally felt compelled to flee the commotion being generated in the very space that had previously so nourished my spirit. I am naturally more at home among Quakers than Episcopalians. Yet despite my personal proclivities, I think it is fair to say that as a people, Americans tend to find silence and "doing nothing" unwelcome and uncomfortable. The *yin-yang* concept probably could not have originated on American soil.

Self-Help and the Common Good

Still, religions have often called people to inner reflection. And in their personal spiritual journeys, seekers through the ages have turned to their religious traditions, whose function, at the least, is to educate the soul in how to make life's journey. When culture changes, that part of religious instruction that is wedded to and embedded in a previous iteration of the culture loses some of its efficacy because the context has faded, and so the language of religion must be rethought and reinvented for a new age. Either one explains anew in contemporary idiom what the old language means—Kathleen Norris takes this tack in *Amazing Grace*—or one finds an altogether new language. The impact of Buddhist psychology on the American public—in fact, the intrusion of so many wisdom traditions— is part of this reaching for a new language. Psychotherapy has provided yet a different articulation.

But whatever the path of the inner journey, always a new challenge arises when we step again outside the door: to act from the insight and wisdom as we move through the world. The Christ and the Buddha, Carl Jung and Lu Xun, and all the heroes, mentors, teachers, and spiritual guides could only point the direction because they had taken their own journeys. But they did not rest content in suburban enclaves hoarding their insights, doing yoga, reciting mantras, saying the rosary, sitting peacefully on their cushions or snug in their pews. They intentionally entered their sacred learning into the world. And the depth and suffering of their journeys that had radically transformed their inner beings of necessity informed the nature and quality of their actions. To rest complacent with one's own inner peace is to cut the journey short.

The current plethora of spiritual self-help books poses a dilemma for me for two reasons. Every person who grows clearer about the shadow side, who becomes wiser in owning up to overlooked currents or the demons within, inevitably slips a bit of much needed peace into the world. Yet in my unscientific survey of these shelves of books, I have noticed that only some counsel investigation into the maiming sufferings of one's life and even fewer reach beyond the healing of the individual self to consider the impact of that healing on the community in which the self resides. In fact, many pitch their wisdom as utilitarian tools for addressing the material world as it is, with nary a hint of any moral imperative to transform it for the better. Perhaps it was the publisher who insisted on naming a Deepak Chopra book on the spiritual life *The Seven Secrets of Success*. The title implies "success" in its usual American, material context, and the book, which does not speak to community transformation, conveys relative indifference to the struggles of other pilgrims in this life.

I find myself missing a commitment of service to the group. There also seems to be no apperception of the larger premise, embedded in the Confucian tradition and implied in Lu Xun's inquiry into the Chinese shadow, that heaven, earth, and humans are ideally in alignment and that there is a continuum of the moral issues from the individual through the family and community to the nation and the globe. The wisdom traditions, on which the self-help genre frequently draws, embed their insights into the lives of communities. Through institutions or rituals or teachings, these traditions in their lived environments construct social contexts in which the spiritually rich are invited to share the wealth with those less advanced on the journey. The current American tendency to focus on the independent individual in isolation has, perhaps, abrogated the fullness of these insights and left the new literature of spiritual transformation the poorer for it.

The embrace of "individualism" helps make "freedom" and "choice" superficial watchwords, perhaps appropriately praised in the context of quotidian realities but misleading in the context of psychological truths. Without the deepening journey, we have compulsions, not choices, constraints, not freedom. Even in a comfortable middle-class life, how persistently we are not free, prey to our addictions, our angers, and our fears and unconsciously responsive to societal manipulators. Deep listening is the necessary though not sufficient condition to gain freedom from inner compulsions and external manipulators, those advertisers of goods, ideas, celebrities. Most people also need guides to help distinguish authentic voices of the soul from fraudulent expressions of a damaged spirit. For the great heroic spirits, their inner journeys prepared them for action on the world stage. Having vanquished their inner demons by making allies of their shadows and incorporating these dark figures into their own armies, these heroes of spirit became exemplars and champions of freedom for their communities. Then history offered up an opportunity for them to paint freedom on a large canvas, and they chose to change the world.

Elie Wiesel and others have testified to the capacity of the human being to retain internal freedom even in the face of unremitting, catastrophic extremity. Some rare spirits have made of prison an extended sabbath: Wiesel himself, Mahatma Gandhi, to a degree Malcolm X (whom I think has been much misunderstood), Nelson Mandela, and legions of others through the ages. Today's young people may not recall that until 1990 when Nelson Mandela and F. W. De Klerk stepped across the divide, most observers anticipated that the abolition of apartheid would require a racial bloodbath. That apartheid would be broken by the spiritual power of Mandela and his companions was beyond imagination.

As I noted earlier, one of the lessons from high school, delivered of course on a very minor scale, was that my emotional participation in the events around me was my choice, and I could claim a small space of freedom. There I experienced the first inklings that no one could coerce me into behaving in certain ways if I did not permit it; no one could know my experience if I chose to withhold that knowledge. My capacity to discipline my feelings so that people "could not make me feel a certain way" came much later. To observe the inner sabbath even in secular terms is to push back the unbalanced insistences of a 24/7 culture and reclaim the sources from which freedom, clarity, calmness, and compassion may arise. We can adopt this as a posture of resistance, a kind of "just say no" or, as an affirmation, "just say yes" to the needs of the soul, *yin* as well as *yang*, however loud the worldly clamor.

Taoism Revisited: Wuwei

As returned heroes, we have an ethical obligation to find the love, compassion, and courage to support the journey of others who are wandering as we once did. How, then, might we proceed?

The first imperative is always to tend one's own garden, against the odds given by modern life to nurture a personal contemplative life, always recalling that every action in the world bears the footprints of your soul. The constant renewal of spirit through a personal contemplative or religious practice, ideally one also nurtured in a spiritual community, is a necessity.

In a 24/7 world, we are led to believe the mantra of common sense: the faster we run, the sooner we get there. This disregards whether "there" is where we really want to get, and it defies the wisdom of the Tao Te Ching that doing less may result in accomplishing more and that doing nothing except being rightly aligned may in fact accomplish the most. This concept, *wuwei,* which is typically translated as "doing nothing and everything is accomplished," was indecipherable to my undergraduate mind and lay dormant until experience caught up with education. Two decades later it began to make exquisite, mysterious sense. In this madly dashing world, I must frequently remind myself that the Tao Te Ching has sometimes won hands down over the linear plotting of outcomes.

In some respects the Chinese concept of *wuwei* may perhaps be another way of thinking about Christian grace. It may be that as we clarify our spirits and align ourselves with divine purpose, we draw to us what we need. This process is not entirely mysterious, at least in the fully human realm. We have "merely" to remove all of those impediments that block the action of grace in our personal and communal lives. We have "merely" to acknowledge and so remove the power of our anger, fear, doubt, vengeance, greed, grasping, and so on—those elements that Buddhism calls demons and the Christian church dubbed the deadly sins. Easy to say, impossible to perfect, but quite "doable" in a modest way. With sufficient attention to the inner dimensions of soul, it is quite possible to loosen if not remove the stranglehold that these negatives can have on our spirits. Or in the language of the heroic quest, we have to defeat the monsters and dragons in order to secure the boon. If we manage this somewhat in our personal lives, we may yet fall prey to the powers of sin in the world we inhabit. There are no guarantees. But through inner purification we can at least avoid contributing to the turmoil around us. If you are not part of the problem, you can allow the solution to emerge. Whether it does or not may lie beyond our control.

In any case, I have been the recipient of enormous amounts of personal good fortune that seem to go beyond mere chance. Although I would not make too great a claim to clarity of spirit, I have succeeded to a large extent (and I say this conditionally, since I have no idea what challenges will arise tomorrow) in eliminating inner turmoil from my life. I have repeatedly had only to stretch out my hand in need, even sometimes in frivolous desire, and what I wished arrived at my door without any overt action on my part. Or my need is met through such an improbable chain of events that I could not possibly have plotted the path to the outcome. In this way I have summoned up objects and people. Some have been so minor that I suspect that the spirit of the universe designed their delivery to make a larger theological point. Others have been grand: I dreamed my current house ten years before I saw it. More recently, needing a caregiver for my ninety-plus-year-old mother, I planned to advertise. But something did not feel right, so I procrastinated. Without my spreading the word, an excellent person came walking in my door seeking employment. I met my second husband scant weeks after I decided it was again time to have a mate. Many would call this chance, but it has occurred so consistently in my life that others around me, friends and family, have taken note and asked, "How do you do that?" Some while back I fussed to my oldest son about needing something I did not have. I no longer recall what it was. He advised, "Why don't you do what you usually do?" "What's that?" I said forgetfully. "Summon it up."

The Contemplative Mind in Society

As I was exiting my decade of intense exploration of my inner life, I was also feeling very lonely in that enterprise and inarticulately wishing for a community of companions on the path. A most improbable chain of events, more *wuwei* it would seem, led me into a circle of people who share the common dedication to "integrate contemplative awareness into contemporary life in order to help create a more just, compassionate, and reflective society."[5] In my inner journeying I had finally met an opportunity for action and service that would foster the very knowledge I had so recently acquired. Through a working group that then evolved into the Center for Contemplative Mind in Society, I joined a community of like-minded people who are reclaiming and reframing the essential insights of the world's wisdom traditions and nudging these into the present world using a new language for this time, one that is not local to any particular wisdom tradition, whose vocabulary reaches past the rituals and theologies of specific religions. Christianity, Judaism, Islam, and other major world religions nearly all contain strains that promote contemplative practices, that may even invite mystical experiences, and provide a means for quieting the spirit, increasing concentration, and moving the soul closer to God. In secular American society, where many people feel alienated from their religious roots, meditative practices arising from certain strains of Buddhism provide, it seems, a neutral entry point to inner exploration without commitment to a particular theology. The presence of Buddhist influence in our society is doing more than causing a few mainstream Americans to consider embracing Buddhist contemplative practices. It is also prompting mainstream religions to revisit contemplative strains within their own traditions. So the Center for Contemplative Mind in Society is encouraging a version of "just say no" to the excesses of 24/7 and building an awareness that changing our insides is the essential step to ameliorating the violence and harm that are running amok in ourselves and in our world.

Out of our own experience in joining the contemplative dimension of our spirits to our activist propensities, we hope to offer something of value to the world. In several sectors of society we have broached the possibility that the contemplative practices that we had used to reshape our own lives would be similarly transformative for others. Among our most immediate and interesting challenges as an organization has been to tend our own gardens, to create a new genre of group meeting that embodies the spirit that we hope to foster in the world, and to balance the need to get things done against the requirement that the means we employ in our lived interactions with one another embody the ends that we seek to nurture in the world. By devoting considerable time to meditation and other contemplative practices during our meetings, we have usually avoided the intrusion of ego needs, insecurities, and the full varieties of irritating behaviors that so typically undermine the noble missions of all too many human enterprises. When we have faltered in the execution of "skillful means," it has often been because we momentarily lost the gentle self-discipline of the contemplative container. Shadow forces crept in. At each turn we have lived collectively with the knowledge that one cannot bring forth into the world what one does not possess, and so we return to the spiritual well repeatedly throughout our working times together.

When we began in the early 1990s, we sensed that there were rumblings of spiritual longing in the society that were largely unnamed, except perhaps in the field of mind-body medicine, through the work of Jon Kabat-Zinn, Herbert Benson, and others that was just beginning to receive broad notice. So we took as our challenge bringing forward into other arenas the means for people to experience and practice their professions from a contemplative foundation, or at least to open the discussion of what that might mean. By reason of deliberate choice and opportunity, we began working in academia, law, business, the environment, and philanthropy. My deepest engagement has been with the academic side, and so I will speak to that.

Our perception was that the university had lost the understanding of earlier centuries that educating the young means training both the mind and the spirit, or in our age of rapid obsolescence we might better say opening the way for the whole person to enter into life readied for whatever might arise. Academic institutions have concentrated on developing students' intellect—skills of analysis and synthesis that most certainly are required in the modern world—but they have lost touch with the earlier insight that contemplation is a way of knowing and that knowledge of the spirit is precious and necessary to a balanced life and a balanced world. The contemplative dimensions in education have been neglected even when the content is rich in that knowledge. This can be seen most dramatically, but by no means exclusively, in departments of religion, which will teach theology and the history of religion but address neither the contemplative strains within religious traditions nor help students understand experientially these dimensions of religious life.

Generously funded in its early years by the Fetzer Institute and the Nathan Cummings Foundation, the Center for Contemplative Mind in Society established a fellowship program for faculty members at colleges, universities, and professional schools to develop courses and conduct research that would teach contemplative practices as objects of inquiry as well as make available the subjective experience of contemplation as another kind of knowing. Over the life of the program, both have happened, usually in the same course. To date we have given one hundred fellowships to faculty working in a wide range of institutions, large and small, public and private, in liberal arts colleges and professional schools, all over the country. I could summarize the official evaluations, but in this context I find the anecdotal evidence more persuasive. One fellow, who is a deeply religious Christian and a nun, used contemplative practices in the secular classroom as a tool in teaching the literature of horrific events— slavery, the Holocaust, and apartheid. The contemplative container made it possible for students to absorb the knowledge of these atrocities without becoming self-protective and disengaging emotionally. The quality of the classroom encounter was deepened and transformed.

Another fellow, Marilyn Nelson, whose poem I cited at the beginning of this essay, used various contemplative practices at the opening of each class in poetry that she was teaching to plebes at West Point Military Academy. In an environment where discretionary time was severely limited by a tightly regimented schedule, students were required to meditate fifteen minutes a day, and each class began with five minutes of silence. Repeatedly students testified to the preciousness of this empty time. On the last day of class, because there were so many concluding tasks to accomplish, Marilyn announced that they would not meditate. The students protested respectfully, but she insisted that there was no time in the schedule. Later in the class period, she noticed that one student was inexplicably missing. She found him seated under the table in meditation.[6]

Disengaging the Ego

Not only do I struggle daily to retain some semblance of a contemplative life so as to keep at least one eye on my inner demons and sustain a peaceful spirit, but I have also noticed increasingly that knowledge of my shadow influences my professional work in the world through how I behave, with greater challenge through how I manage my emotions, and finally through the professional work I choose to do.

Although my own spiritual practice is scarcely exemplary, it has enabled me to retain my psychological equanimity, if not always my political position, in the power plays and skirmishes of institutional work life. Exercising spiritual awareness in the world of daily business provides ongoing tests, for some kinds of behavior and patterns of thought must be resisted, and refusing to indulge them often excludes one from the camaraderie of influential groups who wield considerable power. One example: there is a powerful tendency in institutional life to engage in rivalries that pit "us against them," an option that is simply not available to me as long as I stay mindful of my all too human tendency to take that path. I know that the ugliness I see in others at best lies dormant in me in all its destructive potential. The lessons of high school have stood me in good stead: being both insider and outsider is a familiar, powerful, albeit often painful position. So the daily return to the self-reflective honesty of the spiritual well is necessary to the exercise of the Hippocratic oath, which is popularly quoted, perhaps not accurately, as "first, do no harm"—or at least refuse to participate in gratuitously harmful thoughts and actions.

Perhaps the greatest challenge in the workplace is disengaging the ego and cultivating sufficient inner freedom and equanimity that no one, not even one's superiors, can make one feel bad. When I disappoint myself, I can have a bad day. But I have learned, more through failure than success, that I have no obligation to let anyone make me feel bad or good. No one can have that power unless I yield it. This posture is easier to maintain in the federal government than in private enterprise because less is at risk. Unless one behaves egregiously or is grossly incompetent, job loss is unlikely. Marginalization is quite possible, but the paycheck will still arrive. So I work hard because my work is good, noble work and is worth doing well, but I strive unceasingly, and with increasing success, not to permit my standing in the institution's pecking order, which rises and falls with the political winds, to affect what I do or how I feel.

I am reminded of a story that Jack Kornfield tells of a confrontation between a brutal general and a Buddhist master. Having terrorized province after province and caused all to flee before him, the general encounters the lone remaining inhabitant of a village, a Zen priest going about his business. "Don't you know who I am? I can run you through with my sword without batting an eye," howls the military man. "And I, sir, am one who can be run through with the blade without batting an eye," replies the master. The general, of course, is overcome by such spiritual power and bows down in respect and awe.[7] The same principles apply to institutional life. I have scarcely approached the master's equanimity, nor does a bureaucrat need to, but I know in which direction it lies. It is an equal challenge, when things are going well and ego gratifications abound, to refuse to be seduced by appreciation and awards. The workplace can be a fickle lover. So I give my love to the mission but withhold my soul and retain my inner freedom. I hope my equanimity makes me a better colleague.

In our interior lives, we recognize that what the shadow most often requires of us is acknowledgment and incorporation. In the international world, the exemplary model for incorporation is the post-apartheid government of Nelson Mandela, and most symbolically the Truth and Reconciliation Commission established by Archbishop Desmond Tutu, as the inspired strategy for coming to terms with the past and preventing violence. Each time we encounter some deeply disturbing force in our communities and nation, we have the choice between a mode of response that Lani Guinier characterized so trenchantly as "control and punish, control and punish,"[8] or we can choose to listen and learn. That is, there is a choice to silence and expel or to listen and try to incorporate the knowledge or grievance into our understanding. This decidedly does not mean allowing the perpetrators of vicious deeds to go unpunished and unrestrained. Justice does need to be served. But we also need to inquire deeply not only of the perpetrator but also about the forces that fostered his or her emergence. In short, we also need an inquisitive, compassionate approach to the generating sources of the violence.

No Solomon is required to anticipate some of the places in contemporary America from which the shadow forces are likely to emerge. Each of us could scout the landscape and probably identify a few potentials. At the top of my list are the white supremacists, the aggrieved, white, lower-class, mostly males who seem to believe that the one source of respect guaranteed them is their whiteness, which is now slowly eroding as a sure-fire symbol of status. Ironically, they are joined in the dissidence, obviously around a different set of issues, by a large, disproportionately black male prison population, a shadow archetype of mythic proportions if ever there was one. Both groups have been created in part by unacknowledged American violence, institutional racism, and faulty gender definitions.

The approach through compassionate understanding is hardly a new thought; the strengths and pitfalls of loving responses to antisocial or violent behavior are well known. "Turn the other cheek" may be a profound strategy in the spiritual realm, but it requires considerable wisdom to exercise it in daily life. What is useful, perhaps, is to look at the implications of the shadow as they play out in unsuspected places.

Islam, the New Shadow

In late 1999 I found myself increasingly irritated by the news media's repeated use of the phrase "Islamic terrorists," as if it were one word. Even on relatively highbrow nightly news programs, I rarely heard the adjective "Islamic" applied to any other human activities. My responsibilities for the foreign-language collections of the Library of Congress, materials written in some 460 languages from all over the globe, made me exquisitely aware that Muslim societies are highly varied and geographically diverse. They stretch from Africa through pockets in Europe to Central Asia, the Middle East, South Asia, and Indonesia. And Muslims have been in the Americas since the Atlantic slave trade brought literate, Koran-reading cargo to the new world.[9] As human beings, can Muslims really be so very different from others in their fundamental needs and aspirations? Yet all of these millions of people were being tarred with the same ugly brush. This gross distortion was being drummed daily into the minds of the American public. Given the murmurs of unspecified ferment in the Middle East, it surely spelled trouble. Although history never really repeats itself, thoughts about the conflicts between China and the West a century ago still echoed in my memory: the unknowingness on both sides, the parameters set by history, misunderstandings, faulty judgments, confusion, pain, violence, cultural conflict.

In essence my apprehension was not so very different from my experience of my own shadow, which sometimes speaks to me through some unspecified, inner restlessness that disturbs my mental peace. I have a range of preferred strategies that I employ in such situations, all tools for helping the shadow find her voice. Hearing murmurs of my teenage method of addressing pain through academic inquiry and of Lu Xun's intellectual project of spiritual cure, I constructed a new intellectual project as a tiny step toward healing a gaping cultural wound.

In early 2000 I secured modest funding from the Rockefeller Foundation to develop a series of symposia on the human impact of globalization on Muslim societies around the world. It was my attempt to complicate Americans' understanding of this grand variety of peoples. Most of the symposia were "webcast" over the Internet via the Library of Congress's homepage and are still available for worldwide viewing. Even the fact of offering the symposia immediately garnered gratitude from the Washington, D.C., Arab American and Muslim intellectual communities, including notice from the embassies. From the perspective of anyone who has reflected on what it means to be the shadow in society or who had found oneself the shadow for others, a position that I as a black person have occupied, this appreciation was perfectly predictable. Subsequently, the Rockefeller Foundation provided a large additional grant to fund fellowships on the same subject. The first installment arrived in June 2001. It was the right impulse but too little too late. Along came 9/11.

But Lu Xun had also taught me that we have no right to despair because "hope lies in the future," and the future is unknown, or as my brokerage firm never tires of telling me on its statements, "past performance is no guarantee of future results." We do what we can with as much wisdom as we can bring to the moment. The consequences are not ours to know. So at the Library of Congress, we have continued to develop a project in Islamic studies that serves an American audience and also says indirectly to the Muslim, Christian, and other worlds that we are genuinely interested in bringing forward greater understanding of the deep cultural and historical roots of this unhappy moment in world history. We want all to know that the Library of Congress has the intellectual resources, with its collections encompassing the intellectual heritage of the world's peoples, to support that inquiry. As we have talked with our colleagues in other federal government agencies, we have too often found an interest only in getting the American message out and minimal awareness that the American message also communicates the American shadow. For example, freedom can appear to be license when its responsibilities are neglected. And part of the anger at us is the message our shadow is performing on the stage behind our backs.

We also find that one message of the Islamic studies program—that we should be practicing deep listening—is sometimes met with blank stares. If we as a people had learned to listen to our own deepest aspirations and to the voices of the shadows within our own nation, had we listened to the struggles of the poor, the angers of minorities, the rages of white nationalists and brought these people into the daylight and incorporated their grievances into our understanding, would we have found it so hard to listen to those from beyond our own borders? Would we not have known that as a nation, we needed to know the languages Muslims speak, their cultures, their histories, long before a crisis arrived at our doorstep? As the world's most powerful nation, we have an imperative to ensure that what is hidden from our view is made known to our people.

Acknowledging our own limitations in no way removes the onus from "the other" to similarly engage in deep inner exploration. But each side can only exercise inquiry and action in the arenas of its own purview. It is too easy to point the finger only outward and never inward. In my own life, the end result of identifying my own culpabilities has been personally very freeing. The arenas of my responsibility are where I can most assuredly effect change.

In the immediate aftermath of 9/11 many African Americans held odd and unusual feelings as we watched Arab American neighbors in our national community demonized and cast as alien to the American polity. We who had been "the other," perpetually seeking and usually failing to become fully acknowledged as Americans, not hyphenated Americans but just Americans, suddenly felt ourselves to be unproblematically part of "we the people." It was a very nice feeling. White America might not have liked us any better or worse, but even those of us with dreadlocks and baggy ghetto styles were at least familiar and less fearsome than the suddenly emerged Muslim "other." I checked my perception of "something fishy" with other black people and found it confirmed. For that moment in time, we were no longer part of the shadow. My sister, with insight honed from decades living not just as a woman but as an African American woman and schooled in the nuances of performing the unsought role of shadow, put it all neatly in ironic perspective: "Don't worry," she reassured me. "It won't be long before we blacks resume our rightful place at the bottom!"

If being marginal increased the likelihood of my empathy for the pain and anger of another widely and unconsciously disparaged group, I felt empowered to move understanding into action because my project fit so well within the direction set by the librarian of Congress, James H. Billington, who is a great visionary and a wise intellectual. On February 3, 2000, he gave a speech that articulated particularly well his own concern about incorporating the shadow. (I doubt that he would characterize it that way because I do not think he endows the unknown with "otherness." It is merely unknown.) He had made these points earlier, but this is a particularly eloquent expression of them:

We [Americans] have . . . a profound special need to understand better the three great cultural belts of Asia—each of which is now aggressively asserting itself on the world scene: the Confucian- and
Buddhist-based cultures of East Asia, the Hindu-based cultures of
South Asia, and the long corridor of Islamic nations stretching from
Indonesia through Central and West Asia to North Africa. Each of
these worlds contains more than one billion people who speak languages and profess beliefs that few of us have even begun to understand. But if you do not learn to listen to people when they are
whispering their prayers, you increase the risk of meeting them later
when they are howling their war cries.

How unfortunately prophetic his words turned out to be.

Returning to the Well of Spirit

When in my mind's eye I replay images of the World Trade Center after
the second plane struck, in addition to all of the other layers of meaning
that we have considered over the months, including those that demand
accountability from the warped spirits who caused such horrendous suffering, I also see this symbolically as the eruption of shadow forces into
the awareness of the ego. Americans have been complacent, imagining
that we could withdraw into the gated compound of our vast continent,
ignore the distress of others, and escape the consequences. Neither domes-
tically nor internationally is this a viable option in the long term. Label-
ing "the enemy" as "the axis of evil" and seeking its destruction models
the pattern "control and punish, control and punish," and announces a
Manichaean notion of a world divided between good and evil, us and
them. But the evil is also in us, and there is good somewhere there inside
the enemy, however difficult it may be to detect. I worry as I write this
that the president and other American leaders are out of touch with their
own shadows, believe that the United States is only pure and good, and
that anyone who challenges this "truth" is surely bad. It is not merely a
matter of seeing shades of gray, although pragmatically that is essential
to policy and negotiation, but of retaining the capacity simultaneously to
see both white and black at once, to see ego and shadow, one eye on God
and one on the devil.

If I had been President George W. Bush on September 11, 2001—and
how grateful I am that I was not—after I had conferred with all of the
appropriate military and foreign policy officials and consulted various
heads of state, I would have also placed phone calls to Vaclav Havel,

Nelson Mandela, the Dalai Lama, and perhaps several other great heroic spirits. In times of peace but especially in times of crisis, the world needs people who are fully grounded in their own inner worlds of spirit, aware of their inner demons; who have known fear and grown wise enough not to act from it; who know that they too are sinners and therefore are slow to consign to oblivion those still in sin's grip; people who also know the world and its political realities and so can bring deep spiritual wisdom to the dangerous, consequential world of political leadership.

The United States is a great nation. There are good and just reasons why people from all the cultures and civilizations of the world want to come here, why we promise to welcome "your tired, your poor, / Your huddled masses yearning to breathe free, / The wretched refuse of your teeming shore,"[10] and why they risk their lives and their fortunes to accept that offer. I believe that the analogy with the personal does hold. If we want to deepen the American dream for our citizens and extend it to others, if we want to stand as an inspiring vision in a tumultuous world, we must be prepared to listen to the voices from the shadows, whoever they are, whatever they speak. We must summon the courage to acknowledge what is unwelcome and incorporate it into our understanding. If the United States is to move toward being its best self and remain a beacon of hope for others throughout the world, it must embody its deepest spiritual values, not solely its values of self-defense, as it acts in the world community. It must live the ideals that it seeks to promote.

Time and again we see that the initial response to the shadow, whether in the arena of nations, of communities, or of our own hearts, is fear, denial, and suppression. Certainly such impulses arise for credible reasons. Without them those parts of the human psyche and the human family would never in the first place have been consigned to a sphere beyond our awareness and concern. If we have taken our own, deep hero's journey, we know that fear and rejection, "control and punish," are only a shallow, temporary solution to our troubles. If we have taken our own, deep hero's journey, we know that responding out of compassion for our own frailties and for those of others is the harder but surer path to peace. Struggling for a more comprehensive view, trying to bridge the divide between "us" and "them," seeing in a way that affirms the hopes and aspirations of others, even when their methods for achieving these are faulty or even appalling—these modes of addressing the human condition require great self-knowledge and discipline of spirit.

Although few of us are called to statecraft, in our own smaller arenas each of us has no less a moral imperative: to integrate into our frantic 24/7 life a private sabbath of *yin* "nondoing" so that we may be purer of heart; to keep a watchful eye "in" as well as "out" for the shadow figures, which, left unrecognized and in exile, may be up to no good; in short, to water our souls afresh each day from the well of spirit so that what we bring into the world is untainted by unsuspected darkness. We do this for our own sake, because it feels better to be at peace than to allow interior wars to rage. And we do it in preparation for stepping outside of our own doors and taking right action in the world, because the world's wisdom traditions tell us that the journey is cut short until we share the boon.

Ultimately, however much we may try to hide our nature, who we are will manifest in what we do, and any good works we execute will be colored by the spirit we bring to them. When we go into the world of action and when we leave it through death, whatever remains after we pass by will be the footprints of our souls. This has been true since the dawn of humanity and is not likely to change in our time.

NOTES

1 Marilyn Nelson, "May Your Love Convert Lucifer," in *The Fields of Praise* (Baton Rouge: Louisiana State University, 1997), p. 151.

2 Martha Ronk Lifson, "The Myth of the Fall: A Description of Autobiography," *Genre*, Spring 1979, pp. 45–67.

3 This nonstandard analysis of Lu Xun's short stories forms the core of the research I am preparing for future publication.

4 Joseph Campbell, *The Hero of a Thousand Faces*, 2nd ed. (Princeton, N.J.: Princeton University Press, 1968).

5 This is the mission statement of the Center for Contemplative Mind in Society.

6 Marilyn Nelson, "Aborigine in the Citadel," *Hudson Review*, Winter 2001, pp. 543–553.

7 Jack Kornfield, *Seeking the Heart of Wisdom: The Path of Insight Meditation* (Boston: Shambhala, 1987), pp. 75–76. I have taken minor liberties in the retelling.

8 Lani Guinier, "Where Do We Go from Here? Chaos or Community? Black America's Vision for Healing, Harmony, and Higher Ground." Smiley Group Forum, Panel 2, Feb. 23, 2002. [http://video.c-span.org:8080/ramgen/kdrive/mis022302_smiley2.rm].

9 Scholars are beginning to study slaves brought to the Americas whose religion was Islam. Many might well have been literate as a consequence

of the imperative to read the Koran in Arabic. One of the most unique
manuscripts to have surfaced in recent years is the autobiography of Omar
ibn Said from Senegal. Writing in Arabic, he complained of being enslaved
to an illiterate master. His manuscript was displayed at a symposium at the
Library of Congress on January 29, 2002.

10 Emma Lazarus (1849–1887), from "The New Colossus" (1883), which is
inscribed on the Statue of Liberty in New York harbor.

PART TWO

SUFFERING THE
AMERICAN DREAM

CREATED EQUAL

EXCLUSION AND INCLUSION IN
THE AMERICAN DREAM

Elaine H. Pagels

WHEN I REFLECT on the American dream, the first words that come to mind are these: "We hold these truths to be self-evident, that all men are created equal, that they are endowed by their Creator with certain un-alienable Rights . . ." We know that these statements expressed a vision, for certainly this was not the waking reality of those who wrote and signed the Declaration of Independence—some, of course, like Thomas Jefferson, were themselves slave owners living in a colony ruled by British monarchs. How, then, could they declare that human equality is "self-evident"? Anything *self-evident* should be obvious through simple obser-vation; yet empirically minded observers, from ancient times to the pres-ent, often have deduced the opposite. Certainly Aristotle, the most empirically minded of ancient philosophers, inferred from his own obser-vation that nothing was more self-evident than innate difference. As he saw it, among humans, as among every litter of lion kits, puppies, and baby chickens, those endowed with superior strength, speed, and intelli-gence naturally dominate those born weaker. Wherever Aristotle would have looked, from the forum where those ruling the city debated policy to his own household, with segregated and smaller quarters for women and children, or in the kitchens and the fields where hierarchies of slaves labored to clean the house and prepare dinner for their owners, he could find verification for his conviction that such a social order is natural and essential. Two and a half millennia later, any of Jefferson's contempo-raries, walking through his estate at Monticello, might easily have come to the same conclusion.

Many historians have wanted to claim that the Christian movement changed all that—changed, for example, the status of slaves from that of property, with no capacity to engage in legal proceedings of any kind, whether marriage, divorce, ownership, court testimony, or inheritance, to the status of human being. Yet this was not the case. We have noted already that many who signed the Declaration, themselves raised as Christians, took for granted that slaves (and perhaps non-Caucasians as well) were not included among those "created equal" (although some had had qualms about the question). Most, of course, would have excluded women as well, whatever their race or class. Even into the nineteenth and twentieth centuries, many still agreed with Aristotle that the particular virtue (literally, "excellence") of the male master is to rule, just as the appropriate response of those who were, in various ways, their subjects—women, slaves, and children—is to obey.

If human equality is by no means *self-evident,* what about the claim that all human beings "are endowed by their Creator with certain unalienable Rights"? Advocates of human rights have often wanted to claim this as an innate and universal idea, and some have made extravagant claims for nonexistent precedents. The book prepared for World Law Day, for example, says: "The idea of the inalienable rights of the human being was often articulated by poets, philosophers, and politicians in antiquity."[1] This grandiose—and, I suspect, intentionally vague—statement is followed by a single specific example: When Antigone, in Sophocles' play bearing her name, written in 422 B.C., says to King Creon, "All your strength is weakness itself against the immortal, unrecorded laws of God," she invokes the higher law, the natural rights of man.

One might add—just as anachronistically—that she also speaks for the rights of *women.* But what Sophocles actually invokes in *Antigone* has nothing to do with any kind of "natural rights of man"; instead, the "higher law" Antigone invokes is *divine*—the law of the gods—and concerns *blood loyalty among family members*—in this case, their duty to bury their dead. Nothing Sophocles says involves any idea of a universal natural law, much less of human rights.

Some people have suggested that the idea of human rights can be traced back to the ancient law code of Babylonia, instituted around three thousand years ago by the famous lawgiver Hammurabi. Those who make this claim point out that the legislation attributed to Hammurabi specifies certain legal protections against mutilation and torture. What they fail to point out, however, is that these exemptions applied only to aristocrats; the law code not only allows but assumes that mutilation and torture would be routinely applied to lower-class people and slaves. Any "rights"—or, more accurately, privileges—conferred by Hammurabi's code not only depended on social status but were also derived entirely from society (their authors would probably have said from the gods) and not from any quality intrinsic to any individual.

The same was true in Rome, where, as in the ancient Near East, the emperor ruled as the son of the gods and against whose will there was no recourse—except, of course, assassination. Only Roman citizens, a small percentage of the population, had specific rights, and these were minimal indeed: citizenship protected a person from torture and being condemned without a trial—commonplace events for slaves and other noncitizens. Furthermore, if condemned to death, the citizen had the privilege of being privately beheaded, rather than publicly tortured and killed in the arena, as noncitizens were. This legal system, too, is based on the premise that rights are conferred—or withheld—by the state.

But if the idea of human rights is rare and late, historically and geographically speaking, its opposite is virtually universal—namely, the idea that *society confers on its members whatever rights, privileges, or exemptions they enjoy.* Traditional societies take for granted that the sociopolitical order reflects a universal, inviolable divine order, from which all value derives. The laws of the Hebrew Bible make similar claims for their laws and later for their rulers; Muslim society would follow a similar pattern. Such leaders, therefore, rule by divine right: they can make claims on any member of the society, but no ordinary individual has any claim on *them,* since social and political hierarchy, along with whatever rights it conveys—or withholds—also are rooted in the divine order.

Nor was this pattern of deriving rights from society culture-bound— bound, that is, to Western culture. On the contrary, it has prevailed in non-Western countries as well. Among the tribes of Australia, Africa, and North and South America, tribal hierarchy and custom are understood to be sanctioned by the divine order, or by nature. A similar pattern has prevailed for centuries in Hindu societies of India, Cambodia, Nepal, and Pakistan: the social and political order reflects the divine order, which the ruler embodies. The caste system, endorsed as the reflection of that order, fixed the ranks of society into the three upper classes, defined by their respective privileges; the fourth class consisted of people to whom were allotted minimum rights, and below these were the "untouchables," who remained outside any system of rights. The social orders that prevailed for centuries in China, Japan, Korea, Mongolia, Burma, and Ceylon (now Sri Lanka) similarly revered the ruler as the embodiment of divine order and allowed no recourse for what we call "the individual." To this list we may add Marxist societies, which inverted the religious pattern and claimed that the social order reflects inviolable natural laws analogous to the laws of biology and physics. Yet here again, value resides in the social order: only as one contributes to the community can one derive benefits from it.

In Western history as well, of course, this pattern is not just ancient history but the form of political theory that has dominated Christian Europe since the fourth century. One's social position, whether serf or aristocrat, was understood to be arranged according to God's will. Serfdom, and later slavery, as well as the negligible legal situation of women, were sanctioned in the same way, as was the persecution of Jews and Muslims. The Holy Roman Emperor and the Catholic and Protestant rulers of Europe all claimed to rule by divine right.

More accurate than any sweeping claims for the antiquity and universality of human rights, then, is Condorcet's observation that "the notion of human rights was absent from the legal conceptions of the Romans and Greeks; this seems to hold equally of the Jewish, Chinese, and all other ancient civilizations that have since come to light. The domination of this ideal has been the exception rather than the rule, even in the recent history of the West."[2] What the Declaration of Independence proclaimed in 1776, then, was something relatively—and radically—new: the conviction that the individual has intrinsic rights, claims on society and even *against* society, which any state, in order to be legitimate, must recognize and is obliged to protect. Thomas Jefferson and his bold contemporaries were, of course, well aware how radical their Declaration was—in fact, of course, they aimed it directly against the claims to divine right by King George III, whose royal descendents to this day claim as their family motto "Dieu et Mon Droit" ("God and My Right").

Where, then, did we get the idea that supports this central theme of the American dream—the idea that ultimate value resides in the human person, independent from—even prior to—participation in any social or political collective? What could possibly have made its statements sound "self-evident" to its authors, much less to their hearers? The language in which they wrote offers clues: "that all men *are created* equal" and "that they are *endowed by their Creator* with certain unalienable Rights." Far from being inferences drawn from observation, much less facts, these are statements of faith—drawn directly from the creation account of Genesis 1, which tells how God made *adam*—in Hebrew, humankind—in his own image and endowed humankind with his own power to rule over the earth in God's place. The story proclaims, then, the religious conviction that even before the construction of any society, the original human, fresh from God's hands, so to speak, bore intrinsic and sacred value.

Yet American revolutionaries were by no means the first to find political as well as religious meaning in this ancient story. Probably written down about three thousand years ago, this story had been told and retold by Israelite storytellers for perhaps hundreds of years before that. These people, whose ancestors had lived as nomads and settlers at the margins of the great agrarian empires of the ancient Near East, no doubt told this story to challenge, among other things, the prevailing political ideology of the ancient theocracies among which they lived. Tellers of this story had in mind, no doubt, the experience of Israelites forcibly deported to Babylonia, who had heard and seen in the great public festivals celebrated in Babylonia every New Year—that the sun god Marduk, having vanquished all other gods so that now he ruled them all, had delegated his power *over the whole earth* to the king of Babylonia, who embodied that power to rule over human society. Similarly, Israelites who had lived in Egypt would have heard how the sun god, in Egypt worshipped as Ra, had bestowed his power on the pharaoh; and many would have seen in splendid and solemn processions through the streets of Karnak and Alexandria how the pharaoh, clothed as Ra in brilliant regalia, bore the signs of divine sovereignty and ruled as Ra's living image on earth. Thus the political ideology—and the theatrical pageantry—of ancient empires presented each of the actual rulers, bearing the scepter and crowns belonging to gods, in the image of the god whose power each embodied.

When Israelite storytellers insisted, then, that on the contrary, their god had actually *created* the sun—which was, they declared, *not* a god at all but simply a "big light" their god had set in the sky to regulate the daytime, they were challenging Babylonian and Egyptian theology—and the political theory with which it was inextricably involved. And when they went on to say that their god, to crown his creation, had finally created *adam*—humankind—and commanded *him* to "rule the earth, and subdue it," they, no less than Thomas Jefferson, were effectively declaring their own independence from foreign claims of divine kingship. For, we recall, the story tells how God created Adam "in his image and likeness"—not like the monumental stone or bronze statues of Marduk or Ra, as Babylonian and Egyptian rulers were depicted, but as a living, breathing manifestation of God on earth, and solemnly invested him with "dominion over the earth." Thus the story shows, in effect, that "*any one of our men bears the image of our god and so is equal to your king*—indeed, is greater than your king; for both you and your king foolishly worship the sun, which is only a lamp made by our god to serve humanity!"

Thus as Thomas Jefferson intuitively understood, the Genesis creation story not only interprets human nature but also bears direct implications for human society and politics. Even thousands of years ago, many who heard this creation story went on to ask what it meant. If Israel's God for-bade his people to make images of him, what can it mean to say that Adam was made "in his image"? Some storytellers suggested that *adam* was created in the image of the divine light that appeared in that moment before creation, when God spoke into vast darkness, as "a wind (or spirit) from God swept over the deep waters" (Genesis 1:2) and commanded, "Let there be light!" This was no ordinary light, since the world had not yet come into being; rather, this light was a form of divine energy. Those who read the oracles of the prophets Isaiah and Daniel, who wrote that they had glimpsed God in heaven, dazzling with light, suggested that what appeared in the primordial light was "a human being, very marvelous," a being of radiant light, shining like a thousand suns—shining like God himself. Some suggested that this primordial Adam shone with the radi-ance of the divine light and that perhaps it was he whose presence awed the prophets, including Ezekiel, when he was brought up into heaven in a chariot of fire to glimpse God's throne. For Ezekiel says he saw on that throne one who looked "like a human form," flashing with the radiance of fire and rainbows, and "a splendor all around . . . the glory of the Lord." This glorious image, who appears to be somehow both divine and human, later became central to Jewish mysticism, and is often called the "light Adam," who reflects the glory of God himself. Kabbalistic teach-ing suggests that this divine light is the energy from which the entire uni-verse came forth and which still shines, although often hidden and unknown, within everyone.

We may recognize this as a kind of dream image that has come from Midrashic tradition centuries old, which suggests that our mythical ancestor—and so, by implication, we ourselves—have come, as Words-worth says, "trailing clouds of glory do we come from God, who is our home."[3] (In Wordsworth's use of "glory," he echoes the Hebrew term *kabod* for God's appearance that connotes "shining light, radiance.") This vision of divine light as a secret link between God and humankind is what inspired George Fox, who founded the Quaker movement, to pro-claim that the "inner light" shines in everyone—even, as he took care to point out, in the illiterate, the Delaware Indian, the African enslaved in Virginia—and energized his "Society of Friends" to work to abolish slav-ery and war. William Blake, who learned of this tradition from Kabbalis-tic groups in London, embodied it in his poems and paintings.

But every dream, of course, is susceptible to different interpretations. In the case of the dream that inspired the founding of the United States, an essential question is, *Who is included?* That is, when we speak of "our people," whom do we actually have in mind?

Answering this question is no simpler today than it was at the time of the American Revolution. Then as now, some people (and, of course, some politicians) see "all men" (potentially, at least) as representing *everyone;* others do not. From the time the creation story was first told, in fact, this question has proved explosively controversial. Over a thousand years ago, some rabbis argued that the vision of Adam represents everyone, for, they pointed out, the Hebrew term *adam,* though often taken to be the proper name it later became, originally was a generic term that simply meant "humankind." But others—more often the majority—declared instead that Adam, being the original, ideal human being, must have been the very best of his species, which can only mean, many believed, *people like ourselves.* Thus in ancient times, a majority of rabbis agreed that Adam must have been a *freeborn Jewish male.* And while a dissenting minority suggested that women *married* to such freeborn Jewish men might *also* share, by association, in Adam's glory, even these more liberal rabbis assumed that Adam's prerogatives would not apply to any *other* women—much less to slaves or Gentiles. Within the varied writings included in the Jewish Bible, some passages seem to express a universal vision and others a sectarian one. While certain passages, including some oracles of the prophet Isaiah, for example, envision God's blessing finally coming upon all humankind, upon "all nations of the earth," many others suggest that God, having given up on the human race as a whole, now has chosen to bless Israel alone.

Since the idea of Israel's exclusive election could hardly appeal to many Gentiles, it is no surprise that the first widely successful version of Jewish teaching aimed at non-Jews—the teaching of Paul, who saw himself as the missionary of "Jesus the Christ (Messiah) to the Gentiles"— proclaimed a much more inclusive message. Although Paul himself had been educated among rabbis to believe that he, being a free Jewish male, was gifted with divine prerogatives above all slaves, Gentiles, and women, he declared that now he had come to see Jesus as nothing less than a "new Adam"—the prototype of a new and transformed human race. "In Christ," he declared, membership in God's people is no longer restricted by gender, class, or even ethnicity, for "in Christ there is neither Jew nor Gentile, slave nor free, man nor woman; but all are one in Christ Jesus." This phrase is not original with Paul; in fact, he had probably heard these same words pronounced over his *own* head when he was initiated into the group of Jesus' followers. Thereafter, when he and his fellow missionaries baptized others, they solemnly pronounced this formula over the heads of new members of their small—and marginal— groups of converts.

Those attracted to this message—and, no doubt, especially the slaves, women, and Gentiles among them—took this to be very *good news* indeed (which is what the term *gospel* originally means). One of our early "gospels" about Jesus, the Gospel of Thomas, depicts Jesus, rather as Paul did, as one who speaks as a voice from the primordial light—the divine energy that brought the universe into being, like the radiant "light Adam" called into being even before the creation of the universe. But the Gospel of Thomas takes the tendency toward inclusiveness further than Paul and depicts Jesus telling his disciples that because they, too, come from the same divine source as he himself, they may therefore find the same divine light within themselves as well as in him. So, he says, "If [people] say to you, 'Where do you come from?' say, '*We come from the light*; the place where the light came into being through its own power.' And if they say to you, 'Who are you?' say, '*We are children (of the light)*, the chosen of the living Father.'" Thus this gospel teaches that the "good news"—the gospel—is that every one of us can discover that divine light within ourselves, since we all come from the same divine source. However, as Buddhists also taught, many people remain unaware of their relationship to the divine Source and so live "in darkness" or, as Jesus here interprets it, "in poverty—and you *are* that poverty."

The Gospel of Thomas takes Jesus' teaching even further: here "the living Jesus" goes on to say that this divine energy that infuses him also pervades *all things that exist*—not only all human beings but everything in the universe, from the sun and stars even to logs and rocks. Thus, according to this gospel, Jesus says:

> I am the light that is before all things;
> I am all things; all things came forth from me; all things ascend to me.
> Split a piece of wood, and I am there;
> Lift up a rock, and you will find me there.

Although some scholars have read Thomas as an elitist tradition, which, like certain Buddhist teachings, speaks primarily to the few who seek enlightenment, in ancient times such a tradition, like Buddhism, was often understood as recognizing all people—potentially, at least—as capable of attaining it.

Strikingly, a related story in the Syrian *Acts of Thomas* shows that some Christians who followed such teaching not only proclaimed human equality as a matter of religious conviction but also insisted that it be put into *practice*. The anonymous author of the *Acts of Thomas* reports, for example, that when the Apostle Thomas was preaching the gospel in a crowded marketplace in India, Mygdonia, the wife of one the king's relatives, was so eager to see the apostle that she ordered the slaves bearing her litter to press their way through the enormous throng. When they failed to make headway, she sent a slave home to bring back a posse of her household slaves, who came on the run to force the crowd to give way to their mistress, hitting and beating those who stood in her way. But when Thomas saw this, the apostle challenged and rebuked her: "Why do you trample on those who come to hear the word? For [Jesus said] to the crowd who came to hear him, '*Come to me, you who labor and are heavy laden, and I will give you rest.*'" At this point, Thomas pointedly ignored Mygdonia and turned instead to address the slaves bearing her litter:

> *This blessing . . . is now for you, who are "heavy laden."* For it is you who bear burdens hard to bear, and you are driven at her command. And although you are human, they place burdens on you as if you were irrational animals, and *those who have authority over you think that you are not humans like themselves. And they do not know that all are alike before God, whether slaves or free.*

Our evidence shows, moreover, that some women converts similarly drew practical conclusions about gender equality from Christian teaching. *The Acts of Paul and Thecla,* a story widely told and loved in the ancient world, tells of the young Thecla, who, having heard Paul preach, eagerly accepted his teaching, abruptly refused to marry her fiancé, and abandoned her widowed mother in order to follow Paul. After a man tried to rape the solitary young traveler, she cut off her hair, put on men's clothes, and confronted overwhelming obstacles—even obstacles raised by Paul himself. For the *Acts* says that Paul, shocked by Thecla's unconventional behavior, refused to baptize her, lest he encourage, much less endorse, what she was doing. This account, embroidered with legend but based on a true story, ends only after Thecla, refused baptism by Paul, baptizes herself and becomes a renowned and revered holy woman and healer, revered to this day as a saint among Eastern Orthodox Christians.

Yet most of us familiar with the Christianity of the New Testament have never even heard of *The Acts of Paul and Thecla* and the Gospel of Thomas—or of other writings like them. When I began to ask why Christian leaders did not include such writings within the canonical collections they called the "New Testament" or the "apostolic fathers" of the church, I began to wonder whether some Christians set aside these writings because they rejected the radical—and practical—conclusions to which such teachings might lead. We know, after all, that even Paul himself, soon after he began to preach that "in Christ there is neither man nor woman, slave nor free, Jew nor Gentile," discovered—apparently to his distress and chagrin—that certain converts had taken him at what they thought was his word: some slaves and women took him to mean that they were now equal to their masters and husbands. Realizing this, Paul decided to write the letter we call 1 Corinthians, in which he explains to Christian slaves and women that despite their equality "in Christ," for the duration of the present world (which Paul thought would be short), and for all practical purposes, wives must remain subject to their husbands and slaves to their owners.

Furthermore, Christian leaders of the second and third century, who realized how popular and authoritative Paul's letters were for many believers, took care, when they began to assemble the collection that we call the New Testament, to add to Paul's authentic letters a *second* group of letters *attributed* to Paul but actually written by others—the so-called deutero-Pauline letters, which to this day most Christians accept as if they actually had been written by Paul. These deutero-Pauline letters not only address virtually all the practical questions raised among Christian groups during the earliest communities but also, in every case, emphasize the most *conservative* elements in Paul's teaching. The deutero-Pauline letter to Timothy, for example, has "Paul" reinforce and intensify women's subjugation to men, as its anonymous author declares that

> a woman must learn in silence, with complete submissiveness. I permit no woman to teach or to have authority over men; she is to remain silent. For Adam was formed first, not Eve; and Adam was not deceived, but the woman was deceived, and became a sinner. Yet woman will be saved through childbearing, if she continues in faith and love and holiness, with complete modesty. (1 Timothy 2:11–15)

While Paul, in his authentic letters, advises widows and other single women to "remain single, as I do," adding that this is not a divine command but only his opinion (1 Corinthians 7:25), the pseudo-Paul of the letter of Timothy, on the contrary, tells single women to marry and bear children and urges them to occupy themselves exclusively with household obligations (1 Timothy 5:4, 14).

Furthermore, the same letter (and others like it) has "Paul" strongly insist that Christian slaves are not to imagine that they are now equal to their masters "in the world." On the contrary, they are to realize that for the duration of this world, they must remain in subjection:

Let all who are under the yoke of slavery regard their masters as worthy of all honor. . . . Those who have masters who are believers must not be disrespectful on the ground that they are "brothers," but rather they must serve all the more. (1 Timothy 6:1)

Another pseudo-Pauline letter has the apostle order slaves to "obey your earthly masters with fear and trembling, in singleness of heart, as [you obey] Christ" (Ephesians 6:5).

Because the compilers who shaped the final structure of the New Testament canon placed the deutero-Pauline letters along with the authentic ones, generations of Christians for two millennia have taken "Paul" to be saying that although women, slaves, and Gentiles may, through baptism, become "one in Christ" with men, with their masters, and with Jews, such equality "before God," so to speak, has nothing to do with present social and political reality. Since virtually all Christians, for over two thousand years, have assumed that *all* of the letters that bear his name are genuine letters of Paul, such decisions have profoundly shaped Christian tradition as we know it.

At the same time, the canon of the New Testament also excluded, for example, the Gospel of Thomas, with its teaching of the divine light hidden within all humankind. Instead, Christian leaders included the Gospel of John, which depicts only the small group of Jesus' followers as God's beloved, ranged against a vast, hostile mass of outsiders on whom will fall God's wrath. Although the process of compiling this collection has left few records, we can trace the influence of certain church leaders like Irenaeus of Lyons in the second century and Athanasius of Alexandria in the fourth, who wrote down the first known list of the twenty-seven writings they declared divinely inspired. Both bishops championed the Gospel of John, which rejected the universal vision of "divine light" found in the Gospel of Thomas and replaced it with a sectarian one.

We have seen, too, that the authors of *both* of these gospels, Thomas and John, no less than Thomas Jefferson, were interpreting the same Genesis creation story—Thomas interpreting it *inclusively* and John *exclusively*. For while the Gospel of John agrees with Thomas that the divine light called forth "in the beginning" is manifest on earth, it declares that this light is not to be found—even potentially—in all people but only in one *particular* human being. John declares that Jesus of Nazareth, whom he believes to be God incarnate, alone embodies "the true light that comes into the world"(John 1:5), and John pictures Jesus saying, "I am the light of the world" (John 8:22).

When John wrote this gospel, about forty years after Jesus' death, he wrote it to show that the few who, along with himself, believe in Jesus—and they alone—share in God's light, but all who do not believe are "sons of darkness," already divinely condemned to hell. Written in the first century by a member of a persecuted sectarian group, John's gospel has been loved throughout the centuries—and still is—by groups of Christians who see themselves as the few who are "God's own" in a dark and hostile world.

By the time the collection of writings we call the New Testament was compiled, then, Christians were tending toward their *own* form of sectarianism, suggesting, for example, that the divine light *no longer* dwells in Jews—much less in pagans—but only in those who follow Jesus. Thus many Christians now proclaim that they alone (and, many would increasingly emphasize, only certain *kinds* of Christians) are the *only* people whom God favors. This tendency toward exclusion may surprise people who assume that religious language—generically speaking—is benign, inclusive, and unifying. But when we actually investigate a wide range of religious traditions, we often find the opposite. More often than not, in virtually all cultures, religion has served to sanction the claims of one's own people, tribe, or nation—often above, and usually *against,* any perceived as "others."

When Israel's traditions came to be adopted by people of many cultures in many parts of the world and read in thousands of languages, innumerable people interpreted its blessings and promises to apply to themselves—none more consequentially that those who came to America. Recall, for example, how the Puritans who read the story of God's promises to Abraham cast themselves in the role of a "new Israel" to whom God had given this continent as their own Promised Land. In God's command to Abraham to purify the land of Canaan by killing all its previous inhabitants, many Calvinist Christians found their own divine commission to purify America by destroying its previous inhabitants, who were, they believed, pagan savages. At the same time, however, in the early seventeenth century, the radical Christian George Fox received visions that impelled him to reject both catholic and "protesting" Christianity and proclaim a different message. Fox founded the Society of Friends, more often called the Quakers, a "society" based on the conviction that since every human being comes forth from God, each one has the "inner light" within. Fox fearlessly preached his message from one British town to another and from settlements in the American colonies from Massachusetts to the Carolinas, seeking to demonstrate that divine light shines within every person, from every British peasant to the king himself, from every African slave to members of Dakota tribes, whether educated or illiterate, male or female. Repeatedly imprisoned, beaten, attacked, and threatened with death, Fox traveled on both sides of the Atlantic, tirelessly proclaiming the "inner light" and urging anyone who would listen to work to abolish slavery and war. Some three hundred years later, Martin Luther King Jr., in his famous "I Have a Dream" speech, read the biblical promises of a new land as a vision of America healed from racial hatred and transformed by justice and righteousness.

We recognize, then, the "American dream" expressed in the eloquent words of the Declaration of Independence, for what it is—a religious vision inspired by the Genesis creation story. Our history reminds us, however, that we cannot take dreams at face value. From the story of Daniel interpreting the dreams of the king of Babylonia to the writings of Sigmund Freud and his successors, we have learned how elusive dreams can be and how they lend themselves to many possible interpretations. What, then, do we make of this dream in waking reality? How shall we take this vision to shape our sense of who we are—as a people, a nation, a community?

Today, especially as we hear religious rhetoric increasingly invoked in public, we need to know—and take responsibility for—the ways we interpret the dream expressed in our Declaration. More than ever we need to ask, Whom do we include in the "American dream"? We hear many, most of them Christians, who claim the right to declare themselves, or specific groups they have in mind—groups often defined through religious affiliation, race, ethnicity, economic or legal status, or even sexual orientation—as the true heirs of America's legacy. We have even heard our Christian legacy invoked for the purpose of waging religious war.

We cannot, then, take for granted an inclusive understanding of the American dream. On the contrary, maintaining one requires us to contend against a natural human preference to associate with "people like ourselves"—a tendency that, when embodied in our politics, often leads people, consciously or not, to carve out exclusive groups and set them against others—a tendency certainly as alive today as it has ever been. Anyone who glances at the front page of the newspaper can see that claims of exclusive loyalty to one's own blood relatives, to one's clan, tribe, or coreligionists—loyalty allegedly endorsed by divine sanction—still stirs the passion of millions of people throughout the world and explodes into deadly conflict throughout the world, from Serbia to Palestine, from Rwanda to Uzbekistan, from Kashmir, Egypt, and Israel to Newark and Buenos Aires.

Yet we can also see how many people, not only in this country but throughout the world, share a vision of human equality, of the intrinsic value of each person "in the eyes of God." Utopian as this may sound in the tumultuous world we inhabit today, it must have seemed much more so to the men who wrote out the drafts of that Declaration, aware that they were taking irreversible steps to instigate a revolution that required them to risk everything on the stifling heat of that July day in 1776 when they signed it, "pledging our Lives, our Fortunes, and our sacred Honor." As we recall what they bequeathed to us at such cost, let us deepen our understanding of the "American dream" and commit ourselves to extend it to all people worldwide who would share in its promises, blessings, and responsibilities.

NOTES

1 World Peace Through Law Center, *International Legal Protections for Human Rights* (Washington, D.C.: World Peace Through Law Center, 1977), p. 17. Published for World Law Day, Aug. 21, 1977.

2 Cited in Isaiah Berlin, "Two Concepts of Liberty," in *Four Essays on Liberty* (New York: Oxford University Press, 1969), p. 169.

3 William Wordsworth, "Ode," *Intimations of Immortality,* ll. 65–66.

THE GRACE AND
POWER OF CIVILITY

COMMITMENT AND TOLERANCE
IN THE AMERICAN EXPERIENCE

David M. Abshire

THIS ESSAY DRAWS FROM both the great moments and the nightmares of the American experience. It tracks how two elements of our political culture can appear to be contradictory and yet at the same time be recognized as major characteristics of the American experience. The elements to which I refer are a passionate, driven commitment to a cause or idea and the tradition of tolerance, compassion, and inclusiveness.

I argue that in the great historical accomplishments of America, these apparent opposites—commitment and tolerance—are bridged by civility. Civility, as used here, is not simply following rules of etiquette and decorum for the sake of tradition or in order to coat over any differences. In its deepest sense, civility means respect, listening, and dialogue. It does not mean watering down or giving up cherished principles. Indeed, civility has often been exercised in the American experience in order to move to the higher, common ground. In his writings on civility, Stephen Carter reminds us of "two of the gifts that civility brings to our lives: first, it calls for us to sacrifice for others as we travel through life. And, second, it makes the ride tolerable."

In the American experience, civility has not always prevailed, and its role in our political culture cannot be taken for granted. Accordingly, we must review some of the nightmares of incivility in American history to warn of the severe national polarization that could paralyze us in the coming years. We must take lessons from the past to face such challenging issues as the global war on terrorism; conflict in Iraq, Afghanistan, and other parts of the turbulent Middle East; the threatened solvency of Social Security and Medicare; the need to reduce the looming national deficit; the K–12 crisis in public education; widespread anti-Americanism; and the erosion of character-based leadership in the United States in almost all walks of life: in the clergy, in our schools, in heads of business, and even in the presidency.

If we can listen to each other with humility, the positive—almost sacred—accomplishments and qualities of the American experience can enrich and fortify us to live the fullness of the American dream.

The Public Climate: The Determined Choice of Trust over Cynicism

A 2003 poll by the Pew Research Center showed a nation "profoundly polarized between two political camps that are virtually identical in size but inimical in their beliefs on virtually all major questions." How has this come to pass? Why has a political void grown to the widest it has been since the center began polling sixteen years ago despite the unity following the attacks of September 11, 2001? Why is our country more polarized than ever and cooperation less and less common? Is it because the very fiber of our society—the institutions of governance, the engines of the economy, civil society, and our concept of individualism—has been lost to partisan, economic, racial, and religious schisms? Certainly, at the time of this writing, we have faced one of the most contentious presidential campaigns in our history, and even members of Congress speak of their own legislative body as dysfunctional.

But we must look beyond today's events to understand this new age of incivility and disunity. Since the end of the Cold War and the emergence of the present state of world affairs, America has suffered from an identity crisis. Even in its moment of triumph as the world's only superpower, the United States has at times floundered, realizing that global leadership requires certain commitments but remaining divided as to what those commitments should be. Often perceived as too unilateral and sometimes as a bully, the United States has witnessed rising anti-Americanism around the world and the slow defection of some of its oldest allies. At home, the American people are more ideologically divided than they have been in decades. Pollsters now describe the Union in terms of "red and blue states."

Yet even in our present crisis of division, we see hope in a vision of the American identity that was never really lost, only misplaced in the tumultuous modern world. As I will recall several times in this essay, on September 11, 2001, we were a people united by our common beliefs—our need for security, our love of freedom, and our resolve to respond effectively to this outrageous crime, not just against America but against civilization itself. We remain bound, whether we show it or not, by certain principles that are elusive but powerful. On September 11, we remembered who we are and we chose civility.

The images were powerful: the president at ground zero surrounded by first responders, then at the Islamic Center declaring Islam a religion of peace, then at an ecumenical service at the National Cathedral. Our nation was bound by a new connectivity. In the words of Alan Wolfe, we found ourselves "one nation, after all." This memory shows how our nation can unite to achieve great things in a great moment. It is a tragedy that those few months of national, moral, and spiritual unity were so soon lost.

Yet even in an increasingly uncivil Congress, there remain many examples of civility. For instance, the chair and ranking members of the Senate Foreign Relations and Armed Services Committees (Senators Richard Lugar, Joe Biden, John Warner, and Carl Levin) are close and work together regularly on issues of common concern. It is worth noting that for several years, Senators Bill Frist and John Kerry have chaired the Center for Strategic and International Studies' Commission on Global AIDS, which improved President Bush's legislative support. But clearly the cases and occasions are fewer than they could be, especially in the House of Representatives.

Drawing on the "American experience," which, then, is the true America? The America of division or the America of unity? The America of the red and blue states or the America symbolized in the harmony of red, white, and blue in its flag? The America of endless public and partisan warfare or the America of cooperation, civility, and common purpose? The America of many or the America of one?

America's History

A decent respect for the opinions of mankind.
          —The Declaration of Independence

In fact, America has two histories, the history of commitment and the history of tolerance. The better-known version of commitment is the one written by the winners, those who through strength of arms, power of mind, and sureness of purpose wrenched thirteen colonies away from their imperial masters and forged a nation unique in the history of the world. This is the passionate America born of courageous principles—commitment to the fundamental principles of life, liberty, and the pursuit of happiness. This is the America of the revolution that defied King George III, the America of the Declaration of Independence, the America of the "greatest generation" that defeated Hitler's tyranny, and, if I might add a personal note, the America that I experienced fighting for freedom in Korea.

But there is another history and another force that has seen America through some of its most difficult challenges. This story is less glamorous, to be sure, but perhaps even more important. It is marked by countless unsung instances of peaceful disagreement resolved in a spirit of give-and-take and fair play. The foundations of our government that still persevere today were laid during this period. This is the America of compromise and collaboration in the face of differences when strong personal convictions were balanced by a willingness to work for the common good. It is the America of Lincoln's "malice toward none and charity for all."

Neither history tells the whole story because it is the interaction of these forces, of commitment and tolerance, of passion and civility, that has been the hallmark of the American experience. Indeed, while commitment without tolerance produces a sort of zealous, destructive fundamentalism, tolerance without commitment entails a moral reserve that can degenerate into moral vacuity or paralysis ("One man's terrorist is another man's freedom fighter"). In the balance of these forces lies the genius of the American experience. As words, *tolerance* and *civility* carry a certain semantic baggage, the product of use and sometimes misuse. As is often the case, the best definition is a clear statement of what the word does *not* mean. It must be clear that tolerance is *not* a surrender of conviction. Tolerance does not require one to sacrifice personal ideals or water down beliefs to a toothless "least common denominator." As Michael Novak points out, "To be tolerant is by no means the same thing as to believe that any proposition is as true as any other. . . . Our Constitution does not reduce tolerance to some form of moral equivalence, to degrade the truth of things." At its best, tolerance promotes a marketplace of ideas where diverse viewpoints collide to create a higher level of understanding.

Former Senate Majority Leader Howard Baker also expressed the importance of tolerance in leadership, when speaking about his "Baker's Dozen," a list of rules for Senate leadership. Two of his rules contain elements essential to tolerance, to "have a genuine respect for differing points of view" and to "listen more often than you speak."

Senator Baker asked that we remember that "every Senator is an individual, with individual needs, ambitions and political conditions. None was sent here to march in lockstep with his or her colleagues, and none will. But also remember that even members of the opposition party are susceptible to persuasion and redemption on a surprising number of issues. Understanding these shifting sands is the beginning of wisdom for Senate leaders."

Senator Baker admitted to having been admonished by his late father-in-law, Everett Dirksen, to "occasionally allow yourself the luxury of an unexpressed thought."

As we later review the characteristics of civility in American leadership, it will become clear that successful leadership tends to exercise the virtue of inclusiveness. This has been a mark of our greatest presidents. Their gift for coalition-building and marshaling the resources of the nation in times of war and peace required inclusion rather than exclusion of the very best and most creative minds in the country. The civility element of tolerance also involves incorporating the best and most innovative ideas, regardless of differences of politics.

In the realm of religious rights, an area where the necessary balancing act between tolerance and commitment is perhaps most dramatically evident, tolerance does not mean freedom from all religion or banishment of religion from the public square. Rather, for America's founders, it meant freedom to practice devoutly the religion of each person's choice, or not to practice religion at all, without fear of censure from members of another faith or the government. Tolerance does not require that we accept the *absence* of God but rather the *mystery* of God. Tolerance requires that we, to paraphrase Benjamin Franklin, be willing to doubt a little of our own infallibility.

Furthermore, tolerance means more than simply permitting opposition. In a letter to the Hebrew Congregation of Newport, Rhode Island, George Washington noted the importance not just of tolerance but of respect for the conscience of others. Indeed, tolerance requires respect for the presence of opposition and demands listening, common goodwill, and an acceptance of personal frailty—what I call civility. It is this civility that, in the words of Professor Ted Gup, produces an "ennobling effect upon those who rise above themselves." Only with mutual respect can tolerance and civility become an engine of constructive exchange helping all parties see further into the heart of a problem.

Tolerance and civility are not easy. Gup continues, "Some may never wish to break bread with those whose conduct, though lawful, they find loathsome, whose beliefs they find heretical, and whose message they think traitorous. And yet they are called upon to suffer them because *that is who we are as a nation*—not a people bereft of private values but *a people enriched by a stubborn willingness to endure each other*" [emphasis added].

Tolerance and civility, in other words, lie at the very heart of what it means to be an American citizen and at the very heart of the message that we must communicate about ourselves as individuals and as a political culture. Frankly, this is what makes us different from so much of the world. This is the image of America that we must communicate overseas, in place of the current one of a too often arrogant America. Our Declaration of Independence itself called for a "decent respect for the opinions of mankind," which means global leadership with modesty, the very traits that George W. Bush called for in his first election campaign.

The Colonial Period

We must be knit together in this work as one man.
—John Winthrop

Echoes of this particularly American emphasis on civility and tolerance are everywhere, from the early colonial days and the founding of the Republic to the resurrection of the Union. We need only listen.

What a sense of awe they must have felt, those early Puritan settlers, as they courageously sailed out of England on a March morning in 1630, leaving behind years of religious turmoil en route to establish their vision of God's kingdom on earth. They were deeply devout people, committed to reforming the Church of England from within and establishing in America a "city on the hill" which would be to the entire world a beacon of Christian righteousness. Ronald Reagan—ever the optimist—so admired the story that three centuries later, he attempted to improve a bit on the Bible and the Puritans by calling America a "shining city on the hill." These were not small goals, and they were not small people. Theirs was a commitment so intense that American history would be forever shaped by their deeds. But contrary to popular myth, it was not just commitment that drove Puritan society. For all the caricatures painted of the Puritans—the self-righteous reformers, the nosy neighbors, the witch-burning zealots—their communal ethic is one that required no small amount of civility and, yes, even tolerance.

"We must be knit together in this work as one man," wrote John Winthrop, first governor of the Massachusetts Bay Colony, as his ship crossed the Atlantic, "that we, and our seed, may live; by obeying His voice." The New England town would quickly become the very epitome of a tight-knit society that made civility a precondition to daily survival. Each town agreed to establish a covenant that formally articulated consensual agreements on most matters affecting public and private life. Disputes were handled through arbitration, first by a group of neighbors and then, if necessary, by the town, assembled weekly at the now iconic town meeting. This was an intentionally nonlitigious society where social harmony was achieved through consensus, not conflict.

To be fair, though, the Puritan "Bible commonwealths" had many short-comings. Not all dissent was handled quietly at town meetings or tolerated for the maintenance of unity. Roger Williams, perhaps the best known of the rebellious Puritans, criticized the Massachusetts settlement for its lack of religious purity. He had qualms with the mingling of church and state, by which civil officials could increasingly influence religious matters. He preferred a complete separation from the Church of England—"perfection," in his view, was not simply purification of the faith. Thus when Williams established freedom of the individual conscience and religious toleration in Rhode Island, he did so to promote what he saw as an even truer Christianity than the Puritans sought in Massachusetts.

Williams sought freedom to worship, not freedom from worship, and in doing so established a model of religious society that would later inspire the founding fathers and the U.S. Constitution. Perhaps it was his commitment that assured the mercy of Governor Winthrop, who, by the standards of the time, could have punished Williams far more severely. Instead, in an act of tolerance, Winthrop let him depart for Rhode Island.

Another colonial experiment with religious toleration took place in Maryland, led by the second Lord Baltimore, Cecilius Calvert. After receiving a joint-stock company charter similar to Winthrop's for Massachusetts Bay, Calvert sought to establish his colony as a Catholic refuge in the new world. He quickly found that "Catholics could survive in the English world only as a tolerated minority; they were in no position to impose their will on others." To *protect* his religion, then, Calvert passed the Toleration Act of 1649, what scholars have called a "bold move for that era." The act even anticipates our modern constitutional statement on religious freedom and deserves quoting: "No person or persons whatsoever within this Province . . . professing to believe in Jesus Christ, shall from henceforth be in any ways troubled, molested or discountenanced for or in respect of his or her religion nor in the free exercise thereof within this Province."

This "free exercise" clause is one predecessor to our First Amendment clause outlawing legislation "prohibiting the free exercise" of religion. Even though the Maryland act extended freedom of worship only to Christians, it was nonetheless a historic step toward the preservation of religious diversity and commitment.

Following on these early traditions of religious toleration, Thomas Jefferson, a deist, drafted in 1779 for the Virginia State Legislature the "Act for Establishing Religious Freedom." Like Roger Williams, Jefferson declared the awareness that "Almighty God hath created the mind free" and that "all attempts to influence [the mind] by temporal punishments or burdens . . . are a departure from the plan of the Holy Author of our religion." Here again, religious freedom is meant to preserve the true meaning of the "Holy Author," not to dilute or usurp it. Jefferson, in fact, was so fond of this act that he had a reference to it engraved on his tombstone along with the better-known inscription, "Author of the Declaration of American Independence." He makes a similar argument for religious freedom in his "Notes on the State of Virginia," where he writes, "Had not the Roman government permitted free [religious] inquiry, Christianity could never have been introduced. Had not free enquiry been indulged, at the era of the reformation, the corruptions of Christianity could not have been purged away. If it be restrained now, the present corruptions will be protected and new ones encouraged."

Neither is this ethic of tolerance with commitment strictly for the religious. The American religion has become as much a civil religion as a spiritual one and is as important in politics as it is in theology.

As James Morone concludes in his book *Hellfire Nation,* America's colonial religious foundation created a "nation with the soul of a church," a "brawling, raucous, religious people" whose moral fervor inspires dynamic revivals in its faiths—political, social, and religious. Around the world, that fervor gave us a providential mission as a redeemer nation. At home, fervor drives two great moral paradigms from opposite sides of the political spectrum: first, an individualistic ethic of "strength, patriotism, and manliness" and the politics of good versus evil, and second, a new social gospel of communal responsibility and corporate solutions. Though both sides are deeply rooted in different moral convictions, Morone maintains, we "remain Puritans all."

The Founding

Different interests necessarily exist.

—James Madison

Roughly a century after the seeds of community had been planted on American soil, another generation—perhaps the greatest generation—of deeply committed yet practical leaders emerged. "They had great gifts," writes philosopher Jacob Needleman of our founding fathers, "and due to fate or chance or perhaps providence, great currents of human and social energy passed through them." They had first the gift of commitment to forming a new kind of nation, not of a distinct tribal, ethnic, or racial identity but of a philosophical identity holding liberty, justice, and freedom as the nation's fundamental principles. Needleman says, "America was an idea," and our founders' commitment to that idea brought forth on the continent a *new* nation—new not just in years but in character. Some historians have labeled the founding period the "Age of Passion"—a "decade-long shouting match" filled with "shrill accusatory rhetoric, flamboyant displays of ideological intransigence, intense personal rivalries, and hyperbolic claims of imminent catastrophe." True to the present thesis, however, none of our founders' great achievements would have been possible were it not also for their gifts of civility and tolerance. Quite literally, the founders regularly broke bread together even while locked in what must have seemed like political battles to the death.

Many authors have argued that this powerful civil religion bound the founders together with a sense of common purpose despite their divergent interests. Catherine Albanese suggests in *Sons of Our Fathers: The Civil Religion of the American Revolution* that "the American Revolution was in itself a religious experience"—the thread that would knit this next generation of Americans together. If that was the case, it was a powerful religious experience indeed, for the founding period is filled with example after example of compromise and collaboration.

The most dramatic collaboration of the federal period was between James Madison and Alexander Hamilton. Of the principal founders, Hamilton was the most nationalistic, almost a monarchist. He wanted to install a president-for-life and to delegate almost no power to the states. At the Constitutional Convention, Hamilton made an exhausting speech advocating a lifetime chief executive with complete power to veto state laws. The shock in the hall was so great after his four-hour exposition that the next day he recognized that he had made a political blunder. Fortunately for the Republic, Hamilton realized that he would have to compromise, accept some ideas and wisdom from others, and work within more temperate and pragmatic constraints. His partner in this enterprise became thirty-six-year-old James Madison, who talked of an "adjusted federalist" system.

In the scorching summer of 1787, Madison took his so-called Virginia Plan to the fifty-five reform-minded delegates who had gathered in Philadelphia to reshape the government of the young nation. They faced the seemingly impossible task of rectifying the "principles of '76," which rejected centralized authority, with the need for a stronger national government that could unify the states. Madison's plan, endorsed by Hamilton, called for a strong national government.

George Washington had tentatively agreed to preside over the Constitutional Convention. After four months of closed debate, the delegates worked through a laundry list of sticking points until they came to two major areas of contention—the clash between the small and large states and the clash between the agrarian south and the commercial north.

Fierce debate marked the process that ultimately ended in a compromise document. Madison, who outlived the other founders, eventually became the last authority on the "original intent" of the framers and was frequently quizzed on the matter. His standard response was to refer others to the debates at the time of ratification. "Everything," he said, was argued out then.

Madison had won over Hamilton, who came to see the strategic value of dropping the word *centralization* and cleverly captured the word *federalist,* forcing his opposition to be cast as antifederalist. This was an extraordinary coup, since the term *federalist* was a popular word but not yet a coherent notion. Hamilton had learned from the more agile Madison how to seize the political high ground. Even though the Constitutional Convention was not fully in line with Hamilton's ideals of greater centralization, he knew that the perfect should not be the enemy of the good.

Thus to ensure ratification, the unlikely team of Hamilton and Madison, along with John Jay, launched a massive public relations campaign under the pseudonym "Publius." Madison, who was to become one of the most passionate Jeffersonians of all time, and Hamilton, who was surely the most ardent federalist of the period, came together in the *Federalist Papers* to argue for a strong constitutional government. While arguing for national unity, Madison, in *Federalist* No. 51, also recognized the importance of diverse interests. "It is of great importance in a republic . . . to guard one part of the society against the injustice of the other part," he wrote, for "different interests necessarily exist." It was Madison more than anyone else who consistently demonstrated his exceptional ability to pull together "different interests" into a working whole. "He was so obviously gentle," writes historian Joseph Ellis, "and so eager to give credit to others, especially his opponents."

Madison's creed was humility with passion, civility with devotion, and tolerance with commitment. It is appropriate that we should call him the "father of our Constitution"—the document that represents the fruits of enlightened compromise. It is interesting that in this act of civility, each author tried to blur his individual authorship by sharing the *nom de plume* Publius, an example so different from the constant search for "celebrity" in the politics of today.

At the conclusion of the Convention, Benjamin Franklin, by then an elder statesman of eighty-one, rose to give his blessing to the new document. Franklin conceded that the Constitution was not perfect but a compromise document created by fallible men. Then he called for ratification:

"On the whole, Sir, I can not help expressing a Wish that every Member of the Convention, who may still have Objections to it, would, with me, on this Occasion doubt a little of his own Infallibility, and, to make *manifest* our *unanimity*, put his Name to this Instrument."

This, then, was Franklin's definition of civility—the ability to doubt one's own infallibility. And therein lies the lesson of the Constitutional Convention: no human or human creation possesses "all truth," but by melding the passions of fallible men, something of great worth can emerge.

In retrospect, and indeed in the high courts of the land, the Constitution has become "sacred scripture." At the time, all participants in the Convention had conceded on certain cherished beliefs and felt therefore that the Constitution was imperfect but the best that they could do. However, two stubborn Virginia men, eminent in their own right, Richard Henry Lee and George Mason, eloquently noted the omission of the provisions of the Bill of Rights and refused to lend their signatures. Jefferson criticized the document from Paris. All were uncomfortable with the issue of slavery, which defied the Declaration of Independence's statement that "all men are created equal." But the genius of the American experiment is that the Constitution was composed and ratified with the understanding that it was merely a foundation on which to build, and in time, the "miracle at Philadelphia" became admired around the world.

First Presidents

The mutual sacrifices of opinion.

—Thomas Jefferson

The great success at Philadelphia was made possible by the character of George Washington, a leader of impeccable integrity who felt that private and public virtue should be the same. The inner life of the mind and the outer life of service were, in him, in total harmony. The "father of our country" became revered as the great servant-leader who did not seek power or reward, but it was not always so. As a cocky lieutenant colonel in the colonial forces during the French and Indian War, he constantly argued with the royal governor about his pay. When his small command was surprised and forced to surrender, he was written up in the London *Times* as a disgrace to His Majesty's service. Then Washington experienced a transformation. Fighting under General Braddock, he survived a shower of bullets and emerged changed, believing that he was under the miraculous care of Providence. The once-cocky colonel refused a salary as commander of the Continental Army. After the war, he rejected the proposal of disillusioned officers and men who summoned him to become a new American king.

No wonder, then, that Article II of the Constitution, which outlines the role of the executive, was written with this revolutionary icon in mind. His characteristic reluctance to rule exemplified servant-leadership, and Washington was elected our first president in 1789.

His very inclusive first cabinet brought together nearly all of the patriotic personalities that had played pivotal roles in the revolutionary period: John Adams as vice-president, Thomas Jefferson as secretary of state, and Alexander Hamilton as secretary of the treasury. James Madison was the vocal leader in Congress who initially supported Washington but soured on the president's agenda when it included Hamilton's ambitious financial plans. Madison then began his defection to the Republican Party that would come to be synonymous with Thomas Jefferson. For all Washington's accomplishments as America's first president, forming a functioning government from such diverse personalities must have been one of his greatest achievements.

Washington sought the counsel of men whom he considered more brilliant than himself and stayed "so far above the battle that he often saw everything more clearly," according to historian Joseph Ellis. He did this while letting the genius of Madison, Hamilton, Jefferson, and others meld to create precedent-setting public policy. Washington gave both Hamilton and Madison a chance at drafting his famous farewell address, "just as he struggled to allow the opposing geniuses of Hamilton and Jefferson to operate in his cabinet, under his reconciling eye."

Washington captured the importance of collaboration in his farewell address by warning that the spirit of partisanship would make "public administration the mirror of the ill-conceived and incongruous projects of faction, rather than the organ of consistent and wholesome plans, digested by the common counsels, and modified by mutual interests." He encouraged Americans to see their "immediate and particular interest in union" where all would find "greater strength, greater resource, [and] proportionately greater security from external dangers."

The party tensions that had begun in the early days of Washington's first term escalated throughout his presidency as relations between Hamilton and Jefferson—and between the Federalists and the growing Republican opposition—became more strained. The rift began after another great American compromise was brokered. In his staunch advocacy of the assumption of the states' debts and the creation of a national bank, Alexander Hamilton tightened the ranks of the Federalist Party. Hamilton begged Jefferson to give his support to the assumption legislation that was before Congress, but Jefferson opposed the broad constitutional interpretation that would have permitted the national bank's existence and worried that the southern states would receive unfair compensation for federal bonds bought by northern speculators. In one of the great moments of civility in our history, Jefferson requested a dinner meeting with Hamilton and Madison. "I thought it impossible," he wrote, "that reasonable men, consulting together coolly, could fail, by some mutual sacrifices of opinion to form a compromise which was to save the union."

He was right. The men agreed to change certain votes so that Hamilton's measure would pass. As a consolation to the southern states, it was agreed that the permanent capital of the United States would be located in the South—along the Potomac in what would become the District of Columbia. The "mutual sacrifices of opinion" made by deeply committed leaders held George Washington's administration together at a time when the Federalists and the Republicans seemed to be embarking on irreconcilable paths.

Adams succeeded Washington as president in 1796. Fresh on the heels of Washington's farewell warnings against the dangers of party, a great rash of incivility polarized not only the government but the nation as a whole. Bernard Bailyn describes an environment in which basic courtesies had been abandoned: "Every aspect of American life—business groups, banks, dance assemblies, even funerals—became politicized. People who had known each other their whole lives now crossed streets to avoid meeting. As personal and social ties fell apart, differences easily spilled into violence, and fighting broke out in the state legislatures and even in Congress."

War with France was imminent, and internal dissent, according to the British ambassador, had the "whole system of American Government tottering to its foundations." The Adams administration was in many ways doomed from the outset. Still, despite his unflattering portrayal in history books as pompous and vain, Adams, a man of enormous intellect and strong commitment, showed himself capable of reaching across party lines and personal convictions. He steered the nation through troubled waters in the "quasi-war" with France, the Alien and Sedition Acts, and the XYZ affair. In 1799, Adams sent a second peace envoy to France and kept America out of what would have inevitably been a devastating and divisive war with France.

Following these years of incivility, by 1801 the new president, Thomas Jefferson, was able to speak for unity in his inaugural address: "Every difference of opinion is not a difference of principle. We have called by different names brethren of the same principle. We are all republicans— we are all federalists." Joseph Ellis writes that his inaugural address "signaled that the bitter party battles of the 1790s would not continue, . . . that the incoming Republicans would not seek revenge for past Federalist atrocities, . . . and, most significant, that Jefferson's understanding of 'pure republicanism' did not mean a radical break with Federalist policies or a dramatic repudiation of the governmental framework established in the Constitution."

Many Americans are inclined to look back on the founding generation and its Age of Passion with deserved reverence. But though they are revered today as miracle workers, their powers, as Madison reminds us, were the powers of men, not angels. Their gifts were also plenty and diverse. As the greatest and most productive generation in our history, and perhaps in world history, we must learn from the examples of these men— their ability to hold ideals so strongly and to maintain their convictions while still listening to opposition and making allowances for human failings and compromise.

A House Divided

"Bleeding Kansas" placed sectional animosities on grim display.
—Gary Gallagher

By the time Jefferson left office in 1808, the man who had opposed nationalism had nearly doubled the size of the country. From thirteen original coastal colonies, America was rapidly expanding westward as streams of settlers sought new opportunities in the territories. But the territories would also provide the catalyst, and in many cases the battlegrounds, for the greatest era of incivility that the country had yet known. Unfortunately, for all their insight and brilliance, the founding fathers had been silent on one divisive issue: slavery. It was what Joseph Ellis calls "the tragic and perhaps intractable problem that even the revolutionary generation, with all its extraordinary talent, could neither solve nor face." This problem served as a warning to our nation of the dangers of intolerance and incivility.

History suggests that drifting so far apart can only produce calamity. To mollify the South in the midst of growing sectional tensions, the Compromise of 1850 contained a provision to toughen the Fugitive Slave Law, which mandated the return of any slave, whether found in a free or a slave state, to his or her original master. Enraged by the law, Harriet Beecher Stowe penned *Uncle Tom's Cabin,* a fictional narrative criticizing slavery that quickly became a best-seller on both sides of the Atlantic. Southerners reacted with equal rage, banning the book and trying desperately to offer a proslavery response. The slavery debate was becoming a central dimension of the sectional tensions that threatened to split the Union.

Political divisions followed, especially after the passage of the Kansas-Nebraska Act, which guaranteed popular sovereignty to the territories to decide the slavery issue for themselves. The Whig Party fell to pieces, and the Republican Party emerged as the primary rival to the Democrats by 1856. That year, three major candidates ran in the sectionally charged election, which pitted the proslavery Democrat James Buchanan against the antislavery Republican John Fremont and against Millard Fillmore, the proslavery "Know-Nothing." Buchanan won by carrying all but one slave state while Fremont carried much of the North.

These political rifts widened, particularly when the situation in Kansas slid from disagreement to distrust to violence. As the historian Gary Gallagher writes, "'Bleeding Kansas' placed sectional animosities on grim display." Violence between proslavery and antislavery factions in Kansas also marked a collapse of civility that would escalate to civil war.

In one glaring example of the utter disintegration of mutual respect and tolerance among public officials, a proslavery southerner, Preston Brooks, brutally caned Massachusetts Senator Charles Sumner on the floor of the Senate because Sumner had delivered a speech critical of the proslavery movement in Kansas. Now the blood was literal, and the Republicans took up the slogan "Bleeding Kansas and Bleeding Sumner" to remind the public of the offense.

Political divisions did not mark the extent of the bleeding, however. The slavery debate played out even in churches—the longtime mediating institutions in American life. Across the country, churches were scrambling to find a moral high ground amid a flood of political and sectional controversy. The Methodist church held a firm antislavery stance until 1844, when the Methodist Episcopal Church of the South split off to adopt the defense of slavery as a positive good. The Baptists divided a year later after the church convention refused to appoint slaveholding missionaries, and although the Presbyterians avoided a formal division, the church suffered sectional divisions that produced an "Old School" proslavery faction and a "New School" antislavery faction. Differences in the churches quickly became irreconcilable as opponents ascribed the worst possible motives to one another.

Along with the collapse of the Whig Party and its roots in both the North and South went its great compromiser, Henry Clay. The violence and divisions accelerated as reciprocity and trust vanished. Something had to be done to stop the bleeding; the unfinished work of the founders could no longer be ignored.

Rebirth of Freedom

We are not enemies, but friends.

—Abraham Lincoln

By 1858, the new Republican prairie lawyer, Abraham Lincoln, knew that the time to end the divisions had come:

> A house divided against itself cannot stand. I believe this government cannot endure, permanently half slave and half free. I do not expect the Union to be dissolved—I do not expect the house to fall—but I do expect it will cease to be divided. It will become all one thing or all the other. Either the opponents of slavery will arrest the further spread of it and place it where the public mind shall rest in the belief that it is in course of ultimate extinction; or its advocates will push it forward, till it shall become alike lawful in all the States, old as well as new—North as well as South.

These words introduced to the country his "antislavery ideology that combined fixed purpose with a respect for constitutional restraints," an ideology that won him the presidency in the election of 1860.

When Lincoln rose to deliver his first inaugural address in 1861, South Carolina had repealed its ratification of the Constitution of the United States and seceded from the Union. The other southern states were soon to follow. Still, Lincoln preached reconciliation. To the last, he believed that war could be avoided if only all could remember their common "bonds of affection." He said, "We are not enemies, but friends. We must not be enemies. Though *passion* may have strained, it must not break our bonds of affection. The mystic chords of memory, stretching from every battlefield and patriot grave to every living heart and hearthstone all over this broad land, will yet swell the chorus of the Union, when again touched, as surely they will be, by the better angels of our nature."

Lincoln knew that the sectional controversies of the previous decade did not represent the true American identity. He committed his presidency to winning the "second American Revolution" by which he sought to restore to the country its mediating ethics of tolerance and civility—its "better angels." To accomplish this goal, though, the very shrewd Lincoln also knew he had to move slowly, showing the southern states tolerance with commitment to return them to the federal government. Thus as evidenced in his first inaugural address, Lincoln made the preservation of the Union, not the abolition of slavery, his war goal.

His seemingly hypocritical move away from his "house divided" speech, in which he forecast the "ultimate extinction" of slavery, showed Lincoln's deft timing and practicality. It was a tactical concession to maintain unity of effort, without which Lincoln knew he could not win the coming war. He had to hold the border states, where many citizens kept slaves, and maintain loyalties among the Democrats, who were willing to fight a war to maintain the Union but not for abolition in the North. Although Frederick Douglass and other abolitionists pilloried Lincoln as a moral relativist, it was thanks to Lincoln's calculation that abolition ultimately came. The president proved willing "to temper firmness with restraint" so that his other goals might, in time, be realized. He had that extraordinary leadership ability to set a clear goal but also the insight to know that the best path is not always the shortest.

Before long, though, Lincoln knew the time for America's second revolution was at hand. Thus when Lincoln realized that his plan for gradual and compensated emancipation in the border states was not likely to materialize, he made a bold move. After the modest and bloody Union victory at Antietam in 1862, Lincoln moved forward to prepare his immortal Emancipation Proclamation, declaring that slaves "within any State . . . in rebellion against the United States shall be . . . thence forward, and forever free." "Although restoration of the Union remained his first priority," writes the historian James McPherson, "the abolition of slavery became an end as well as a means, a war aim virtually inseparable from union itself."

He had brilliantly struck a critical blow against the South: this provided the Union with an additional 180,000 black troops and gave the North the moral high ground from which to secure European sympathies. As both a war strategist and a political leader, Lincoln was unsurpassed in American history. On the moral level, it was only after witnessing their gallant fighting that he recognized African Americans as fully his equal. The decisive stroke of his proclamation also allowed Lincoln to make an important redefinition of the cause for which so many had already given their "last full measure of devotion." As one studies presidents as war leaders, or military strategy in general, timing is everything, and Lincoln's was simply brilliant.

With his Gettysburg speech in November 1863, Lincoln went from being a "transactional leader," who had until then carefully managed the national crisis, to a "transformational leader," who would envision and bring about for America "a new birth of freedom." Realizing the founding vision of a "nation conceived in liberty and dedicated to the proposition that all men are created equal," he was in the process of completing his revolution.

By 1864, weary of war, many northerners were inclined to support the Democratic Party, led by the good-looking General George McClellan, who promised a negotiated peace settlement even if that settlement meant southern independence. For Lincoln, this was unacceptable, as it would compromise his first goal of preserving the Union. Suddenly buoyed by Sherman's decisive victory in Atlanta and other northern victories that summer and fall, Lincoln, to his surprise, easily won reelection.

Even while remaining committed to a total offensive against the South that would cost thousands of lives, Lincoln preached reconciliation and civility. Before the victory of the North was assured, Lincoln rose in his second inaugural address, as the sun suddenly broke through the clouds, to call famously for "malice toward none" and "charity for all." Far from a moral relativist, he balanced this call for civility with an equally emphatic call to maintain "*firmness* in the right as God gives us to see the right."

And as at so many other crucial points in the American experience, it took faith to negotiate this passage. Unlike President McKinley, who felt that he had received direct authorization from God to go to war with Spain and take the Philippines, Lincoln never assumed that he was in lock-step with God or that the Almighty directed all that he did. Rather, Lincoln was a constant inquirer and keenly aware of his own fallibility. He noted that both sides read the same Bible and that the prayers of both would not be answered fully, for God had his own purposes. Lincoln never claimed to speak for God. He used the conditional throughout his speech: "If God wills that . . ." After his second inaugural address, the president's former critic Frederick Douglass told Lincoln, "That was a sacred effort." Douglass was referring to the speech, but he could just as easily have been referring to Lincoln's transformational leadership over the preceding five years. Sacred indeed. Ironically, the savior of the Union was slain on Good Friday in 1865, some said to atone for the sins of both the North and the South.

The Best-Laid Plans

He serves his party best who serves his country best.
—Rutherford B. Hayes

Lincoln's tragic death dashed any hope of a smooth national reunion. In the later years of the Civil War, the Great Emancipator had advocated a plan that would have allowed the rebel states to rejoin the Union with minimal repercussions. The so-called "ten percent plan" stipulated that as soon as ten percent of the voting population of a state swore an oath of loyalty to the Union, that state would be free to set up a loyal government and be readmitted. Radical Republicans in Congress resented this approach as overly generous and sought instead a fifty percent loyalty requirement and increased power given to the federal courts to enforce emancipation. Congress passed these plans in the Wade-Davis Bill of July 1864. Not wanting to prematurely commit to any one plan for reconstruction, Lincoln exercised a pocket veto of the bill. Tragically, he was slain before he could clarify his intentions for reconstruction.

Lincoln's successor, the Southern Unionist from Tennessee, Andrew Johnson, wanted every state to pledge an oath of allegiance. He also urged southern states to declare secession illegal, repudiate the Confederate debt, and ratify the Thirteenth Amendment abolishing slavery. The former rebel states did this begrudgingly, intentionally writing loopholes into their new constitutions to keep rights, particularly voting rights, from blacks. Southern state legislatures enacted the "black codes," which placed further restrictions on the freedoms of former slaves. Congressional Republicans also resented the election of several prominent ex-Confederate leaders to Congress in 1865 and decided to take the reconstruction agenda away from Johnson. After Johnson subsequently—and stubbornly—vetoed two relatively modest Republican bills, moderate Republicans in Congress joined their more radical brethren in opposition to the president.

Proud and intolerant of opposition, Johnson refused to reconcile with his party and took to the stump in his infamous "swing around the circle campaign" of 1868. He argued against the majority of Republicans and campaigned for his own newly created National Union movement. The campaign, along with Johnson's opposition to the Fourteenth Amendment, further alienated Congress and the public, and the election gave Republicans two-thirds of the seats in both houses of Congress. Thus Congress was in a position to begin its own harsh reconstruction program.

Johnson began dismissing members of his administration who supported Radical Reconstruction. An equally uncivil Congress responded with a number of measures meant to curb the president's power to hire and fire employees, and before long, they snared Johnson in a violation of the new laws. Sensing their opportunity to remove an obstacle, the House impeached the president. He was acquitted by a single vote in the Senate. Johnson's lack of civility and intolerance drove people to extremes, polarized the country, and nearly cost him the presidency. This was a low point in American history.

In 1876, shortly after the nation celebrated its centennial, the struggle of Reconstruction had officially ended, but the disputed election of Hayes and Tilden in November was threatening to become violent. It was much worse than the disputed election of 1800, for some governors began to mobilize militia. Congress set up a special commission to determine how to award the electoral votes from four states (three still under federal military control), and a political deal was struck. Candidate Hayes received the disputed votes, no doubt as a result of a deal whereby a Democratic senator, David Key, and a former Confederate colonel would come into the Republican Hayes's cabinet. Union troops would be withdrawn from the occupied southern states, and southwestern railways would receive subsidies. President Hayes spent his four years in office trying to rebuild the civility of the nation and bringing the North and South together again. His motto was "He serves his party best who serves his country best."

The America that emerged in the decades following the Civil War was an industrial giant, a rising global power, and a nation of ever more immigrants. Many new arrivals fled not only poverty but also religious intolerance. This was the era during which the Statue of Liberty, a centennial gift from the people of France, erected in 1886, took on its global significance as the protector of the downtrodden, the weak, the huddled masses who could not find education, material wealth, or political power in their native lands.

A new generation of leaders emerged to guide America into this new world. The most notable was the adventurous "Rough Rider" Theodore Roosevelt, called the accidental president. He led the Progressive movement, became the first environmental president, busted trusts, and turned the United States into a great power. In global affairs, he carried "a big stick" but "spoke softly" and even negotiated a peace treaty between warring Russia and Japan for which he won the Nobel Peace Prize. The warrior turned diplomat.

The Beginning of an Age

> *It was a case of too much too late.*
> —John Cooper, on President Wilson's outreach
> to ratify the treaty of Versailles

The next important chapter in American history was written by President Woodrow Wilson, who ran for a second term in 1916. Though he campaigned on a ticket to keep the United States out of the European "Great War" then raging, in 1917, he led America to intervene in that conflict.

Suddenly, dramatically different people and cultures had a more immediate impact on American affairs, and tolerance became an even more important virtue, as did American commitment to the republican principles of liberty and the rule of law. Despite rising discrimination at home against German Americans, the enemy in Europe, Wilson, the scholar and idealist, recognized our responsibility not just to the nation but to the world. "We are at the beginning of an age," he said, "in which it will be insisted that the same standards of conduct and responsibility for wrong done shall be observed among nations and their governments that are observed among individual citizens of the civilized states."

Wilson, the former head of Princeton University, developed perhaps the most extensive international reconstruction plan ever created and the grandest postwar vision of "making the world safe for democracy" in his proposal known as the Fourteen Points. Wilson, like Lincoln, had vision. Unlike Lincoln, he was ineffective at blazing a pathway to achieve that vision. His lack of civility, practicality, and inclusiveness produced what John Cooper calls "perhaps the greatest presidential failure in the politics of foreign policy." It is instructive, then, to discuss the rise and fall of the Fourteen Points.

At war's end, Wilson, the moralist, hoped to lead the Paris Peace Conference to adopt a new world system that would prevent the eruption of war by removing its impetus. The keystone of his plan was the creation of a League of Nations to mediate between its member states. Even before the conclusion of the war, there was general public support for such a league, but Wilson made few attempts before the Paris conference to extend the base of support for the issue beyond his own party. Because of personal animosity, Wilson did not invite a key Republican, Senator Henry Cabot Lodge, to be a part of the discussions. He also failed to include a single Republican in the peace delegation—neither former President Taft nor former Secretary of State Elihu Root nor his former presidential opponent Charles Evans Hughes. Thus when he returned from Europe and undertook a whirlwind campaign to convince the American public to embrace the League, it "was a case of too much too late." Finally, it was Wilson's refusal to entertain compromise with the Senate or court the necessary coalitions that would not just weaken but actually destroy the viability of his Fourteen Points.

Like Wilson, many American presidents have failed not at creating a vision but at implementing it. In our system, compromise, inclusion, and some tolerance of dissenting views are essential to developing a practical pathway to success. The lesson to be taken from Wilson's failure might have special significance for President George W. Bush as he tries to implement his vision for postwar Iraq and democracy in the Middle East.

The miracle of the Constitutional Convention and of Abraham Lincoln's presidency is that the leadership qualities of civility and commitment, coalition building, and inclusiveness coincided at precisely the right moments. Tragically for America and for the world, there was no such miracle after World War I. Indeed, a strong League of Nations with the United States as its leading member would have involved us directly in the international crises of the 1930s. Hitler might have been stopped early on. An American leadership presence in Europe might have deterred his rise in the first place.

The New Deal: "Dr. Win the War"

In a play on his initials, F. D., fellow students at Harvard called this handsome, young patrician a "feather duster"—a lightweight. Franklin Delano Roosevelt was nonetheless appointed assistant secretary of the navy during World War I, following in the footsteps of his cousin, former president Teddy. All expected he might become an important political figure one day, but in 1921, Roosevelt was suddenly cut down by polio. His son James referred to him as the father with the dead legs. Roosevelt's protective and domineering mother wanted him to retire to Hyde Park. Instead, with the support of his estranged wife, Roosevelt transformed himself into a towering leader who could overcome all odds. He would later say to the nation, "All we have to fear is fear itself." He led us out of the Great Depression and later to victory in World War II.

Unlike Wilson, Roosevelt had both the bold vision and the practical ability to experiment, change course, and build coalitions. Notes James MacGregor Burns, "FDR entered office without a set program or even a definite philosophy of government. Roosevelt said that he was perfectly aware that he might have to try first one thing and then another—the pragmatic implication was that 'what works' would be the decisive question, although it was not always clear what worked." Elected first in 1932 during the high tide of the Great Depression, Roosevelt knew he faced nearly impossible odds but spoke as a truly great communicator with compassion and hope.

In his first term, he assembled a "brain trust" to advise his presidency. Having won all but fifty-nine electoral votes, Roosevelt built a remarkable coalition to launch the most expansive legislative initiative ever undertaken. His "first hundred days" saw the passage of fifteen major bills that covered multiple facets of the Depression crisis.

His dramatic achievements in these turbulent times were a testament to his moderation and flexibility. By installing a social safety net in the form of the New Deal, Roosevelt rescued the free enterprise system from a crisis. While he was attacked from the right for his liberal social policies, the onslaught from the left was even more severe as charismatic figures like Governor Huey Long and Father Coughlin argued for what amounted to American socialism. Roosevelt's deft compromises with these competing ideologies kept America from going socialist, as many European nations did.

Roosevelt was far ahead of the nation in recognizing the threat from Hitler and personally pursued both covert and overt efforts to aid the British. Even before Pearl Harbor, Roosevelt formed a unity war cabinet by appointing two experienced Republicans, Stimson and Knox, to head the War and Navy Departments. He enlisted the help of the scientist-engineer and head of the Carnegie Institute, Vannevar Bush, to mobilize the university scientific research community behind the war effort. He also used Wendell Wilkie, his presidential opponent in the election of 1940, as a messenger to Winston Churchill. In his own words, FDR had moved from "Dr. New Deal," the partisan, to "Dr. Win the War," the nonpartisan. Roosevelt's war leadership also showed his superb balance of commitment and tolerance to unite with Republican business leaders to accomplish the nearly impossible. Roosevelt did not always agree with them, but he joined forces with them to win the war.

Like Washington and Lincoln, Roosevelt believed in a divine design that had taken care of a cripple like him. He respected the mysteries of that design and never pretended to have a direct line to heaven. Unlike Lincoln, he was a conventional Episcopalian who believed, almost playfully, that the Lord would occasionally make small things happen to encourage him onward.

Roosevelt's wartime example of inclusion extended into the Cold War through the successive administrations of Harry Truman and Dwight Eisenhower. These practical presidents maintained working relations with Congress and the opposing party as they faced the new challenge of the Cold War. Despite his domestic fights with Congress as "Give-'em-Hell Harry," his 1948 campaign against what he called a "do-nothing Republican Congress," and his courageous drive for civil rights legislation while facing an election campaign, Harry Truman, the domestic partisan, was a master of civility and inclusion on the foreign policy front.

The Marshall Plan

We are the first great nation to feed and support the conquered.

—Harry S. Truman

The Marshall Plan was the greatest success of the Truman administration. It was a post–World War II European reconstruction plan as bold as Wilson's ill-fated Fourteen Points but far more successful.

The first reason for success was Truman himself. Like Washington, this plainspoken man from Missouri surrounded himself with eminent advisers. Truman admired his secretary of state, George Marshall, more than he did Churchill and Roosevelt due to Marshall's role as the organizer of victory in World War II but even more because Marshall was totally selfless, a listener rather than a talker. These were qualities needed to woo the Republican Senator Arthur Vandenberg and other members of Congress, including the Taft isolationists. Truman knew that Marshall would solicit and incorporate Vandenberg's views on the plans, formulation, and implementation of European reconstruction. This $12 billion program, which came to be known as the Marshall Plan, won bipartisan approval.

A few days after the plan passed, Truman wrote, "In all the history of the world, we are the first great nation to feed and support the conquered." The plan emanated forgiveness, healing, and reconstruction worthy of the Puritans' "city set on a hill." It was a shining hour for America. Truman, Marshall, and Vandenberg were worthy of the founding fathers.

By the time Truman left the White House, the great institutions responsible for winning the Cold War were in place: the National Security Council, the Department of Defense, the CIA, the Marshall Plan, and NATO. Even here, Truman resurrected Republican President Herbert Hoover to lead important commissions on better government performance.

President Dwight D. Eisenhower came to office having commanded the grand coalition of often difficult generals that won the Second World War. His more subtle style of leadership exuded honesty, civility, and optimism. The boy from Kansas, who led the Allies to victory in Europe, was an incarnation of the American dream. He was comfortable in his own skin, especially with his quiet inner faith. He never criticized an adversary by name. He appointed members from both the internationalist and isolationist wings of his party to the cabinet and established for the first time in the American presidency a congressional liaison director, Bryce Harlow. The president acted with great deference and decorum toward Democratic leaders in Congress. When facing an international crisis, he believed in first going to the Hill, knowing that unity added to presidential success at home and abroad.

The early period of the Eisenhower era was marred only by the opportunistic scare mongering of the uncivil Senator Joseph McCarthy, whose investigation of and public hearings on suspected Communists in government became indiscriminate and mean. During one dramatic hearing, the secretary of the army asked McCarthy, "Sir, have you no decency?" The Senate agreed in its resolution to censure the senator.

Eisenhower skillfully changed course from the liberalism of Roosevelt and Truman without upsetting the system they created, including some New Deal and Fair Deal programs. He championed the monumental national highway legislation that transformed the country and laid infrastructure for the greatest expansion of wealth seen in our history. Like George Washington, he tried to be a mediator rather than party leader or chief legislator. For all the conservative rhetoric, Eisenhower was truly a practical leader, and his great organizational skills equipped the White House with a national security process to better manage the ensuing forty years of Cold War. A true grand strategist, he created the United States Information Agency to explain the best of America and thereby win the battle of ideas and perceptions. He created the science advisory system to maintain scientific superiority. He was inclusive in his outreach for professional talent.

Young and charismatic John F. Kennedy came into office with inspirational rhetoric that mobilized the country's idealism and united the nation and many peoples longing for freedom everywhere with the challenge, "My fellow citizens of the world, ask not what America can do for you, but what together we can do for the freedom of man." An inclusive Kennedy enlisted a prominent, highly respected Republican secretary of the treasury in Douglas Dillon, who stimulated investment with tax cuts. After the Bay of Pigs fiasco, for which Kennedy publicly and immediately accepted responsibility, the president brought in a second highly respected Republican, John McCone, as head of the CIA. He soon announced that America would go to the moon. The peak of his career was the careful handling of the Cuban Missile Crisis. Throughout his brief presidency, Kennedy came through as a man of civility, as a uniter, not a divider of the nation. He inspired the youth of our country to public service.

The Vietnam War: The Great Divide

Unfortunately, the principles of civility, bipartisanship, inclusion, and unity of purpose that Roosevelt, Truman, Eisenhower, and Kennedy had championed to lead America in the immediate post–World War II period would not last. Increasing support in America for the "containment" of communism worldwide led President Kennedy in the early 1960s to commit U.S. aid and advisers to the South Vietnamese in their struggle against the Communist north. Later, under Secretary of Defense Robert McNamara's influence, Lyndon Johnson committed more ground troops in an Americanization of the war. Lacking clarity of purpose and an effective strategy, U.S. operations became bogged down in the quagmire of South Vietnam. In stark contrast to the incredible national unity that won World War II, the Vietnam War sundered America. Some sons of the rich obtained college deferments from the draft, while the poor went to fight. Antiwar sentiment mushroomed, and across the country, angry citizens jeered, "Hey, hey, LBJ, how many kids did you kill today?" The unexpected 1968 Tet Offensive—a spate of coordinated surprise attacks on U.S. bases and the Saigon Embassy—had minimal military repercussions but delivered a bruising blow to public opinion on the American home front.

Johnson saw the harm the war was causing, both at home and abroad, and shockingly declared that he would not stand for reelection so that he could devote his full energy to a negotiated settlement. This story of Johnson and Vietnam is truly a presidential tragedy. LBJ was an extraordinarily successful domestic president who effectively built coalitions in areas such as civil rights. It remains a mystery why he could not better apply these skills to Vietnam.

In 1968, the new president, Richard Nixon, brilliant, shrewd, and insecure, recognized the disastrous nature of the Vietnam conflict and pursued a policy of détente with the Soviet Union. In a series of masterstrokes, Nixon hoped to end the Cold War with the Soviets, open China, and "Vietnamize" the war. But well into his first term as president, the conflict raged on, and with his failure of character in dealing with the Watergate break-in and subsequent cover-up, Nixon ruined his chances at successful leadership. The nation suffered both from the tragic end of the war and the near impeachment and resignation of a sitting president.

A man of great civility as Republican leader in the House, President Gerald Ford did much to use his two-year tenure to heal the nation. He was hindered by his courageous but controversial pardon of Nixon. He said that he wished only to spare the nation the sight of a protracted trial.

In this period of both domestic and international suffering, another transformational leader emerged, not in the halls of government but in the pulpit. For the nation at large, Dr. Martin Luther King Jr. was a transformational figure throughout the 1960s. More important, he embodied the kind of committed yet tolerant leadership consistent with the founding of our Republic. Speaking in biblical tones not heard since Lincoln, King called on America to "live out the true meaning of its creed" that "all men are created equal." King's uniting vision gave millions of Americans genuine hope in the American dream. He believed that people should be judged "not by the color of their skin but by the content of their character." King, following on the model of Mahatma Gandhi in India, advocated principled nonviolence in pursuing his goal. This was especially important as the incivility and violence escalated in both the civil rights and antiwar movements. King encouraged his followers, including Vietnam War protesters, to show civility and restraint in the face of extreme mistreatment. Much as Roosevelt warded off socialism at a moment that transformed our political culture, King warded off violence in a nation divided. He called the nation to find common ground.

Civility on the International Stage: Jimmy Carter, Ronald Reagan, and George H. W. Bush

Our next three presidents—Jimmy Carter, Ronald Reagan, and George Herbert Walker Bush—were very different. Each had striking international successes that were achieved only through exemplary civility. These successes were due to their common styles in manifesting civility in their negotiations and coalition building.

Though Jimmy Carter was a man of character, devoted to human rights worldwide, he lacked the visionary skills and charisma of Kennedy. His presidency was marred by double-digit inflation and the Iranian hostage crises. His defining moment, however, was at Camp David, where through unusual skills of civility and careful handling of negotiation details, he brought together President Anwar Sadat of Egypt and Prime Minister Menachem Begin of Israel to agree to a remarkable Middle East settlement. After his single term, Carter continued such reconciliation work by building his presidential center into an institution in Atlanta that mediates conflicts worldwide with a keen understanding of compromise and civility. He appropriately received the Nobel Peace Prize.

Ronald Reagan, the Great Communicator, rode into office on a landslide victory, increased military spending and created large budget deficits, launched the Strategic Defense Initiative, and branded the Soviet Union an "evil empire." When Mikhail Gorbachev came to lead that nation, Reagan, ever the Cold Warrior, recognized an opportunity to make a U-turn toward engagement, dialogue, and negotiation, especially in view of the weakened Soviet economy. In 1985, the leaders of the world's two superpowers met in Geneva, where mutual fascination and deep discussions on how to move forward proceeded in civil exchange. Before his advisers, Reagan saw the opportunity to work with a man he liked on a new course of disarmament between the two superpowers. Together he hoped they could bring to an end the "overnuclearized" strategy, which Reagan loathed.

In the autumn of 1986 in Reykjavik, Iceland, the two leaders came together in intensive armament negotiations in which Gorbachev demonstrated startling flexibility. Then Gorbachev suddenly declared his concessions contingent on Reagan's shelving the Strategic Defense Initiative, and the meeting broke apart. Contrary to the public alarm at this time, Gorbachev later wrote that this was the decisive turning point of the Cold War. The following year, Reagan and Gorbachev reached a dramatic agreement that for the first time eliminated an entire class of intermediate-range nuclear missiles worldwide and included serious negotiations toward reducing all long-range nuclear missiles by half. The end of the Cold War was in sight. The two leaders truly connected in what Gorbachev has since called "a miracle."

Reagan's successor, the experienced George H. W. Bush, called for a kinder, gentler America, but he lacked the Gipper's magic touch. When Iraq's Saddam Hussein suddenly invaded Kuwait, however, Bush swiftly and masterfully built an international coalition. He conducted personal consultations with leaders of many countries, including even radical Syria, and carefully laid out a unified military strategy and burden-sharing with coalition partners, who assumed over eighty percent of the cost of the ensuing brilliant military victory. The entire effort is a case study in civility: two-way discussions with partners and allies to move to higher ground in an extraordinary unity of effort.

The Current Challenge

Civility is not a tactic or a sentiment.

—George W. Bush

Democrat Bill Clinton's popular two-term presidency was politically charged: he took over some Republican programs and wrapped them in compassion, believing he had to govern from the political center to meet the great economic challenges we faced. America enjoyed great prosperity during his presidency. Clinton had an uncanny ability to identify with individuals and to "feel their pain." He and the newly elected midterm speaker of the House, Newt Gingrich, leader of the 1994 Republican electoral revolution, formed a pact with a handshake. They later opposed one another over the shutdown of the federal government due to Congress's failure to provide funding, a confrontation that boomeranged against the Republicans and set the stage for Clinton's political revitalization. However, the president's sordid affair with an aide, Monica Lewinsky, the attempted cover-up, and his ensuing impeachment resulted in the first trial of a sitting president since Andrew Johnson. Open hostility in Congress plunged the country into partisan divisions. The resulting incivility and polarization have stayed with us to this day.

Indeed, the congressional actions on the impeachment and trial of Bill Clinton are an example of the harm that can be done by incivility and partisanship within Congress. Unlike the bipartisan congressional handling of the Nixon-era Watergate affair and the Reagan administration's Iran-Contra scandal, the 1998–1999 Clinton episode is far more reminiscent of the political civil war between Andrew Johnson and the radical Republicans. In Congress, Senator Dianne Feinstein offered a constructive way out of the controversy with a resolution stating that President Clinton "gave false and misleading testimony and his actions have had the effect of impeding discovery of evidence of Judicial Proceedings." This resolution drew seventy-nine senators into bipartisan support but was blocked by Republicans who wanted a conviction they could not obtain. A civil bipartisan outcome to heal the wound was out of reach, and America was once again so split and Congress so polarized that by the turn of this century, redistricting hardened the battle lines into red and blue states. The loss of a middle ground often left Congress dysfunctional or merely passive. In 2000, divisions were exacerbated by the third disputed election in our history, this one going to the U.S. Supreme Court for resolution.

George W. Bush, a self-labeled "compassionate conservative," had campaigned on the platform that he would bring the country together, as he had done with his state as governor of Texas. He lost the popular vote but came to office, proclaiming civility, after the Supreme Court awarded him Florida's electoral college votes. Review the call for civility in his inaugural:

> America, at its best, matches a commitment to principle with a concern for civility. A civil society demands from each of us good will and respect, fair dealing and forgiveness. Some seem to believe that our politics can afford to be petty because in a time of peace, the status of our debates appear small. But the stakes for America are never smaller. We must live up to the calling we share. Civility is not a tactic or a

sentiment. It is the determined choice of trust over cynicism, of community over chaos. And this commitment, if we keep it, is a way to
shared accomplishment.

From the start, George Bush led boldly, as if backed by a majority man-
date. He pressed forward with deep tax cuts and then joined with Democratic Senator Ted Kennedy on a bipartisan education bill under the mantra
"leave no child behind." In a gracious act, Bush named the Department
of Justice building after Robert F. Kennedy, the former attorney general
and brother of the former president.

When the September 11 terrorists struck in 2001, President Bush led
the nation with courage and wisdom as an inspiring war leader. As noted
earlier, his presence at the Twin Towers site, at the Islamic Center, and at
the National Cathedral memorial service with past presidents, exemplified a national unifier. Putting together a sixty-nation coalition for the war
on terror in the next four months and executing an agile attack on the
Taliban and al-Qaeda in Afghanistan, he was a model war leader and
stood for these months alongside Lincoln and FDR, America's two greatest war leaders.

But in the first months of 2002, his diplomacy became less inclusive
and things got somewhat off track. The Bush administration tried to
mobilize resources for a determined move against Saddam Hussein in
Iraq, but damage had been done by unnecessary talk of preemption and
unilateralism, despite the fact that Article 51 of the UN Charter allows
for the right of such self-defense and obviously had to be reinterpreted in
an age of weapons of mass destruction and terrorism. Under dire circumstances, our nation has always operated unilaterally, even preemp-
tively, as in the Cuban Missile Crisis.

The use of such extended rhetoric as a doctrine and talk of unilateralism only increased anti-Americanism worldwide, further strengthening
the image of America as a bully rather than a wise and judicious world
power. Bush's advisers, including Prime Minister Tony Blair of the United
Kingdom, as well as the U.S. Congress, stressed the importance of going
to the United Nations. Bush consulted the UN Security Council, where he
received unanimous support for a resolution to disarm Saddam Hussein.
France, however, threatened to veto a resolution approving military action
and, in the end, the United States, our staunch ally Great Britain, and a
limited coalition moved to a full offensive without the Council's final
approval. The ensuing "Operation Iraqi Freedom" culminated in Bush's
declaration of military victory just a few weeks later, on May 1, 2003.

Although the war resolution received bipartisan support from Congress, the political side of Bush's postwar reconstruction strategy did not involve the kind of expert and inclusive marshaling of expertise as under FDR's postwar planning or in Truman's execution of the Marshall Plan. Hussein's tyrannical regime had been toppled, but maintaining the perception of moral superiority was complicated as an undermanned occupation force dealt with an increased insurgency, mounting casualties, and the involvement of American reservists in the Abu Ghraib scandal. Anti-Americanism soared around the world, and our relationships with longtime allies became strained. With the midsummer transfer of sovereignty to the provisional Iraqi government, the United States began to move away from its role as a dominant occupying force toward one as part of a larger peace-keeping mission.

In contrast to these troubling developments overseas, Homeland Security Department Secretary Tom Ridge has been dedicated to civility, outreach, and inclusion as he has organized the resources needed to fight the war on terrorism at home. Ridge created broad advisory structures to draw on a wide range of bipartisan talent from across the nation, somewhat analogous to what FDR had so brilliantly done in World War II. Of course, Secretary of State Colin Powell has been another model of civility in all of his endeavors, as is evidenced by his extraordinary public standing. With the costs of Iraq continuing to challenge us, the need for leadership demonstrating such inclusion on domestic and international fronts is clear if we are to succeed.

Mistakes have been made. But as the master strategist Napoleon said, in war it is not he who makes no mistakes but he who makes the fewest who prevails. The test is how leaders deal with their mistakes. This too has something very much to do with civility and humility, which George W. Bush spoke so well about in his presidential campaign and his inaugural. This lesson of humility applies to whoever leads the White House and Congress in the coming years.

Spirituality as a Bridge

Surely some revelation is at hand.
                                        —William Butler Yeats

Most of this essay has focused on the attributes of civility, on civility's roots in traditional and civil religion, and on the many expressions of civility (and incivility) during various American presidencies. It has noted that the greatest presidents have tended to be inclusive, to be uniters rather than dividers.

I want to turn, first, to the current political and social scene and raise a fundamental question about our religious nation: Are civility's religious and spiritual roots a unifying force for our country? Or, as some would argue, has religion, now so mixed with politics and the mass media, itself become a wedge issue? Second, I want to apply the historical lessons of civility to current events and to the diversity of religious beliefs in America. In doing so, I believe that we will find that even in these troubled times, civility is the vital component to our democratic form of government and must also be applied in the religious sphere between and within denominations and faiths. Indeed, civility is needed to infuse creativity and common purpose in our government and its several branches and throughout the nation.

Today, as our nation and the world confront new and great perils, the paralyzing forces of incivility and intolerance could threaten our country. Divisions in Congress reflect divisions in the country. The wedge issues appear endless: pro-choice, right to life, death penalty, gay marriage, stem cell research, tax cuts and raises, and now, on top of everything, the war in Iraq and the overextension of our citizen soldiers, National Guard, and reserves. As mentioned earlier, we also face long-term challenges to our nation: the deficit, the rising cost of Social Security and Medicare just as the baby boom generation enters retirement, and rampant anti-Americanism overseas, which can create more terrorists. All of these factors contribute to our domestic discord. These challenges, if allowed to divide the nation, might deny the next generation the prosperity and civic culture that we have inherited.

A house divided against itself cannot stand, intoned the biblical-sounding Lincoln. True, we have not reached the great national downslide of the 1840s and 1850s, leading to the Civil War, but today we are at "one of the low points," the political scientist Ross Baker noted, observing the lack of civility in Congress. As the *New York Times* writer Sheryl G. Stolberg notes, Benjamin Franklin once said that "Congress should be a mirror image of the American people, and it is, in the sense that Americans are terribly divided and their elected representatives are unable to transcend those divisions."

The words of the poet William Yeats come hauntingly to mind:

> Things fall apart; the centre cannot hold;
> Mere anarchy is loosed upon the world,

the blood-dimmed tide is loosed, and everywhere
the ceremony of innocence is drowned;
The best lack all convictions, while the worst
Are full of passionate intensity.
Surely some revelation is at hand.

But what is this revelation? The question still stands: Is religion in America a divisive force, or can American spirituality and the civil religion of the founders help unite the country? The central idea in this essay is that American spirituality can be a uniter, if the same principles of civility I have enumerated are also practiced by different religious groups. For we often ignore the fact that pure religion in its spiritual core involves both commitment and tolerance.

America is indeed a spiritual nation, a people whose spirituality goes well beyond the regular attendance at church, temple, and mosque. Indeed, for the mid-nineteenth-century French visitor Alexis de Tocqueville, the intense "religious atmosphere of the country was the first thing that struck me on my arrival." This tradition should be embraced, as America is increasingly a nation of many faiths, each with its own deep commitments, but interlocked in civic virtue and the need for tolerance. A uniting spirituality can keep us humble and remind us that we are but small parts of a greater plan. If civility and interfaith dialogue are practiced among religious groups, common spirituality will unite us.

Rabbi Ronald Sobel, the leader of the largest Reform Jewish congregation in America, eloquently notes that "beneath the theological differences that separate us—profound and serious—there is a far greater 'depth theology.' And when we penetrate beneath the surfaces of our differences, what we find is that we stand not on opposite sides of the fence but rather on the same side."

Many faiths experience this same core spiritual revelation. Michael Novak touched on this theme in his book *On Two Wings: Humble Faith and Common Sense at the American Founding.* His title reminds us of the connection between the inner self and outer practice that the founders took for granted, for their spirituality and their very character were mixed with a sense of the practical and respect for the individual. The best among our founders lacked arrogance and self-righteousness.

The genius of American religious culture and its relationship to our political culture is, as de Tocqueville noted, that America's spiritual and practical elements express both our religious nature and our individualistic personalities. Dogmas that divide theologians, scandals in the church, and the politicization of religious issues often shrink before the individual expression of an overarching spirituality. Alan Wolfe's book *The Transformation of American Religion* captures the nexus of this relationship. Wolfe writes, "Understanding more about the ways Americans practice religion also helps. . . . Americans are more likely to identify with their faith, which they consider personal to them, than with institutions, including denominations and congregations, that have historically represented their faith to them." It is the revitalization of these spiritual roots of civility that we sorely need.

Crossing the Bridge

The consonance of faith and reason.
—John Witherspoon and Samuel Cooper

Whenever religion in America angrily divides us, that division violates the spirit of the world's great religions, as well as the convictions of our nation's founders. It is also against the teachings of our more thoughtful religious leaders. Inclusiveness, especially in a religious context, is not new. For instance, early in the Christian tradition, even the Apostle Paul struggled to contain the deep division in the early Jesus movement between the Jewish Christians, who demanded circumcision for all the followers, and the Gentiles, who vehemently opposed this and other Levitical requirements. Yet in his epistles to the Romans and the Ephesians, time and again Paul told each movement to support its individual belief on such matters. Do not compromise the details of your belief but "welcome all." "May the God of steadfastness and encouragement grant you to live in harmony with one another. . . . Welcome one another, just as Christ has welcomed you." This teaching is filled with the search for civility and inclusiveness.

At a meeting of fellow evangelists, the Rev. Robert Schuller recently lamented, "What upsets me about religious leaders of all faiths is that they talk like they know it all, and anybody who doesn't agree with them is a heretic." To take Schuller's words a step further, too often religious leaders believe—a bit arrogantly—that they have at last solved the mystery of God. Likewise, we are approaching an era of partisanship that echoes this mind-set of absolutism that can close off dialogue and mutual respect, if we are not able to reclaim our civility.

In dealing with religious differences, we must remind ourselves of the tradition set by our first president, George Washington. An Anglican, Washington conversed alike with the Jews at the synagogue at Newport, the Quakers in Pennsylvania, and the Catholics in Maryland. He epitomized the American genius of unity in diversity. This is a political unity that coalesces around common political philosophy—our religious traditions, rising from the Judeo-Christian and later incorporating other traditions, that acknowledges these "self-evident truths" to allow unity in diversity. Washington and other early American leaders were influenced by the leading preachers of their time and also by the Enlightenment and the Age of Reason. It is important to recall that John Witherspoon of Princeton and Samuel Cooper at Harvard emphasized "the consonance of faith and reason" that they held together as friends from different religious traditions.

Abraham Lincoln, our most articulate and spiritual president, knew much of the Bible by heart. He was even called the "redeemer president." Not only was he possessed of extraordinary humor, but he also had an uncanny ability to penetrate to the core of the human condition and its hypocrisies. When Lincoln was asked why he had not formally joined any church, he replied, "When any church will inscribe over its altar as its sole qualification for membership, the Savior's condensed statement of both Law and Gospel—'Thou shall love the Lord thy God with all thy heart and with all thy soul and with all thy mind, and thy neighbor as thyself,' that church I will join with all my heart and all my soul."

Lincoln saw the love of God and people around us as fundamental. Certainly, all religions require and are enriched by creeds, liturgies, commandments, and rules, but when those crowd out Lincoln's core beliefs, they are, as the Apostle Paul laments, of tongues that speak but do not love, merely "sounding brass or a clanging cymbal" (1 Corinthians 13).

As we turn to present events, Lincoln's words are well heeded. Clearly, religion in America—and certainly spirituality—cannot be categorized into states or platforms because it pervades them all. In modern times, the first president to express his faith so openly was not George W. Bush but Jimmy Carter. In recent years, Democratic Senator Joe Lieberman, an Orthodox Jew, has talked more than any other public figure about the historical and current importance of religion in the public square. Not just Republicans but almost every Democratic presidential candidate has addressed religion in his life. In Congress, congressional prayer breakfasts bring Republicans and Democrats together and probably remain the best and most unobtrusive avenue in an often partisan Congress to promote nimble dialogue and civility.

Today, our national connectivity, even as it enhances our individual beliefs, comes from getting to know and admiring people "different from ourselves," whether in terms of politics, skin color, culture, sexual orientation, or religion. I must say that the most deeply selfless and spiritual business leader I have ever known is the one-time Buddhist monk from Kyoto, Dr. Kazuo Inamori, founder of the Kyocera Corporation. He was awarded the Andrew Carnegie Medal of Philanthropy in 2003.

This brings us back to our central question: Which America will we be today—the America of one or of many? Will "things fall apart" and the center not hold, or will we see a new revelation to meet the challenges with unity of purpose? Will we "nobly save or meanly lose the last, best hope of the earth" (house divided speech), the last great cause born of the unique American dream whose preservation Lincoln believed so crucial for the future of humanity? Can we reclaim the civil religion and civil unity of the founders? The answer lies at the heart of our national motto: *E pluribus unum.* We are many, but we can also be one in mighty purpose. America's civic identity can, paradoxically, bridge the forces of commitment, difference, and tolerance.

We must live this identity to its utmost if we are to engage in the respect, listening, and dialogue required to unite us and fulfill the promise of our revolutionary Constitution. On September 11, as the ashes of hate, destruction, and doubt settled across our nation, a renewed connectivity, civility, and spirituality arose. Something sacred indeed happened as rescue workers, firefighters, and police insisted on going back to face almost certain death. There was the sacrifice that Stephen Carter noted in his definition of civility. So much of the world joined with us, for people of ninety-one different nationalities died in the Twin Towers that awful but now sacred day. And within days at the National Cathedral, a rabbi, a Catholic cardinal, a Protestant evangelist, and a Muslim imam all spoke from the same pulpit as presidents, Republicans, and Democrats listened.

As Lincoln told the nation during its great travail, "We cannot escape history. . . . The fiery trial through which we pass will light us down in honor or dishonor to the latest generations." It is my hope that this discussion of magnificent triumphs and deep tragedies in the American experience will help refortify the heart of civility. Such a restoration of national character is needed to move the nation toward greater tolerance, respect, and commitment. We need civility to unite the nation in order to act from a higher common ground, that we all might be one step closer to the American Dream.

REFERENCES

Albanese, Catherine. *Sons of Our Fathers: The Civil Religion of the American Revolution.* Philadelphia: Temple University Press, 1976, p. 16.

Bailyn, Bernard, and others. *The Great Republic: A History of the American People.* Boston: Little, Brown, 1992, vol. 1., pp. 237, 286, 578.

Baker, Howard H., Jr. Address to the U.S. Senate in the "Leader's Lecture Series, 1998–2002" [http://www.senate.gov/artandhistory/history/common/generic/Leaders_Lecture_Series_Baker.htm]. July 14, 1998.

Baker, Ross, quoted in Sheryl Gay Stolberg, "The High Costs of Rising Incivility on Capitol Hill," *New York Times,* Nov. 30, 2003, p. A10.

Browne, William H., ed. *The Archives of Maryland.* Baltimore: Maryland Historical Society, 1883, vol. 1, pp. 244–247.

Burns, James MacGregor. "Franklin D. Roosevelt's 'First Hundred Days.'" In David M. Abshire (ed.), *Triumphs and Tragedies of the Modern Presidency: Seventy-Six Case Studies on Presidential Leadership.* Westport, Conn.: Praeger, 2001, p. 20.

Carter, Stephen. *Civility.* New York: HarperCollins, 1998, pp. 4, 207, 331.

Cooper, John M. "The Versailles Treaty." In David M. Abshire (ed.), *T riumphs and Tragedies of the Modern Presidency: Seventy-Six Case Studies on Presidential Leadership.* Westport, Conn.: Praeger, 2001, pp. 54, 56.

Delbanco, Andrew. *The Real American Dream.* Cambridge, Mass.: Harvard University Press, 1999, p. 48.

Donald, David Herbert. *Lincoln.* New York: Simon & Schuster, 1995, p. 284.

Ellis, Joseph. *American Sphinx: The Character of Thomas Jefferson.* New York: Knopf, 1997, pp. 215–216.

Ellis, Joseph. *Founding Brothers: The Revolutionary Generation.* New York: Knopf, 2000, p. 53.

Guelzo, Allen C. *Abraham Lincoln: Redeemer President.* Grand Rapids, Mich.: Eerdemans, 1999, p. 446.

Gup, Ted. "Tolerance Has Never Come Naturally." *Washington Post,* Mar. 14, 2004, p. B–1.

Inaugural Addresses of the Presidents of the United States. Washington, D.C.: U.S. Government Printing Office, 1989.

Jefferson, Thomas. "Notes on the State of Virginia (1787)." In David A. Hollinger and Charles Capper (eds.), *The American Intellectual Tradition: A Sourcebook. Volume 1: 1620–1865.* New York: Oxford University Press, 1989.

Jewett, Robert. *Christian Tolerance: Paul's Message to the Modern Church.* Philadelphia: Westminster Press, 1982, pp. 13–14.

Lincoln, Abraham. "House Divided Speech," June 16, 1858. In Philip Van Doren Stern (ed.), *The Life and Writings of Abraham Lincoln.* New York: Random House, 1940, pp. 746, 742.

Madison, James. *Federalist* No. 51. New York: Modern Library, 2000, p. 339.

McPherson, James. *Abraham Lincoln and the Second American Revolution.* New York: Oxford University Press, 1990, p. 85.

Morgan, Edmund. *The Meaning of Independence: John Adams, George Washington, Thomas Jefferson.* Charlottesville: University Press of Virginia, 1976.

Morone, James. *Hellfire Nation.* New Haven, Conn.: Yale University Press, 2003, p. 497.

Needleman, Jacob. *The American Soul.* New York: Putnam, 2002.

Novak, Michael. *God's Country: Taking the Declaration Seriously.* Washington, D.C.: American Enterprise Institute, 1999.

Novak, Michael. *On Two Wings: Humble Faith and Common Sense at the American Founding.* San Francisco: Encounter Books, 2001, pp. 115, 144.

Pew Research Center for the People and the Press. "Survey Finds Americans Are Increasingly Divided." *Los Angeles Times,* Nov. 6, 2003, p. A20.

Porte, Joel. *Emerson in His Journals.* Cambridge, Mass.: Belknap Press, 1982, p. 129.

Schuller, Robert, quoted in David D. Kirkpatrick, "Bush Assures Evangelicals of His Commitment to Amendment on Marriage." *New York Times,* Mar. 12, 2004, p. A10.

Shi, David E., and Mayer, Holly A. *For the Record: A Documentary History of America,* Vol. 1: *From First Contact Through Reconstruction.* New York: Norton, 1999.

Sobel, Rabbi Ronald. Remarks given at the retirement ceremony for the Rev. Dr. Daniel Matthews of Trinity Parish Wall Street at Saint John the Divine Cathedral in New York City, New York, May 1, 2004.

Stolberg, Sheryl Gay. "The High Costs of Rising Incivility on Capitol Hill," *New York Times,* Nov. 30, 2003.

Tocqueville, Alexis de. *Democracy in America.* J. P. Maier, ed., George Lawrence, trans. Garden City, N.Y.: Anchor Books, 1969, p. 295.

Waldman, Michael. *My Fellow Americans: George Washington's Farewell Address.* Hapeville, Ga.: Sourcebooks, 2003, p. 11.

Winthrop, John. *A Model of Christian Charity,* 1630. Online collection. Massachusetts Historical Society, Boston, 1838 (3rd Ser.).

Wolfe, Alan. *One Nation, After All: What Middle-Class Americans Really Think About God, Country, Family, Racism, Welfare, Immigration, Homosexuality, Work, the Right, the Left, and Each Other.* New York: Viking, 1998.

Wolfe, Alan. *The Transformation of American Religion: How We Actually Live Our Faith.* New York: Free Press, 2003, p. 263.

Yeats, William Butler. "The Second Coming." In Richard J. Finneran (ed.), *The Collected Poems of W. B. Yeats.* Old Tappan, N.J.: Macmillan, 1983.

PART THREE

DEEPENING THE AMERICAN DREAM

BREAKING THE CULTURAL TRANCE

INSIGHT AND VISION IN AMERICA

Robert Inchausti

We are living in the greatest revolution in history—a huge spontaneous upheaval of the entire human race: not the revolution planned and carried out by any particular party, race, or nation, but a deep elemental boiling over of all the inner contradictions that have ever been in man, a revelation of the chaotic forces inside everybody. This is not something we have chosen, nor is it something we are free to avoid.

—Thomas Merton,
Conjectures of a Guilty Bystander

A Diverging Inheritance

AS AN AMERICAN, I sometimes feel like the spoiled heir of an eccentric genius who ignored his family in order to make millions in international finance. What exactly does such an enormous material inheritance mean to me if there is no happiness in the home? Are all these possessions just a very elaborate surrogate for love? Or is there something else going on here? A hidden legacy, a deeper truth that needs to be unearthed, defended, and explained? Today as terrorist threats blow against our lives like an unflagging wind and political controversies infiltrate even the most intimate aspects of our lives, we are being forced to leave our adolescent impatience with complexity behind and, like the prodigal son, come home to a heritage that we never honestly appreciated because it was never truly understood.

The American dream, as our Puritan forefathers imagined it, was not a dream of abundance through which every desire could be fulfilled but a life lived in accord with conscience, a life ruled by the heart, not dictated to by material or political circumstances.[1] "Sanctifying grace," as they understood it, was to grow and deepen as their understanding of God grew and deepened. Conscience, in other words, was not an unflagging absolute but a creature of dialogue nurtured by prayer, scriptural study, and personal sacrifice. It was not Freud's internalized parental prejudices or an unchanging interior compass but rather a work in progress: the most profound accomplishment of a free people.

And so whatever one might say about the historical legacy of the Puritans—the witch hunts, the Indian wars, and the unabashed chauvinism—they did ingrain in the American character a deep desire for integrity and authenticity. Unlike their modern, positive-thinking descendants, the Puritans never thought of this country as a paradise on earth but more as a wilderness where the faithful might journey together toward an ever more accurate understanding of God's will.

The Founding Fathers enshrined this religious conception of life in the Declaration of Independence and the Constitution by foregrounding the principle that we can grow as a people and as individuals only to the degree that we "check and balance" our own inherently self-destructive impulses. This unique synthesis of spiritual aspiration with skeptical, secular authority was not the product of any abstract European political theory per se but rather the outgrowth of a completely different vision of the relationship between civil authority and the spiritual life.[2] The Founding Fathers simply assumed that democratic institutions—like every other human construct—existed within a more transcendent cosmic order. And how one related to that transcendent order could not be directed by any nationalist agenda or curtailed by institutional forces. It was one of those fortuitous accidents of history that by refusing to dictate the terms of religious expression, the United States government actually increased the value of a morally engaged, spiritual life, transforming a life lived in accord with conscience into the much more liberating and demanding challenge of practicing what one preached.

This is why the word *deism* is not sufficient to describe the worldview of our Founding Fathers. It makes it sound as though their innovative synthesis of soul and *civitas* was the expression of some very specific antique creed, whereas the truth of the matter is that the term was simply "made up" to describe the unique dialogue they initiated between faith and rationality. The idea that a government's primary responsibilities were to protect the rights of individuals to follow their conscience and to protect civil society from the tyranny of both majorities *and minorities* had the unexpected consequence of directing religious idealism toward practical human achievements and the quest for a universal ethic.

The unique power of this heady "search for a synthesis" between the theoretical and the concrete was brought home to me a few years ago by a Vietnamese student who just happened to take my American literature course.

After the quarter was over, Thi came by my office to thank me for the class. I told her that no thanks were necessary, that teaching was my job, and I got paid for it.

"No," she insisted, "you don't understand. Ever since I came over here from Vietnam, my parents have been telling me how great America is. But I never could see it. All I could see were shopping malls, bad television shows, and pickup trucks. But after taking your class, now I know what makes America so great."

"Tell me," I asked. "What makes it great?"

She looked me right in the eye and said with reverence, "Ralph Waldo Emerson."

It was a moving moment for me. I teach Emerson all the time, so it's easy to forget how life-changing his vision can be, how heady his bold assertions of human potential, how comforting his acknowledgment of solitude as the natural ally of every true individual. And it's easy to forget that we don't always need new ideas to deepen our lives; the old ones freshly conceived can do the same thing.

Not wanting to be narrow-minded, I asked her if she had read any Vietnamese literature. She said that she had but that she liked American literature better. Vietnamese literature, she told me, was mostly about wars with the Chinese, but American literature, she said, was one long lesson on how to free your own mind.

Then she read me her credo. It was a passage from the introduction to Walt Whitman's *Leaves of Grass* that she had copied out onto the back of her notebook:

> This is what you shall do: Love the earth, the sun and the animals, despise riches, give alms to everyone that asks, stand up for the stupid and crazy, devote your income and labor to others, hate tyrants, argue not concerning God, have patience and indulgence toward the people, take off your hat to nothing known or unknown or to any man or number of men, go freely with powerful uneducated persons and with the young and with the mothers of families, read these leaves in the open air every season of every year of your life, reexamine all you have

been told at school or church or in any book, dismiss whatever insults your own soul, and your very flesh shall be a great poem and have the richest fluency not only in its words but in the silent lines of its lips and face and between the lashes of your eyes and in every motion and joint of your body. . . .

As she read this, I almost cried. She had found in Whitman a succinct summary of the finest American virtues: spiritual largesse and inclusion, the rejection of pretense and status, an admiration for the outcast and the outsider, the love of the earth and the animals—but perhaps most important of all, the need to see the transcendent in the immanent and the Word in the Flesh.

I guess I really shouldn't have been surprised that at the threshold of Thi's discovery of America stood the most revolutionary precursor of them all, "the American Jesus,"[3] the great, gray, gay poet of democracy, Walt Whitman. He was exactly what she was looking for—the confirmation of all her secret wishes, the proof that there was a spiritual tradition in this country after all! America really did possess a self-conscious understanding of its own radical egalitarianism and the brave souls who lived in the light of that revelation.

Thi went on to graduate school at Emerson College in Boston. She went there largely because of its name. I tried to tell her that she didn't need to go to Emerson College to be an Emersonian, but she wanted her external circumstances to reflect her inner reality.

She has since graduated and works for a computer firm in southern California. She sent me an e-mail just a few months ago about her trip to Ground Zero in New York City and about her ongoing attempts to see through the world's pretensions and "dismiss whatever insults her own soul."

Thi's story made it clear to me that one way to deepen the American dream is to take the same approach as the Transcendentalists: contest its one-dimensional materialism, embrace its vision of individual responsibility, and simply dismiss the managed environments and pseudoevents that try to pass themselves off as reality.

Admittedly, Thi was a first-generation American, and so Emerson may have struck deeper chords in her than in her more jaded native-born peers. The idea that each of us possesses untapped potential, that faith is an aid to making that potential actual, and that self-actualization and membership in a revelatory community are the ultimate ends of civilization may not be as inspiring to those who already think of themselves as the envy of the world and have never felt the bitter sting of poverty or institution-alized prejudice. Not that native-born Americans are complacent exactly; if anything, they seem far less secure in their simulated worlds than the immigrant in the new world. Overwhelmed by the multifaceted, multi-layered incomprehensibility of their lives, they willingly embrace various forms of stupidity to protect themselves from the horrors of uncertainty and change and the boredom of a jaded existence. It is not that they lack intelligence; it is that they purposely narrow their consciousness to small, manageable matters in order to pare down the infinity of options that perpetually dwarfs any single choice they might make. Camp, kitsch, and satire seem to be needed as a hedge against all the false promises and empty urgings they must endure.[4]

Native-born Americans are not born culture critics; they are born suc-cess seekers, bent on going their parents and their peers one better—not necessarily by achieving any greater understanding of themselves or the world but by getting more of what everyone else seems to want and mak-ing good on other people's missed opportunities. They are not particularly moral beings. They live on the surfaces of things—ambitious and prag-matic to a fault, alive to the images before them and the external trap-pings of pleasure and success but dull to the ineffable, the indirect, the iconographic, and the implied.

Last year in my modern poetry class, we were studying a poem by Pablo Neruda, a beautiful, tragic lament from *Canto General* about the human costs of living under a dictatorship. One of my students—a home-grown American native of Salinas, California, and a business major—objected that Neruda was biting the hand that fed him: "After all, the dictator was only helping to integrate Chile further into the global econ-omy." The ignorance of this remark didn't really astonish me, but for the first time I saw it for what it was—the product of a bad education mag-nified by the blind impatience of youth, the result of a hurried need to know coupled to the false assumption that answers are more important than questions and that knowledge must always have a material, if not immediate, payoff.

My American-born student couldn't see the power of Neruda's view into the tragic ironies of life because he had heard (no doubt from one of my lectures) that Neruda was a "Marxist," and so—given the ideological bent of our current academic culture—he thought he knew all he needed to know about who Neruda was and what he stood for. Consequently, he could find in the poem only what his labels allowed him to perceive. Neruda's brave protest against the excesses of totalitarianism, his cry from the heart for spiritual liberty and political freedom, became for this impatient, poorly educated, American-born opportunist merely just one more egghead's attack on free market capitalism.

Such are the perceptual lacunae we breed in our young by our unmitigated focus on knowing things. They suspect and dismiss anything that doesn't solve a problem or have the potential to serve as the answer to an exam question. Any challenge to their ideas and linguistic formulations poses a direct threat—not only to their grade point average but to their self-image and hence to their very existence. So they learn very quickly how to avert their gaze from troubling anomalies, unsolvable questions, and potentially embarrassing complexities and in some cases even how to bully others into accepting their own simplistic formulations.

This pernicious identification of their identity with their opinions, talents, and personal accomplishments is one of the most damaging misconceptions in our culture. It overpersonalizes debate, undermines creative speculation, rigidifies community life, and bleeds spiritual energy out of every one of our cultural enterprises, misshaping our educational and religious institutions and sealing the best minds of this generation within a bubble of narrow expectations.

Native-born American youth often have no clue of the cultural trance they live in, so whenever anyone—a teacher or a writer—can make the historically conditioned artificiality of their lives visible to them, these teachers deepen the American dream. This is, of course, not an easy thing to do, for the more widespread the trance, the more true believers must prove its superiority, and so our national success myth carries with it a need for self-confirmation.

One of the reasons my business student couldn't appreciate the poetry of Pablo Neruda, he later told me, was because Neruda wasn't "rich." Why should he listen to a poet when the world is run by financiers? Indeed, why should anyone even attempt to see through the world's illusions unless he or she believed in something as old-fashioned as reality?

As a poet well versed in the surrealist dynamics of modern-day Chilean politics, Neruda understood how difficult it is to remain attuned to the soul's vocation in an ideological age. When we are beset by propaganda and nationalist mythologies, our capacity for human empathy flags; our speech loses its lyricism, freedom, music, and wit; and we devolve into imaginary actors in a staged historical drama so poorly composed that even we have difficulty believing in the parts that we play—not to mention difficulty believing in reality.[5]

"Deepening the American dream," for such success-driven, ideologically primed, homegrown "absurdists," is quite a different thing than it is for American immigrants. The native-born are far less interested in making sense of their situation than they are in acquiring pleasure, status, power, and control. Unlike immigrants, they do not judge their achievements against the moral and intellectual progress of humankind but rather against the accomplishments of their peers and the lives and leisure of millionaires and celebrities. This has the compounding effect of driving them deeper into the media culture and making them more ambitious for public notoriety of any sort, which only makes them even more unhappy, guilty, and self-righteous, all at the same time. It is as if the more empty the experiences, the more of them are needed!

One needn't pursue a psychoanalytical discourse here on the decline of the American character. Academics go too far in their hand-wringing analyses of postmodernism and the decline of values. Besides, Americans are not really occupied from within by corporate media images so much as they are isolated from their own inherent idealism and heroic past in postures of ironic self-defense—living a life of feigned indifference, longing for sincerity but incapable of imagining what it would be like to experience it.

At the close of the nineteenth century, Leo Tolstoy lamented the fact that the Russian middle class and aristocracy were so divorced from the material realities of everyday life that they were no longer capable of experiencing authentic grief, authentic love, or authentic courage. They spent their lives in relative luxury that only heightened their appetites, inflated their ambitions, distorted their affections, and turned the most spirited among them into reckless adventurers or duplicitous success seekers totally out of touch with themselves or the realities of their time.[6]

The same could be said of us and our progeny. Increasingly incapable of discerning love from lust, anger from indignation, fear from grief, or hope from ambition, we seek some sort of map to orient our interior lives. But to the extent that the programs, processes, therapies, and philosophies that are supposed to supply these maps reinforce the centrality of individual accomplishment, we find ourselves plunging ever more deeply into the very dilemmas we hope to cure.

Grief, loss, suffering, and contrition are, of course, the traditional medicines for hubris and self-absorption. But simply waiting for life's honesty to fall on us naturally isn't a particularly forward-thinking strategy for those of us seeking to deepen the American dream by calling it back to its radical democratic roots. Besides, suffering in itself was never worth much unless it was tied to some great ideal, and homegrown Americans already pay an enormous psychological price for their narrow focus on personal happiness and material achievement. Depression and anxiety are at near epidemic levels.[7] And there is a growing clinical consensus that both of these maladies arise from a misguided attempt to control life.

This desire for mastery fosters a fascination with all manner of positive-thinking strategies, miracle cures, tactics, techniques, dirty tricks, and sympathetic magic. Americans are apt to try anything once if it promises them some material benefit—everything from transcendental meditation and the Thigh Master, to the prayer of Jabez, right on up to and including pulling the sheets up over their heads or taking a gun to school. All of these are attempts to halt change, either by forcing the moment to its crisis or refuting its dynamics entirely by sheer force of will.

When such superficial and desperate measures reach a critical mass, cultural narcissism passes into outright paranoia, and then personal security, preoccupations with one's health, addictive routines, material accumulation, sexual experimentation, and military might become the preoccupations of the land and intellectual timidity and vice insinuate themselves throughout the body politic. This reactionary "cocooning" is then further aggravated by apocalyptic radio hosts, misanthropic rock stars, fear-mongering politicians, and all manner of false prophets who exploit our phobias and insecurities. This in turn inflates the national ego and drives the quest for a life lived in accord with conscience even further to the margins of our society.[8] As a people, we have ingratiated ourselves far too willingly into the mechanical extensions of our need for material security—almost to the point of a pathological fascination with means over ends, becoming the tools of our tools.

Immigrants like Thi are less vulnerable to such distortions because for them Emerson's America is as real as the America they experience in the shopping malls or see on television. In fact, Emerson's America is more real because it answers the immigrants' question as to what it means to live in America without losing one's soul—a question homegrown Americans seldom ask because they assume that their souls are safe and they are so busy trying to succeed that they have no time to worry about anything but their families and their bank accounts. As a result, they often forgo their responsibilities as citizens; whereas, immigrants like Thi embrace their civic responsibilities as a unique opportunity to make sure that *their* idealism, *their* heroism, indeed *their very souls*, will not go unregistered in the life of the republic. For Thi, it would be a failure of character not to become the most accomplished person she could be—not just in terms of financial success but in terms of self-knowledge and ethical wholeness as well.

If we wish to inspire homegrown American youth to seek their place within the world historical gestalt, question the culture they live in, or even just seek out an understanding of what it means to live an "examined life," we will need a very different strategy than the transcendentalists' frontal assault on "dead traditions" and worldly authorities. We must first liberate the young from the fears that breed their moral posturing and then free them again from the shame that accompanies their realization of just how little they know. Until this happens, they will continue to linger in the shadows of their own misperceived "success," feeling both superior and ignorant at the very same time.

A Community of Revelation

The vocation of the teacher, like the artist and the statesman, is to awaken us from our cultural trance, our unthinking acquiescence to conventional life, and initiate us into a community of seekers who confirm and deepen our sense of being called. One of the most profound articulations of how this can be done is in William Gibson's Pulitzer Prize–winning play *The Miracle Worker*—which is to my mind the finest play ever written on the vocation of the teacher and the meaning of revelation. The climactic water pump scene alone tells us almost everything we need to know about what it means to move from mere existence to being *alive*.

Annie Sullivan is sitting at the family dinner table, celebrating Helen Keller's return to the family home after living in isolation with Annie for two weeks of intense language training. Helen's father, a traditional Victorian patriarch, is ecstatic because Annie has succeeded in teaching the girl table manners. But Annie is frustrated because the child still hasn't grasped the symbolic connection between signs and things, so although she can sign some words, she still can't use her imagination. She is, in truth, little more than a trained monkey who has not yet made the miraculous leap into her own creative humanity.

In order to see if the rigorous discipline established over the past two weeks still applies in her parents' home, Helen begins to "forget" her manners and drops her napkin. Her mother lets the indiscretion go uncorrected, but Annie demands that Helen pick it up. In defiance, Helen sweeps her arm across the table, smashing the china and sending her mother's roast flying across the room. She even takes a pitcher of water and splashes it in Annie's face. Realizing that all her previous work is at stake here, Annie picks Helen up, carries her outside, and makes her refill the pitcher at the water pump. As she does so, Annie continues, for what seems like the millionth time, to sign words into Helen's hand. "Water," she says, and thrusting Helen's hands to the pump handle, signs, "W-A-T-E-R."

Annie is not doing this because she thinks Helen will learn this time but simply because she doesn't know what else to do. Helen resists—crying, kicking, pushing, and pulling. Then, as instantly as this outburst had begun, her tantrum stops. She becomes quiet, absorbed, and perfectly still. Rapt with attention, Helen finally makes the connection between words and things, signs and experience, and in that moment enters into the human community, the community of revelation. In that glorious scene, Helen says, "Wa, wa," and her world is transformed.

But what happens next is every bit as moving. Helen whirls around the yard trying to touch *everything*, thirsty for the signs that represent her world.

"What's this?" Helen indicates, touching a post. "And this? And this? And this?" Annie calls to her parents: "Mr. and Mrs. Keller! Come! Come! Helen knows. She *knows*!"

What does she know? She knows that she is part of a race of beings who experience a common reality, beings who know and name and share their knowing, and in knowing that they know, they accept one another as intimate coparticipants in what theologians sometimes refer to as the Being of Being. Helen learned from Annie that she was part of the human condition, heir to a bottomless and fathomless subjectivity infinite unto itself, existing within and as part of a mysterious universe of unfathomable value.

Helen's parents emerge from the dining room, and she runs to embrace them—touching their faces and signing their names, knowing them for the very first time, loving them as human beings who share life with her. But then she stops, walks over to Annie Sullivan, and touches her face. "Who are you?" she asks. Annie signs out the word "T-E-A-C-H-E-R." And they embrace. It is what one might call a prophetic moment, for it is clear that from now on, Annie and Helen share something far deeper than signs or sentiment. Annie is not a parent, limited by pity or frustrated by libidinal bonds. Nor is she an agent of culture transferring the conventions of American Sign Language. She is something quite different, something much more profound. She is a teacher, an ally to the heroic possibilities within, a midwife to revelation, what William Gibson calls "a miracle worker."

This inspiring vision of the teacher as prophet and education as revelation parallels many of my own experiences in education. Had I not met a certain dedicated and uncompromising professor my sophomore year at the state university, I might very well have lost my soul. Had he not placed my hand on the works of William Blake and made the signs of life and had he not persisted after I shrugged him off, placing my hands on the novels of Dostoyevsky and then again on the essays of Emerson, I would never have heard the call to a life lived in accord with conscience. But thanks to my teacher, I, like Helen, was now obligated to live a deeper life and to pass on this possibility to others.

Again, the question was how? How was I to connect the vocation of revelation to the largely indifferent, materialistic world in which I found myself immersed? It was as if in waking up to the fact that my life had yet to be fully discovered or honestly named, I had not been liberated at all but rather infected with an incurable disease that forever severed me from my world.

This lack of continuity between my inner life and outer circumstances baffled me for many years. I knew I was called to a life lived in accord with conscience, to a life lived from the inside out, but such a life didn't always seem welcome in the schools I attended or in the television shows I watched or in the jobs I held or even in the career ambitions I was encouraged to adopt. I found it reflected only in the artistic and religious extremes—in the literary masters and mystics, in plebeian revolutionaries and philosophical outcasts.

This bothered me for a long time, for what good was an exalted sense of human possibility if it only alienated you from your society, a society that operated on much less sublime premises? What good were precise articulations of contemporary dilemmas if one's leaders and institutions were simply too coarse or too distant to register them? And what did revelation matter if nature itself absorbed all of our protests into an abyss of sex, death, and indifference?

It wasn't until I met my mentor, Brother Ed, that I understood that these questions were the expression and essence of a great vocation: the sublime calling of a classroom teacher.[9] He showed me that one of the ways I could reconcile myself to these tensions was to dedicate my life to the young by becoming a teacher, a miracle worker, an agent of revelation.

Revelations of the kind that changed Helen Keller's life, he explained to me, were becoming increasingly rare in our schools. They were being replaced by knowledge, professionalism, and other forms of information science, driving the religious aspirations of the young underground and rendering them oblivious to the likes of Emerson, Whitman, and Thoreau. Such figures had been rendered by their teachers into mere cartoons, illustrative examples of outmoded trends and superseded fashions.

Ed told me that in their heart of hearts, American youth wanted someone to rescue them from the false prophets and sophists who have rendered all intuitive knowledge suspect—distorting its power and fatally tainting its significance. Revelation, he told me, is not just some clever invention or insight, like the "Water Wiggle" or "cultural relativism," but a qualitative shift in awareness that links the individual to a tradition, group, or language to which he or she had previously not had access. It is not an increase in information so much as it is an initiation into a community, a quantum leap in point of view that takes us inside a universe of discourse from which we had previously been excluded either by simple ignorance or by misdirected attention.

To the extent that our schools place test scores above these epiphanies, they not only mold young minds in the image of their own narrow professional goals (orderly classrooms, model curricula, and higher than average test scores) but also incapacitate them philosophically and further what Herbert Marcuse once described as "the moronization of the United States."[10] For Marcuse, the focus on instrumental reasoning (to the exclusion of theoretical abstraction) had rendered American culture devoid of general ideas and incapable of abstract thought.

In every moment in every classroom, a choice must be made between control and discovery, between the familiar and the new, between safety and danger, between repetition and revelation. Good teachers, like good martial artists, understand that to meet the needs of the moment, you must live dangerously and move into that zone where the joy of illumination triumphs over the comforting but deadly illusions of the known. Such existential bravery, however, is too often discouraged by technocrats and mid-level professionals who have a material stake in the repeatable process over the creative act and the once-in-a-lifetime breakthrough.

These hardworking, middle-brow managers see the future in continuity with the past and so have nothing to say except to repeat the tired litanies of the known and chart our way into a collective future of more of the same. And most of them are damn good at it. They know what they want and have confidence in themselves and their moral authority. But as Emerson pointed out, such "retained attorneys" are not American scholars and so do not represent the genuine American dream. "There every truth is not quite true. There two is not the real two, there four not the real four: so that every word they say chagrins us, and we do not know where to begin to set them right."[11]

Needless to say, these Philistines don't provide a very inspiring vision of the future to people just waking up to the existential reality of their lives, and yet most of the young are savvy enough (and sufficiently demoralized) to put their disappointments aside in order to navigate their way through the colleges and schools run by such functionaries. They spot the "scripts" being run very quickly and make their way through the posturing with very little complaint, mistakenly assuming that by not making waves and by speaking to form, they can achieve all that they want. This makes classroom teaching a very tricky business, because if you are serious about it like Annie Sullivan, you can't just work your way through the textbook or produce students who score high on the SATs. You must free them from their slavish conformity to other people's expectations so that they can begin to see with their own eyes, speak from their own hearts, and understand with their own minds. What was Nietzsche's wonderful advice to the young? "Be yourself! All that you think, feel, and desire is not really you."[12] This isn't very surprising advice for an immigrant for whom everything in the world has been transformed, but when you are teaching homegrown Americans who think of themselves as living at the apex of history and as the envy of the world, who have been subjected to flattery and hype and patronizing their entire lives, who have been tested and measured endlessly for their capacity to follow instructions and robbed of any access to their own radical intellectual traditions, then more circuitous methods are called for.

Brother Ed taught me a number of them.

First, always insist on existential distinctions that mark the difference between real experience and feigned understanding. Point out that there is a world of difference between talking and speaking, thinking and reasoning, "the performance" and "the doing." Talking, according to Ed, is emotional sharing, a passing back and forth of ideas; speaking is putting one's own unique point of view into words and up for grabs. Thinking is a little like worrying, an essentially associative process, an inward churning of images and ideas into various patterns; reasoning is the thoughtful attempt to sort through things logically. It takes time; it follows a procedure; it seeks internal coherence. And "performance," as the word suggests, is a simulation of achievement by appropriating the form of a thing. It is act, not an action; while "the doing" is an actual creative accomplishment that manifests itself in a new reality in real time.

Second, try to ask questions that have no answers as of yet, so that students will be thrown back on their own developing intellectual resources and brought into the self-created community of true thinkers and spiritual explorers.[13] Third, try to anticipate all the predictable "opinions" before they are even uttered, write them down, and pass them out before any meeting or discussion so that commonplaces can be ruled out right from the start. Doing so cuts off all lines of escape into clichés, truisms, and bromides, thereby making it impossible to evade real thinking.

Fourth, throw away the teacherly agenda altogether and relax into the actual confusion of your students' minds, giving up any and all images of a "successful" lesson, and letting moments of revelation emerge of their own accord. In truth, if teachers and parents would stop force-feeding their children predigested insights and simulated epiphanies, they would have to own up to the truth of their own experience.

Finally, prepare to be criticized and misunderstood by your peers and evaluators. If you do, in fact, throw away the teacherly agenda and attend to the actual confusion of your students' minds, you will be charged with all manner of incompetence by those who want to replace your immeasurable aspirations with their behavioral objectives. Try not to let this bother you; it comes with the territory.

When I taught with Brother Ed, a new principal eliminated—*overnight*— an innovative humanities curriculum Ed had spent more than twenty years painstakingly putting into place. I was so outraged when I got the news that I ran to tell him while he was taking his morning walk around the athletic field. Ed was in his late sixties at the time, and I was surprised that he wasn't upset by the news at all. "They like to change things," he told me. "That's how they justify their pay and prove their professionalism. They move from a quarter system to a semester system to a trimester system and back again about every five years, upsetting everyone's lives in the process. They deemphasize grammar in favor of linguistics, then deemphasize linguistics in favor of literary theory, then return to grammar again in an endless attempt to turn education into something less miraculous than it really is. They don't know what we do. They aren't in the revelation business!" And with that he disappeared into one of those dense fog banks that dotted the track on that cold January morning. Then out of nowhere I could hear him shout back to me, "They can't even see us!"

Such strategies and admonitions are useful to anyone attempting to clear away the half-truths and self-serving programmatic formulations that drive revelation underground. The real enemies of the American dream were never the critics, skeptics, or even the nihilists in our midst but rather the Philistines, opportunists, boosters, and professional elites who foist a surrogate dream in its place, a dream of order, teamwork, hierarchies, and measurable outcomes to replace the dangerous vistas of Whitman's cosmic democracy. Like Helen Keller's parents, they never really cared if their children grew souls, just so long as they ate well.

But teachers, like poets and immigrants, and dissenters, must refuse to be taken in by such agents of the status quo and hold fast to Emerson's dictum that there can be no scholarship without the heroic mind. In other words, there can be no intellectual life without dangerous conversations, outlandish questions, awkward silences, unprofessional outbursts, and the unabashed stupidity that cries out not just for correction but for a loving recognition of its truthfulness.

Renewing the Experiment

One of the sad legacies of the Cold War and its aftermath is that the vision of America as the search for a consensus spiritual reality—a true, universal ethic—has been superseded by an oligarchy of professional sophists, influence peddlers, and political illusionists who value power over process and product over meaning. The Allied victory in World War II may have saved the world from entering a new dark age, but our failure to recognize the waning democratic values that preceded the war and that threatened to collapse in its wake has created the very real possibility that our military successes and national sacrifices are rapidly becoming hollow.

We might very well triumph over our adversaries without carrying into the future any vestige of the religious asceticism, social egalitarianism, or radical democratic individualism that animated our worldview in the first place. Should that happen, the dream of a life lived in accord with conscience would disappear into a new mythos of worldly success, and then the United States really would become an imperial empire, the sober guardians of a disillusioned world order run on a calculus of power, bereft of Helen Keller–like revelations, Emersonian idealism, Thoreauvian epiphanies, or Whitmanesque largesse.[14]

World War II and its aftermath have forced Americans to regard their country more as an economic and military power than as a moral and metaphysical experiment, and this has led to a crisis of personal meaning in the lives of our young that is not sufficiently recognized. To meet the dangerous new power alignments and military threats of the twentieth century, America became corporate, consolidated, internationally connected, militarily ready, and run by professional managers, social scientists, and experts. As a result, the question of preserving its unique democratic character took a backseat to partisan bickering over whose interests the new superstate was going to serve.

Despite Dwight D. Eisenhower's prescient warning to beware of the military-industrial complex and Martin Luther King Jr.'s call to a more universal conception of the Bill of Rights, most Americans continue simply to put their shoulders to the wheel of progress and accept their burdens without asking too many questions. The contrarian (or independent) point of view so eloquently defended by the likes of Henry David Thoreau and Oliver Wendell Holmes, just to mention two, has become so marginalized that virtually all our serious literature focuses on our failed resistance to the pressures of the new psychological totalitarianism. Over the last fifty years, we have made far too great a compromise with the ways of the world. Seldom, if ever, is Annie Sullivan's vision defended, asserted, or even explained.

The emerging global economy does not solve these problems; in fact, it heightens them by presenting us with a vast smorgasbord of conflicting worldviews severed from their origins and thrown together by asymmetrical economic needs. The fundamental questions of existence are so radically reframed that we have even more trouble sorting out fact from fiction, ideology from analysis, wisdom from prejudice, and publicity from product. The hyperpsychological sophistication of advertisers and state propagandists have not only distorted the operation of our free markets but also subverted the epistemological and ontological dimensions of our democratic process.[15] Politics no longer functions as collective decision making but has become an esoteric art of mass manipulation and control—Machiavellian to a fault, tactical in the extreme, and ultimately morally corrupting.

If the history of the twentieth century has taught us nothing else, it has made clear that human culture is not a stay against moral erosion, a revolution in manners, or a Utopian alternative to the violence of history.[16] Human culture is, as T. S. Eliot suggested, what we make of the mess we have made of things.[17] At its best, it can provide a sustained resistance to the ever-changing face of depersonalization and false authority, challenging the complacencies of the middle class, the entitlements of the rich, and the internalized powerlessness of the poor.

The problem isn't that our leaders don't know these things; it's just that they are not original enough in the conclusions they draw from them or brave enough in their attempts to dispel the confusions. They always seem to opt out of paradox for tactical responses and action-oriented solutions. To collapse the ironies of history within the framework of any programmatic analysis, however nuanced or complex, only serves to place knowledge before revelation again and procedural thinking over creative response.

The good news is that most Americans have never bought into the materialist premises that dominate our commercial culture and guide our imperialistic foreign policy. Something in them resists: a residue of hope in transcendent possibilities, an unused idealism that they take home with them after work and hide in the silent, contemplative reaches of their hearts. The fundamentalist Protestant revival of the 1980s, as well as the current popularity of Buddhism, *The Course in Miracles,* and other "spiritual things," are all expressions of this desire to somehow escape from our self-created political house of mirrors into something universal, transcendent, and real.

Perhaps this is why American-born youth are so fascinated with travel and extreme sports. They suspect that maybe China, Mexico, Chile, or

Japan has something more solid to offer them. If not, then a death-defying slide down the side of a mountain will certainly free one's mind, if only momentarily, from the ever-present unreality of commercial hype.[18]

The problem, of course, is that if this desire is going to lead to anything more significant than another conservative retrenchment, we will need a postmythological perspective on human development that goes beyond both consumerism and nationalism to a true solidarity with the poor and with those not at home in our interpreted, quantified, and commercialized world. I am thinking here of some form of cultural expression that will resonate with those perennial carriers of the American dream: the dissidents, the artists, the outcasts, the immigrants, the refugees, the reformers, and the working poor. These "pariahs" remain America's true avant-garde, for their lives embody an instinctive flinch both away from the part of us that is sustained and identified with the powers that be and toward the part of us experienced in times of loss and psychological disintegration when we must gather up all our courage, resolve, and grit in order to reconstitute our lives at a deeper and more inclusive level of reality—like George Washington did at Valley Forge, Abraham Lincoln at Gettysburg, and Martin Luther King Jr. in Birmingham. The inner life of the America soul, its true self, remains hidden in the silences of our unexpressed idealists, our young, our misunderstood outsiders, our struggling immigrants, our martyred firefighters, and our stoic poor. They alone seem to know that we are not who we think we are, that our country remains incomplete without their contribution, and that they themselves, in coming to be who they were meant to become, will fulfill the ideals of our greatest statesmen and most profound poets far better than our privilege class.

Such a refocusing on our coming into being—rather than on our riches and privileges—holds far-reaching implications for how we learn and who we think we are. It shifts interest away from the tactics of successful living toward an existential analysis of individual struggle and honest dialogue over our ultimate concerns. It makes Pablo Neruda more important than Tony Robbins and transforms a news story about how a war in Iraq will affect the supply of oil in Tennessee into the story of how such a shift in resources will affect our lives as democratic individualists committed to making our own destiny not on the backs of others but in the light of our highest ethical and religious responsibilities. Conventional political journalists—especially the more successful ones—will have a hard time making the transition from power assessments of leaders like Henry Kissinger to the soul-searching democratic idiom of the likes of Tom Paine, but it is a transition that will have to be made if we want to find a way back to the visionary promise of America.

My grandfather was a Basque sea captain, an immigrant who fell from his ship in San Francisco harbor, hit his head on an anchor, acquired a progressive skin disease, and ultimately committed suicide in his cabin. The day after his death, all of his friends received in the mail a drawing of two hands clasped. Needless to say, he has become something of a family myth, and I have often wondered what he was thinking about when he sent off those icons of human brotherhood. Was his first-generation American soul too empty or too full? Were his letters apologies or prophecies? Sometimes I feel him grumble inside me, like some great bearish Zorba with an immense love for life and a hero's willingness to die, and I know that I must be a disappointment to him. How could I not be? The further we move away from the hopes and struggles of our ancestors, the harder it is for us to remember exactly what we owe them and exactly what they wanted us to achieve.

Mahatma Gandhi once wrote that all history is "the record of every interruption of the even working of the force of love."[19] Another way of saying this is that history is the accumulated sins of the fathers visited upon the sons, shadows playing on the cave of tainted memories, a nightmare from which we are all trying to awake. And yet if the transcendental source of life's time-bound particulars are inevitably tainted by human greed, and if our shared humanity is always hidden behind a veil of prejudices, wars, and chronicles of strife, this does not mean that a common human freedom is not available to us, only that it is as yet unnamed.

It is in this process of naming our collective identity that the significance of our lives together will be defined, and if we are not careful, if we don't listen to our poets and visionaries or honor the heroism of our precursors and the wisdom of the poor or take seriously the cries of the victims and the outcasts, we will end up oscillating between a preoccupation with our own personal desires and a superstitious faith in nineteenth-century scientific materialism that passes for conventional sanity.

We have to do better than that.

Breaking the Cultural Trance

Whatever our technological achievements or economic gains, it is time that we own up to the fact that this world remains a purgatory—a spiritual diaspora where most people live in abject poverty and the best among us are all too often lost, exiled, left for dead, or buried at sea.

We also now know that our DNA is not that different from that of the higher primates. And I suspect that any qualitative divergence between the animals and us will prove not to be physical so much as subjective, revelatory, and prophetic: the product of a mysterious event, an originating moment, a change in collective perception that initiated the ritual of language, that ongoing dance signifying our belonging to one another.[20]

But if such a revelatory anthropology is going to dismantle the empty talk of ideological wrangling, there will have to be a generation or two of willing outsiders who consciously live in the silences of our epoch, biding their time in communion with the sacred. And I suspect that such souls will look a lot more like stoic firemen, unintelligible scientists, unread poets, and jobless immigrants than well-paid professionals, overpaid CEOs, or politically correct movie stars—not because these folk possess any innate moral superiority to their more successful peers but because their anonymity renders them less susceptible to the cultural trance that dominates the lives of the accomplished.

The young will have to be rescued from teachers and parents who inoculate them against their own nascent inwardness and "mentors" who emphasize the "performances" of experts over the practice of virtue. Such a rescue may require a New Theory of the Classroom or a New Theory of the Book or even a New Theory of the Self [21]—something that will reinvigorate the Emersonian idea that thinking is an act of sustained nonconformity, not a display of intellectual virtuosity.

Contemporary scholars and academics have been very little help in creating such practices or encouraging such contrarian thoughts. The forms of criticism and analysis taught at our universities today just carry dialectics to its ultimate conclusion in deconstruction, the new historicism, and other forms of ideological critique.[22] In fact, the most progressive academics actually argue that we must bring everything into dialogue with ideology.[23] If I am even partly correct in my account of contemporary trends, we need exactly the reverse procedure: to subsume ideology within a more contemplative tradition, perhaps even a return to *lectio divina*, prayer, and meditation as preferred ways of knowing. If anything, we need to place the truths of revelation at the center of our educational and cultural enterprises.

But since such an approach has been advocated by a number of shallow religious extremists, it suffers from the superficial familiarity and special pleading that plagues so many contemporary expressions of Christianity, Buddhism, Judaism, and Islam. Not that these traditions don't have their serious exponents; it's just that the widespread "dumbing down" that all three have suffered hampers them from establishing the kind of serious philosophical foundation that a new humanities needs to ground itself. Without a convincing philosophical anthropology to serve as its base—that is to say, without an inclusive vision of what it means to be a human being—the attempt to put the search for virtue at the center of our cultural enterprises simply cannot take place. Somehow we must find a way to overcome our fascination with scientific and materialist reductionism in order to tap into the pagan, lyric pedagogy that animated the Psalms and all the rest of our poetry without drowning in the heady wine of Dionysian irrationality or popular sentimentality.

Giambattista Vico's *New Science,* written at the turn of the eighteenth century, may seem like the precursor to the kind of thing I am advocating here: a felt and imagined metaphysics to replace the abstract ponderings of our philosophers, a return to divination, "a rational civil theology of divine providence."[24] We can see this kind of speculative poetic thinking in the reflections of people like Joseph Campbell and the post-Jungian psychotherapist James Hillman. But then again, it isn't exactly a new mythopoetics that we need, and despite Robert Bly's spirited attempts to invigorate the tradition of the deep image, his attempt at reestablishing the transcendental roots of American culture remain more instructive as a false start than anything else.

Nor is the neoconservative suggestion that we teach virtue any better. We can't teach virtue without practicing it, and practicing virtue is not a performance or a political stance but a creative breakthrough. It manifests itself in a revelation of the good, not in a repetition of the known. It isn't just Nietzschean relativism that has rendered the modern academy damaging to the souls of the young; it's also the positivist, ahistorical classicism that is offered as its only alternative.

This is why we need a refreshed sense of contemporary culture that takes into account the post-Enlightenment awareness that the "real world" is not only what exists outside of us but also what is within us— at one with our own inner ground.[25] And that we share this ground with other human beings whenever we are present to our freedom and the freedom of others. Without knowledge of this shared metaphysical reality, others remain an impenetrable mystery; the natural world becomes a patient etherized on a table, and we remain an enigma to ourselves.[26]

The difficulties we face as Americans are not the product of a clash of civilizations or the rift between Western democracies and Eastern despots. The conflict is where it has always been: in the clash between our true and our false selves, between our desire to control and manipulate life and our desire to throw off every form of internal and external tyranny, as our forefathers yearned to do. As I get older, I see the young rushing through a world I once rushed through—blinded by their hope of better things to come, in a hurry, always looking forward. And I want to tell them to slow down, that the world they carry around on their shoulders is not the real

world, and that living fully is not a matter of building for the future, col-
lecting memories, or even kissing the joy as it flies. Rather it is a matter
of accompanying existence as a beloved companion whose subjectivity
can never be fully comprehended or sufficiently understood.

Life is not a project to be completed or a debt to be paid; it is a long-
lost relative longing for attention, friendship, and care. I guess I am old
enough now to admit that none of my failures ever really mattered. Or
else their consequences usually turned out better than what would have
happened had I got what I wanted. Defeat humbles us and prepares us to
receive other things down the line. In fact, I think it would be fair to say
that the best things in life always come to us unexpectedly as gifts,
unearned, gratuitous as rain. Whenever I tried to be somebody or force
the moment to its crisis, I suffered the inevitable consequences, but whenever I let life lead me, I wised up.

But before I could wise up, my false ambitions had to be exposed as
illusions, not pandered to. Somebody had to tell me—in words or images
that penetrated my defenses—that the end of all my striving should not
be material success but true life. And that true life was an interior accomplishment, the product of a lifetime of revelations, not the answer to a
question or the end result of an unwavering adherence to some single set
of prescribed virtues.

Perhaps the reason we deepen as we age is that over time we are all
forced to leave parts of our lives behind and become different people.
These losses reveal—even to the most hardheaded among us—the tentative and fictive nature of our own felt identities. Such disillusionment can
breed cynicism, but if we trust that there is a reality behind the flux of
experience—an enduring pattern, a transpersonal transcendental self—
these changes can also be liberating by helping us distinguish fact from
fiction and dream from reality.

It may take years of being drawn into flame after flame of various self-
generated passions before we can acquire the humility to relax into the
life actually given us and accept a destiny more mysterious than any we
could ever have imagined for ourselves—rising from the ashes of our self-
manufactured illusions to become resolute champions of the actual. But
this is possible only to the extent that we see "the actual" in a transcendental light—hence the need for a poetic, visionary rendering of the American dream.

I once heard a speaker remark that the historians had gotten the story
of African America all wrong. The life of Martin Luther King Jr., he said,
proves that blacks were not brought over here by whites to be slaves *but
sent over here by God to change the world*. Such an observation bespeaks

the incommensurable distance between the language of fact and the language of revelation, between America as history and America as metaphor. To deepen the dream, we must hold both truths in our minds simultaneously without immediately reaching after some slogan or theory to collapse the paradox. We are both better and worse than we know, our future is more horrific and more graced than we can ever imagine, and our past is still with us in ways we have yet to surmise. The truths of our religious traditions do not contradict the sciences that diverge from them or the political innovations devised to contain them but rather hold their ground as parts of ourselves still seeking integration into the unfolding "brave new world."

This essay has been, to a large extent, an exercise in pattern recognition and moral invention. I have tried to discern certain emerging forms of conscience and their comings and goings in the minds of Americans caught up in the storms of current social changes. If there is a thesis here, it is that depth is not merely complexity; it is also specificity—an active resistance to vague generalities in a constant search for ever more particular, one-of-a-kind revelations into life, capable of liberating untapped human potential by initiating us into new, hitherto unimaginable, universes of discourse.

The new American history will not be the fragmented story of previously marginalized groups vying for power and recognition, but the story of the excluded universal self finding its way independently and free. The young often experience this self as an untapped energy hovering about them in the antechambers of their lives, waiting to make its appearance in the form of some new lover, superstar, or hero. But it never appears that way because the true self isn't defined from without.

The cultural trance is a product of the mass media, government, Big Money, and terrorism, and so the true self will return, as it always has, in private, inward events inside the souls of particular individuals. It returns only in moments of revelation.

NOTES

1 The key text for this is John Winthrop, "A Model of Christian Charity" (1630).

2 For a more detailed and eloquent development of this idea, see Jacob Needleman, *The American Soul: Recovering the Wisdom of the Founders* (New York: Tarcher/Putnam, 2002).

3 Whitman was given this name by the critic Harold Bloom.

4 In an essay in the April 2002 issue of *Harper's,* "The Numbing of the American Mind," Thomas de Zengotita quotes Nietzsche to describe the psychological pressures experienced by our young: "In the youthful soul the massive influx of impressions is so great; surprising, barbaric, and violent things press so overpoweringly—'balled up into hideous clumps'—that it can save itself only by taking recourse in premeditated stupidity" (p. 33). And in our time, this premeditated stupidity takes the form of MTV.

5 The novelist Milan Kundera calls the phenomenon the "modernization of stupidity" and has written about it in his collection of essays and lectures *The Art of the Novel* (New York: Grove Press, 1988).

6 See, among other works, Tolstoy's "Confession," in John Bayley (ed.), *The Portable Tolstoy* (New York: Penguin Books, 1978).

7 The Substance Abuse and Mental Health Services Administration reported in 1999 that depression and anxiety disorders affect nineteen million Americans annually and that up to one-half of all visits to primary care physicians are due to conditions that are caused or exacerbated by mental or emotional problems. See http://www. samhsa.gov.

8 See Richard Hofstadter, *The Paranoid Style in American Politic and Other Essays* (Chicago: University of Chicago Press, 1979).

9 I tell the whole story of my initiation to the art of classroom teaching in *Spitwad Sutras: Classroom Teaching as Sublime Vocation* (Westport, Conn.: Bergin & Garvey, 1993).

10 Herbert Marcuse, *A Critique of Pure Tolerance* (Boston: Beacon Press, 1965), p. 83.

11 Ralph Waldo Emerson, "Self-Reliance," in Nina Baym (ed.), *The Norton Anthology of American Literature,* shorter 6th ed. (New York: Norton, 2003), p. 543.

12 Friedrich Wilhelm Nietzsche, *Schopenhauer as Educator* (Chicago: Regnery, 1965), p. 2.

13 Norman Mailer once advised President Kennedy that one of the best things he could do for the country would be to go on television and talk off the cuff, in a unprepared, honest way about literature, history, and philosophy in order to demonstrate to the American public what a real "American scholar" looks like. Given Kennedy's popularity, Mailer argued, this would establish a new intellectual standard for American presidents. From that point forward, they would have to demonstrate true intellectual sophistication to the American public, or they would be dismissed as second-rate.

It might even put an end to programmed answers and poll-driven campaigns. Needless to say, Kennedy never took him up on the proposition, and we have suffered the consequences ever since.

14 An argument for this new paganism can by found in Robert D. Kaplan, *Warrior Politics: Why Leadership Demands a Pagan Ethos* (New York: Random House, 2002).

15 The Founding Fathers understood that democracy was not a particularly efficient way to run a country, but it was the best way to process shared experiences and competing revelations in a manner that held open the possibility of checking and balancing the inevitable antagonisms of man. It was a means for the collective naming of things, and the Constitution was a machine for the perpetual legal and periodic mythopoetic reconstitution of the state.

16 I am indebted here to Eric Gans, whose brilliant work in generative anthropology takes off from René Girard's work in new and very promising directions.

17 See Eliot's *Notes Toward a Definition of Culture* (New York: Harcourt Brace, 1949).

18 Andrei Codrescu has written a probing analysis of this phenomenon in his collection of essays *The Disappearance of the Outside* (Boston: Addison-Wesley, 1990).

19 Krishna Kripalani, ed., *All Men Are Brothers* (Ahmedabad, India: Navajivan, 1960), p. 83.

20 Eric Gans argues for this in his book *The Origin of Language* (Berkeley: University of California Press, 1981). But he makes a even more succinct case for this view in *Science and Faith: An Anthropology of Revelation* (Lanham, Md.: Rowman & Littlefield, 1990).

21 This was the central theme of my book, *Spitwad Sutras*.

22 One notable exception here is Parker Palmer's work developing "circles of trust." Based on the Quaker idea of an assisted examination of conscience, individuals come together not to debate or even discuss problems but to help individuals discern what their conscience is telling them. See, for example, Parker Palmer, *Let Your Life Speak* (San Francisco: Jossey-Bass, 1999).

23 See, for example, Sacvan Bercovitch, *The Rites of Assent: Transformations in the Symbolic Construction of America* (New York: Routledge, 1992).

24 *The New Science of Giambattista Vico* (Ithaca, N.Y.: Cornell University Press, 1968), para. 342.

25 I am thinking here of a host of postmodernist philosophers and thinkers as diverse as Paul Ricouer, Hans Gadamer, Emmanuel Levinas, Jacques Lacan, and Jacques Derrida, who agree that the ground of our rationality cannot be simply assumed and that Western metaphysics is the mere beginning of thought, not its grand finale.

26 Huston Smith makes this point in his book *Why Religion Matters: The Fate of the Human Spirit in an Age of Disbelief* (New York: HarperCollins, 2001).

FROM CRUELTY TO COMPASSION

THE CRUCIBLE OF
PERSONAL TRANSFORMATION

Gerald G. May

Sadly, as we were preparing this book for publication, our friend and elder, Gerald May, passed away on April 8, 2005. Gerry was a remarkable being whose clarity and passion touched all he came in contact with. During the winter, he shared with some of us his most recent manuscript, *The Power of the Slowing,* which ends with this passage:

> What the Power of the Slowing taught me is what the Source of All is constantly yearning for: that each of us will know without doubt that we are loved, and that we are intimately, irrevocably part of the end-less creation of love, and that we will join, with full freedom and con-sciousness, the joyous creativity that is Nature, that is Wildness, that is Wilderness, that is Everything.

∞)) ((∞

A SINGLE SENTENCE has haunted me for over a decade. It is the first line of the Dalai Lama's foreword to Zen Master Thich Nhat Hanh's book, *Peace Is Every Step:* "Although attempting to bring about world peace through the internal transformation of individuals is difficult, it is the only way."[1]

On the surface the thought seems simple, almost obvious. We all know that individual changes in people affect larger social systems. But it is those last five words that catch me up: "it is the *only* way." The Dalai Lama's statement is far more than another simple encouragement to love one's neighbor; it is also a critique of all the other ways we human beings have tried to bring peace and justice to the world. It says that they simply do not work.

As I have reflected on the Dalai Lama's words over these past ten years, I find myself sadly in agreement. War, violence, oppression, injustice, and countless other forms of human cruelty are endemic on this planet. They have been with us since the beginning of our species, and they are no less present now than they were ten thousand years ago. With modern technology, the cruelty we humans wreak upon one another is now more devastating than it ever was.

It's not as if we haven't tried to find better ways. It is impossible to count the vast variety of projects and programs humanity has instituted over the millennia to promote peace and justice. How many communities of peace have been established? How many new world orders have been envisioned? How many social, political, and religious systems have been established in the name of peace and justice? One might as well count grains of sand. All have been well-intended and many have encouraged real social change. Some have even created small temporary oases of peace in our troubled world. But the hard fact remains: they have not, individually or collectively, diminished the overall virulence of human cruelty. They have not saved us from ourselves. In this sense, they have not worked.

I am now convinced that our many programs and projects have not worked because they are all systemic remedies. Whether great utopian visions for society at large or simple moral and ethical principles for individuals, they consistently address our corporate ways of living together. But human cruelty is not, at its core, a systemic problem. Political, social, economic, religious, and other collective systems can worsen or minimize cruelty, but they do not contain its roots. Instead, the capacity for cruelty is innate in every human person. Because it is part of our individual human nature, the fault lies within ourselves, not in our collective systems. Any remedy, any depth-change from cruelty toward compassion, must arise within the nature of the individual human being.[2]

I did not come to this conclusion easily. In a quarter-century of practicing psychiatry, I tried to understand people's proclivity to cruelty as the combination of cultural influences and early childhood experiences. My assumption was that aside from certain genetic abnormalities, human beings are born pure, loving, innocent, and just. After birth, a child is subjected to extremely strong cultural conditioning and is formed also by his or her early experiences of trust, care, security, and the like. I assumed that if this early formation occurred in a peaceable and harmonious fashion, the child would grow into a just, compassionate adult. Conversely, cruel and unjust behavior should be traceable to some disorder, some abnormality of nurture.

Looking back, I wonder how I could have been so naive. The evidence of real people in real life in no way supports such assumptions. The undeniable truth is that all children, no matter how well cared for, and all adults, no matter how well adjusted, are capable of terrible cruelty. To be sure, specific patterns of violence (for example, child abuse, rape, and murderous compulsions) are clearly molded by abnormal early experiences. But the violent potential behind such extremes, the primitive capability of and readiness for cruelty are not abnormal at all. They exist within all of us, all the time. They exhibit themselves daily, from small vendettas in workplaces to road rage on the highways, from family feuds to racial prejudice, from terrorism to national warfare. In truth, violence, cruelty, and injustice are horrifyingly normal.

To put it another way, childhood and social conditioning may shape how we express or restrain our capacities for violence, injustice, and other forms of cruelty, but the capacities themselves are inborn, "hard-wired" in our brains.

The Moral and Ethical Dimension of Compassion and Aggression

In the raising of children and the maturing of adults, most psychological wisdom has assumed that it is important that tendencies toward aggression, regardless of cause, be restrained and overlaid by enhanced tendencies toward altruism. Normally this happens by instilling moral and ethical principles, but at a deeper level Sigmund Freud saw it as an ongoing competition between eros and thanatos, the life and death instincts. In his classic, *Conceptions of Modern Psychiatry,* Harry Stack Sullivan characterized healthy adult maturity as a state in which tenderness prevails.

Although it is logical to think that compassion needs to counteract aggression, two fundamental problems arise with a formulation that assumes that the process generally happens through the negative reinforcement of violent behaviors and positive reinforcement of altruism. The first problem is that such conditionings are culture-specific. They conform to local ethics and mores, which determine the behaviors that are to be suppressed and those that are supported. So while it may be wrong to attack someone who has simply insulted you, it may be right to defend yourself against a bully. It may be wrong to attack a family member, but right to brutalize an outsider. It may be wrong to wage war as an aggressor, but right to do so in defense against aggression. Thus arise the endless conflicts in our neighborhoods and our world, in which each of the warring factions feels it is "right."

The second problem with supporting altruism over aggression is more fundamental—it has to do with what happens in the individual. Effective conditioning usually produces people who function well in their cultures, but it does not actually change their basic perceptions or responses. Instead, we simply wind up with conditioned habits and ideas of what is right and wrong. For example, I am certain that it is wrong to lash out at another driver who cuts in front of me on the highway. I also know that to do so is likely to get me into trouble. But when the event actually occurs, my first reaction is hostility, my first impulse is vengeful. It takes at least a second or two to gather my wits and decide to act in a civilized fashion.

What, I wonder, would be the situation if something happened to actually transform my initial responses? What if my immediate reaction were one of sincere concern for the other driver's welfare? What if I felt, right then and there, the desperation or confusion that the other driver must be experiencing? In this example, my outward behavior might not be very different, but it would arise in a completely different way and come from an entirely different place. There would be no suppression of aggression, no sublimating or redirecting violent impulses, no defense mechanisms at all. This, I think, would be an experience of true transformation.

For some, such a prospect raises fear. How would we survive if we did not use aggressive defense? And would not such a realization alienate us from our own culture? For others, the prospect is filled with hope, but it seems simply too idealistic, too good to be true. From my own experience, I can say that the fears that this possibility engenders occur more from thinking about it than from actually encountering it. It is very similar to the way an alcoholic might panic at the thought of never taking another drink—which is why AA so strongly advocates the "one day at a time" attitude. True compassion does indeed require us to relinquish our social and cultural bonds, as well as countless other attachments. But it does not necessarily lead to a sense of alienation. If the detachment occurs in the service of true compassion, the resulting feelings are far more tender than that.

Nor do I think the possibility of immediate compassion is too good to be true. I believe I have seen the inner transformation from selfishness to compassion happening to many people, and I believe I have tasted it within myself. I am convinced that although it is difficult, as the Dalai Lama said, it is a very real and practical possibility. And I am ready to agree that it is the only way, our only hope.

Addressing the Roots of Cruelty

Although systemic programs and projects designed to promote peace and justice do not address the innate causes of human cruelty by transforming the inner lives of individuals, they can be effective in dealing with the consequences of human cruelty. Programs can bring aid to those who suffer those consequences and can, at least for a time, curb the inevitable tendencies of violence to escalate.

An analogy from western medicine may be helpful here. There is a long-standing public health model that describes medical interventions in the three categories of primary, secondary, and tertiary prevention. Primary prevention is real prevention; it disables the initial occurrence of a disease or disorder. Immunization against polio, for example, essentially eradicated the disease. Secondary prevention seeks to identify and treat (and hopefully cure) a disease once it has been contracted. Early screening tests for cancer are a good example. Tertiary prevention comes into play when a disease is fully established and cure is unlikely, as in chronic diabetes, permanent paralysis, or brain damage. Here the attempt is to prevent unnecessary pain and complications, and to improve the length and quality of life insofar as possible.

Using this analogy, systemic programs and projects are the most effective means we have for secondary and tertiary prevention of human cruelty. Just as in medicine, secondary and tertiary preventions are absolutely necessary for minimizing the escalation of cruelty and caring for its victims. But they have never been effective at primary prevention because they do not address the sources. Because the roots of human cruelty lie within each human being, the only hope for primary prevention is through the inner transformation of individuals.

In medicine, primary prevention relies upon a thorough understanding of the exact causes (etiology) of disease. The same is true for human cruelty and its three-part etiology: attachment (the most fundamental cause) and tribalism and revenge, which build on attachment. I emphasize tribalism and revenge not because they are the only expressions of attachment that result in cruelty, but because they create the most widespread and destructive forms of it.

The Tyranny of Attachment

Aristotle said, "It is the nature of desire not to be satisfied, and most human beings live only for the gratification of it." I believe that at the heart of all habitual behaviors is the single driving force that the great spiritual traditions have called attachment. It is at the root not only of all the behaviors we detest but cannot change, but also of many behaviors that we cherish and depend upon daily. And it is the very groundwork of human cruelty.

From a spiritual perspective, attachment is the complex of dynamics that binds our capacity for love and altruism to self-centered desires. The root of the word, *a-tache,* means "nailed to." Spiritual traditions see attachment as nailing our capacity for love to something other than what it was meant for, such as when we make idols of our possessions and relationships. From a biological viewpoint, attachment consists of entrenched cellular patterns that result in behaviors over which we have little choice or control. In large part, our brains and bodies function by establishing attachments: habits to which we become accustomed and which result in significant stress when changed. When the patterns are deeply embedded and the stress of withdrawal from them is too great to bear, we use the term "addiction." I have described these dynamics in detail in my book *Addiction and Grace,* and will give only a brief summary here.

In the brain, attachments are ingrained patterns of nerve cell functioning to which one has become accustomed. I often think of these functional patterns as streambeds, pathways engraved in the brain by the repeated flow of cell activity. Many such attachment patterns are necessary for daily life. Most of these take place without our conscious awareness: rhythms of autonomic activity, digestion and metabolism, habitual adjustments in temperature, heart rate, and the like.

When we do become aware of attachments, we often call them habits. Habits, whether we identify them as good or bad, are patterns of experience and behavior to which we become accustomed, like the expectation of daylight in the morning and darkness at night, the rituals we go through on arising and retiring, the familiarity we develop with our time zone, and so on. Similar habits develop in the ways we relate to one another in families and communities. Although these too are the result of ingrained patterns of nerve cell functioning, they are such a part of our normal lives that we almost never recognize them as such.

Most habit attachments remain automatic and only subliminally conscious until something interferes with them, such as jet lag when we travel to a different time zone, or when a family member suddenly begins behaving in an unexpected way. Then we become aware of the attachment because it causes stress until things return to normal or we adjust to the new situation.

We are very conscious of certain other attachments because we identify them as "bad habits" and struggle to change them. In childhood we learn that we can correct some bad habits by willpower and self-discipline. Others, we discover, are intransigent; they persist no matter what we do. Life teaches us that there are limits to what we can control, even within ourselves. We may come to a realization like that of the Apostle Paul: "The good thing I want to do, I never do. The bad thing which I do not want— that is what I do!" (Romans 7:14ff). We label such unwanted attachments as neuroses, obsessions, compulsions, irresistible impulses, dependencies and codependencies, and so on. At this point it is probably simpler just to call them addictions, for the psychological definition of addiction is any behavior that willpower cannot change. Neurologically, addiction exists when the power of the cell patterns maintaining a behavior is greater than the power of the patterns attempting to change it.

Most spiritual traditions maintain that attachment—even to behavior patterns we identify as good—always represents a certain limitation of human freedom. These traditions say that by compelling us in one direction or another, attachment impedes our capacity for love. We could debate whether attachment to "good" behaviors is desirable or not, but it is very clear that attachment is the foundation upon which all our patterns of destructive behaviors are built.

It is attachment that makes us accustomed to our own kind of people and ways of life—and suspicious of those who are different. It is attachment that makes children refuse to share their toys and adults cling to their lands and possessions. In one way or another, attachment makes fundamentalists of us all, self-righteously protecting our most treasured beliefs and images. Attachment is what blinds us to others' points of view. It is the sustaining power behind racism, bigotry, and all other patterns of intolerance. Attachment fuels all our patterns of grasping, clinging, acquiring, and defending—everything that makes us cruel.

Us and Them: Tribalism

Attachment to one's own in-group in opposition to others is widespread among animals and apparently universal in human beings. As National Council of Churches president Elenie Huszagh said in a recent speech, "In all of recorded human history, and no doubt even prior, humans have always managed to divide themselves into an 'us' and 'them' configuration." Variously called ethnocentricity, xenophobia, or tribalism, it has been extensively studied by social scientists. Studies like the "blue eyes versus brown eyes" games in children and "guards versus prisoners" experiments in adults are classic demonstrations of how quickly tribalism can be stimulated and how easily it can become vicious.

Tribalism is rooted in the pack instinct as seen in dogs, wolves, hyenas, and many other animals as well as primates. A deep, primitive attachment is established at birth between infant and mother. This bond expands to include close family members and finally other members of the pack or herd. Accompanying this bonding is an identification with the group itself and attachment to behaviors and attitudes that are acceptable to the group. Almost inevitably, these wind up being clearly distinguished from behaviors and attitudes directed toward outsiders. As biologist and ecological philosopher Garrett Hardin said, "The essential characteristic of a tribe is that it should follow a double standard of morality—one kind of behavior for in-group relations, another for out-group."[3]

It is easy to understand the importance of in-group attachment and identification; an infant must learn the ways of the herd (family, community) in order to survive. What may be more difficult is why the group itself so commonly needs to define itself over and against others—the "us and them" mentality. This too has been explained on the basis of survival; a group has a better chance of defending against competing groups if it has a pre-existing attitude of suspicion or paranoia. In so-called primal or primitive societies, this may take the form of giving the name "people" to the in-group and considering all out-groups as less than human. Some researchers have proposed that such universal attitudes of paranoia toward others are not only behaviorally reinforced, but also genetically encoded.[4]

Shaped by both nature and nurture, tribalism is directly related to defining one's own group against others, yet it is the result of innate processes within each individual. If for whatever reason an animal does not form such patterns of attachment, it is ostracized from the group or killed. Human beings who fail to form such attachments, as in autism, are generally incapable of effective functioning and require various forms of care.

Although the innate patterns of attachment that manifest as tribalism are clearly important for survival, they form the groundwork for some of the most destructive behaviors of which human beings are capable, from physical oppression, torture, and enslavement to outright genocide. Only when combined with revenge does tribalism get worse.[5]

The Universal Impulse Toward Revenge

In contrast to tribalism, attachment to patterns of vengeance is not necessary for survival. Nor do we share it with other animals. Revenge is, I believe, a trait unique to human beings, and one to which we bring our endless human creativity. Revenge by one individual upon another is always ugly and cruel, but when revenge combines with tribalism the result is holocaust.

Years ago in my book *Will and Spirit,* I wrote of revenge as being the paradigm of human evil. My reasoning was that other forms of destructive willfulness can be traced to some motive of self-preservation or defense, but vengeance seemed to serve no such purpose. Revenge certainly does not prevent recurrence of injury; it only increases violence and escalates animosity. Nor could I find any other way, no matter how depraved, in which revenge might be seen as self-serving. I concluded that it exists for no other reason than to get even. Yet revenge is an almost universal human reaction. Its role is obvious in all levels of human conflict, from ugly divorces through feuds within and between families, to the great ethnic atrocities that have so scarred our world. I have seen it first-hand in Vietnam and in Bosnia, and I have to admit I've felt its ugly movement within myself in my reactions to affronts by others.

The dynamics are obvious. One person or group injures another, who in turn tries to get even, and the conflict escalates. The destruction can become extreme and complex, but the vengeance that drives it arises as simply as a reflex. From the time we first develop self-identity as little children, our capacity for revenge is in place. It is horrifyingly *natural.*

I later learned of some studies of traumatized children in which an attitude of revenge seemed to prevent—or perhaps compensate for—what otherwise would have been paralyzing depression. At last I began to see how, at a primitive psychological level, vengeance does serve a certain self-protective function. It by no means prevents future injury, but it does function as a defense against facing the reality of insults or injuries *that have already been sustained.* In the absence of revenge, we would be left with the bare pain of our loss, the sheer awful *fact* of it. Without revenge, we would have to bear what may seem like bottomless grief and despair. We would have to see ourselves as weak, humiliated, degraded victims. As I have written elsewhere, vengeance stands ready to protect us from such abysmal feelings.

The impulse toward vengeance is a pattern of feeling and behavior that arises from attachment to our images of ourselves as being in control. It occupies our minds and hearts with thoughts about getting even. It consumes our attention with rage. It tempts us with the promise of a renewed sense of power and control if we can strike back and get even. All of this protects us from realizing the power of our injury and the depth of our vulnerability. Child psychoanalyst Anna Freud recognized these dynamics decades ago. "Young children," she said, "react to pain not only with anxiety but with other affects . . . on the one hand with anger, rage and revenge feelings, on the other hand with masochistic submission, guilt or depression."[6] Revenge rises within human beings so quickly that it appears to be a reflex, automatic and without discrimination. The forms it takes may be shaped by conditioning, but the impulse itself seems unconditioned—as likely to occur in children as in adults and ready to become active with every injury, insult, or humiliation.

The vengeance impulse is so primal and automatic that it must be actively restrained or redirected to keep order in any social system. Parents try to train their children to control their temptations to strike back. Moral and ethical education seeks to reinforce this control: "Obey the golden rule," "Turn the other cheek." Society's laws do the same, outlining precise boundaries as to how and when revenge can be extracted. Such restraints are absolutely necessary to allow the continuance of civilization.

But the effectiveness of these restraints is imperfect. As in my simple example of being cut off in traffic, the restraint of revenge may inhibit destructive behavior, but it does not prevent the impulse. Sometimes restrained revenge becomes seething animosity, eventually breaking out like steam from a cracked boiler. This kind of vengeance has created a new terminology for our modern language. A fired employee "goes postal," killing coworkers. A teenager, sick of being picked on, gets a gun and "Columbines" his high school.

Liberation from Attachment

Almost every atrocity and virtually every warlike or oppressive action can be traced to some combination of attachment to tribalism and/or revenge. Almost every enduring social injustice can be traced to this combination of forces, from smoldering class oppression through racial prejudice to the genocide of so-called ethnic cleansing. The same applies to all versions of warfare, from street gangs and drug wars to terrorism and retaliation. All are manifestations of our innate capacities to be cruel to one another, and all are grounded in attachment. The primary prevention of cruelty therefore requires attention to attachment itself and to the destructive patterns it generates.

Throughout human history, the spiritual traditions have most deeply come to terms with attachment. The insights from different faiths reveal a striking similarity. Buddhism is perhaps most forthright, claiming in its Four Noble Truths that attachment (usually mistranslated as "desire") is the cause of human suffering and that freedom from suffering requires freedom from attachment. Other traditions may speak of it more in terms of sin or delusion, but all see attachment as a kind of bondage, limiting the human freedom to be who we are meant to be. In Hebrew, a number of words that connote salvation have a two-letter root: Y and S, *yodh* and *shin*. This root directly implies liberation from confinement or restraint. Thus "being saved," as used in Jewish and Christian traditions, essentially means being set free.

Freedom, however, is relative. Attachment is so much a part of our physical nature that complete freedom is not possible in this life. Since all organisms that possess nervous systems depend upon attachment to maintain homeostasis, total absence of attachment is incompatible with life. But as recovering chemical addicts and the mystics of all traditions know, freedom from *specific* attachments can and does happen. And such liberation, when it occurs, can bring with it an increased capacity for truly altruistic lovingkindness.

When one has experienced even a taste of freedom from significant attachment, it is clear that what has happened was not the result of discipline, willpower, or self-imposed restraint. Nor was it due to the implementation of a new and effective strategy. Instead, something inside oneself has been transformed. I frequently tell the story of an alcoholic man whom I treated in my early days of psychiatric practice. After years of relentless drinking, he experienced a sudden liberation while simply walking down the sidewalk one day. He never drank again. When I asked him to describe what happened, all he could say was, "On the way to the grocery store I discovered equanimity."

One hears many such stories in the rooms of twelve-step programs where recovery is discussed. The explanations vary widely, but they share a common theme. Whatever takes place to empower recovery is not a result of willpower or self-discipline. It is not achieved by strategies and tactics. It comes instead as a mysterious, often unexpected gift of grace. And after receiving it, one is never the same.

In my early years of exploring the nature and treatment of addictions, I spoke with many people who had experienced such liberations. Most said that they were grateful for the various forms of professional help they had received. They valued the support others offered when they had given up on themselves. They appreciated the insights they had gained through therapy. They acknowledged the value of structured treatment and rehabilitation programs. Yet they all maintained that these things, alone or together, were not responsible for the transformation.

The professional help offered to addicted people, like programs designed to promote peace and justice in the world, constitutes secondary and tertiary prevention. Some of the people I interviewed said the medical treatment they received had saved their lives on more than one occasion.

Without it, their addiction would have killed them. But liberation from the addiction itself came from a wholly different source and in a completely different way.

The only word that my interviewees and I could agree upon to describe this source and way was "spiritual." It is an overused and misused term, but it does communicate what people experience. At its core, "spirit" refers to energy, life force, breath of life, the power that both brings us to life and creates all our motivations.[7]

Of course different belief systems have widely varying ways of thinking about spirit. I use it to connote something not so much otherworldly or nonphysical, but rather something most profound and basic to existence. Matters of spirit are beyond our usual ways of thinking and understanding, not because they are above us in some ethereal plane, but because they lie deep within us, as our life source. Regardless of how one might conceptualize spirit, it always comes down to something profound that has the capacity to create and affect the very nature of who we are. It is only at this deeply personal level that the roots of human cruelty can be cut.

Spiritual transformation lies beyond the reach of our strategies and machinations; it cannot be achieved or acquired through willpower, wisdom, or technology. Every person with whom I spoke looked back upon their experience and called it a gift.

Receiving the Gift

Although it is possible to describe the innate causes of human cruelty with some objective precision, I find the spiritual transformation of these roots to be much more difficult to explain. Not only do spiritual matters defy objective description in the first place, but attempts to do so generally must rely on religious and theological terminologies that differ among faith traditions and schools of thought within those traditions. Yet the difficulties are surmountable because there are common themes among the different spiritual traditions that, when taken together, can be very revealing.

For example, many traditions view experiences of liberation from innate attachment patterns as *gifts* rather than achievements or accomplishments. Although this gift quality is understood differently in major spiritual traditions, all of them recognize it. In Buddhism, which is largely nontheistic, the gift quality of liberation might be seen as realization of the essentially compassionate nature of creation. A Christian interpretation might see it as *charism*, a healing or deliverance by the Holy Spirit. A Jewish sense might see it as God's mercy, *chesed*. Similarly, an Islamic interpretation could see it as a benevolent act of Allah, the *ar-Rahman* (all-merciful) and *ar-Rahim,* (all-compassionate). Hindu interpretation as set forth in the *TejabinduUpanishad* could see it as a combination of God's love and the effects of *karma* (". . . to all . . . whose hearts are given to the Lord of Love, He gives himself through his infinite grace").

Despite differences in interpretation, the spiritual traditions acknowledge the inherent giftedness of transformation. When individuals realize this gift quality, it always seems to come as a combination of good news and bad news. The good news is that the essential Source of All is benevolent. It does somehow *give the gift.* The bad news is that we can neither earn the transformation nor achieve it on our own. In one way or another, we must *receive* it.

To put it mildly, most human beings dislike the receptive position. It seems too passive and vulnerable. We would much prefer seeing ourselves as captains of our fate and masters of our destiny. The desire to achieve and preserve autonomy comes from our attachment to a sense of separate self, and it is one of the most universal struggles in the spiritual life. Because of their differing experiences in society and culture, women and men tend to have characteristic reactions to the passivity, receptivity, and surrender associated with the spiritual life, but neither gender likes the idea very much.

As recovering addicts well know, movement into the receptive mode is often only possible after one has exhausted all one's resources and is forced to admit defeat. In recovery circles, this experience is called "rock bottom." In Christian tradition, a similar experience applies to life as a whole. St. John of the Cross called it the dark night of the soul. In either case, it is a confrontation with one's inability to handle life autonomously. And although it may be accompanied by considerable despair, it also gives birth to a fresh openness to receptivity that is far less passive than one might think.

An ancient Christian model proposed by St. Bernard of Clairvaux in his *Treatise on the Love of God* or *On Loving God* may be illuminative in this context. Written in the twelfth century, this work is surprisingly relevant for our time. Bernard described four stages or "degrees" of the love of God. He called the first "Love of Self for One's Own Sake." At the outset, most of us try to use our own efforts and abilities to overcome problems and gain satisfaction in life. Bernard maintains that sooner or later this will end in failure. We discover we are unable to control things enough to get what we want and avoid what we don't want.

However it happens, this realization leads to the second phase, "Love of God for One's Own Sake." Although loving God for one's own sake may sound selfish and not very "spiritual," Bernard does not disparage it. It is part of what he sees as a normal, natural process. The transition from the first to the second phase is very like the beginning of Alcoholics Anonymous's twelve steps: admission of powerlessness and turning to a higher power. For many people, it is also the beginning of a conscious, intentional spiritual life. Experiences differ of course, but Bernard emphasizes that there is always hope to receive some gifts of grace, some help or deliverance. And sooner or later, Bernard says, we *do* experience such gifts. They may not come in the ways we expect or even want, but they come.

The second phase may last for a very long time, with God imaged as savior, comforter, the divine source of help. These are true attributes of God, but most theologies maintain that God desires to be much more for human beings. Primarily, God desires a loving relationship. Thus Bernard says that at some point, again by means of grace, the person receiving the gifts becomes increasingly touched by the inherent goodness of the One who gives them. The love of the gifts themselves changes into love of the Giver.

This third stage, which Bernard calls "The Love of God for God's Sake," is a journey of growing intimacy and deepening devotion impelled not by possible gains or blessings but as a sheer expression of love. Finally, in Bernard's thinking, this love births a new and profound realization. Deeply impressed with God's goodness and deeply feeling the flow of love, people may begin to recognize how essentially good and loveable they themselves are. Here begins Bernard's fourth degree of the love of God: "Love of One's Self for God's Sake."

Bernard's simple model doesn't reflect everyone's experience, but it does have an uncanny similarity to the twelve-step model developed eight hundred years later. It is also consonant with a basic understanding of the Christian mystical tradition, namely that the entire journey toward liberation is surrounded and empowered by grace. Individual will and effort are important, but it is the divine gift that makes everything possible.

Further, Bernard's fourth stage of love indicates a critically important and often overlooked aspect of spiritual transformation. The sense of one's self, rather than being denied or destroyed, somehow takes on a new beauty and worthiness. As this realization begins to dawn, one recognizes that the old assumptions about passivity were completely illusory. I want to take a little extra time to describe this further here, because it seems especially important in our modern era.

Transforming the Sense of Self

A superficial reading of nearly all mystical traditions seems to indicate that one's sense of one's self needs to be abandoned, that the "ego" must be relinquished. This assumption seems to be supported by concepts such as "letting go and letting God," surrendering and becoming passively receptive instead of actively taking charge of our lives. It is also supported by the classical distinction in Christian and other traditions between meditation and contemplation; meditation is what we seem to be able to do "on our own," while contemplation seems to come completely as gift. I believe the primary cause of such misinterpretations lies in the assumptions we make about the relationship between the individual person and God (or, for nontheists, "ultimate reality"). Many of us develop a sense of ourselves as autonomous, independent, and irrevocably *separate* from God and the rest of creation. We may be *connected* in some way with that which is "other," but we feel we must always remain distinct. Our society considers it a disorder or even a disease when this sense of an autonomous self is missing or diminished. To be healthy and whole, there can be no blurring of ego-boundaries, no "codependency," no fading of the inviolate separation between self and other.

The spiritual traditions maintain that although we may usually experience ourselves as separate, we are in truth deeply, profoundly, unbelievably connected—even in union with one another. Christian mystics consistently echo St. Paul's statement that we "live and move and have our being" *in* God (Acts 17:28) and St. Augustine's proclamation at the turn of the fifth century that God is closer to us than we are to our very selves. In sixteenth-century Spain, St. John of the Cross stated unequivocally that "God is the center of the soul." The intimacy portrayed here, and similarly in other traditions, is unfathomable to the rational mind. It clearly transcends the simple discriminations we make between "me and you," "us and them," and even the more intimate "I and Thou."[8]

Although the mystics' affirmation of essential unity challenges our experiences of autonomy and independence, it does not, as is commonly believed, negate the existence of a self. It simply gives the self a new meaning. Further, even while one is experiencing separateness, there is no need to disavow one's sense of self in order to participate in receiving the gifts of grace. A case in point is John of the Cross's frequently cited statement, "Pure contemplation consists of receiving." At a superficial level, this seems to describe a completely passive role in which God "does unto" the person according to God's will. But the Spanish word John uses, *recibir*, does not imply totally passive receptivity. Instead, it connotes welcoming, even welcoming with open arms, as one might receive a beloved friend into one's house.[9]

Even when we understand these reinterpretations, our attachment to autonomy and self-determination is so great that we are still likely to be repelled by the spiritual language of surrender and receptivity. Paradoxically, only when our sense of self begins to be transformed into a realization of essential unity can we appreciate that there never was a threat in the first place—that the process is moving not toward self-destruction but toward self-realization. And the self that one realizes in this transformation is resplendent, inexpressibly beautiful, and, as Bernard proclaims, completely loveable.

Experiencing the Transformed Moment

Another common misunderstanding is that spiritual transformation happens in a linear progression and, once realized, is permanent. The mystics' actual experience belies this. St. Teresa of Avila, who was John of the Cross's most important mentor and spiritual guide, said that the longest time she had ever experienced realized union was "about half an hour." She also cautioned that "No one is so advanced in prayer that they do not often have to return to the beginning."

It seems to me that most people's experience is as Teresa described. There's a sense of spiraling or recycling in which one experiences moments of realization or short periods of freedom and compassion, followed by a return to old habits and reflexes. In the example I gave earlier of being cut off on the road by another driver, I might very well respond with sheer immediate compassion rather than rage. But the next day, in similar circumstances, I might find myself again having to restrain initially hostile responses.

In one sense, it is probably a gift that the transformed moment comes and goes. Only after the fact, between such moments, can we reflect upon and appreciate what has happened. Usually one has a very consoling sense of rightness about the freedom and tenderness experienced. Many describe it as a kind of homecoming. Others call it authenticity, a realization of who one really is, the way one was meant to be. This sense of rightness or authenticity eradicates any possible doubt that the experience was an aberration. One may not be able to describe or explain it, even to oneself, but there is no doubt that it was absolutely real.

There is also always a deep gratitude for the experience, but it is often accompanied by a kind of sadness or regret, even contrition that comes from realizing how unfree and self-centered one generally is in comparison to the transformed moment. It's a feeling of, "Why can't it be this way all the time? Why can't *I* be this way all the time?" This often prompts a prayer for some kind of mercy.

I doubt that anyone in this life ever makes it to a perfect steady state of freedom for unconditional love and realized unity. Such "nonattachment" does not seem possible for embodied human beings. But there is an inner movement going on that has a direction away from the compulsions of cruelty and toward freedom for love. Perhaps just as important, the process builds a growing appreciation of oneself in the world. It could be called self-knowledge, even wisdom. As in Bernard's fourth stage of love, there is a deepening sense of the beauty and preciousness of one's own being and with it a similar appreciation of all creation. At the same time, there is a growing familiarity with one's tendencies toward selfishness and separation.

The process can be likened to walking the terrain of one's own being in the world, learning first-hand the landscape of one's soul. Our growing knowledge and deepening wisdom give us confidence to recognize freedom and to act in love. Such wisdom encourages sensitivity to self-centeredness and the capacity to restrain actions that arise from it. Confidence grows along with humility, and together they encourage deeper dedication, a more radical giving of ourselves to the ways of love. And over time, the moments happen more frequently. They last longer. We appreciate them more, desire them more, trust them more and are increasingly open to welcoming them.

Confidence and Consolation

The confidence experienced in transformed moments can be so consoling, so joyful as to seem ecstatic. It is completely different from the usual self-confidence achieved by shoring up one's sense of personal competence and autonomy. It is a form of self-confidence to be sure, but the whole experience of "self" is changed so that it is no longer secured in separateness but rather is discovered in unity and communion. In much the same way, Teresa of Avila discriminates between the consolations that happen in meditation and those that occur in contemplation. In meditation (the activities we feel we are doing through our own intent and effort) we may often feel a quiet calm, a peaceful centeredness, a sense of being wide-awake and right here. Teresa uses the term *contentos* to describe these good feelings, the consolations of meditation. She says such feelings arise in our senses and encourage us toward God.

As good as these *contentos* may be, however, Teresa says they pale in comparison to the consolations that happen in contemplation, which begins when autonomous effort eases and one becomes more receptive to divine action. She calls contemplative consolations *gustos,* and says they arise not in our own senses, but in the presence of God's very self within us. They arise in God and overflow into our senses, thus becoming our experience. In short, the *contentos* of meditation are sensory experiences achieved by our own calming and centering, while the *gustos* of contemplation are God's own joy, freedom, and love becoming our own.

This description sounds as though experiences of transformation are always happy and pleasant. This is decidedly not the case. To put it simply, whether the experience is happy or sorrowful depends upon the situation at hand. In transformed moments, attachment to self-image is eased and one ceases to see oneself as separate. Thus one *feels with* (the literal meaning of "com-passion") the situation. If the situation is beautiful and harmonious as in a pristine natural setting or in loving and peaceful human relationships, the primary feeling may be one of sheer delight. But if the situation involves angry conflict, injustice, or other sufferings, the feelings will not be pleasant at all.

This is true in any authentic realization of things as they are. As the sense of separateness eases, one joins the surrounding reality. There is no "rising above" anything here. It is instead an "entering into." From a theistic perspective, one joins not only the joy and sorrow of the world, but also to some extent joins God's own joy and sorrow.

Yet even if one encounters deep sadness in a given moment, the sense of consolation, the *gusto,* remains. As one sheds tears of pain with those who suffer, the sense of goodness and rightness in simply being there is wonderful beyond all description. Even in the fear of risking one's well-being in responding to a situation, the rightness remains, the realness remains, and this, I think, is the ground of true confidence. In this confidence there is no sense of being on a mission, no feeling of carrying out God's will, no identified cause for which one might sacrifice oneself. True confidence never rests on explanation, rationalization, or any justification whatsoever. It arises simply, cleanly, as a direct response to the reality at hand.

Humility and Humor

In our usual way of thinking, confidence and humility might seem contradictory, but in the transformation of which I'm speaking they become one. The key lies in *realization*. I have used the term *realization* many times here, and it is important to explain that it does not refer to conceptual understanding or comprehension. Often in fact, it occurs in profound unknowing, in complete absence of understanding. Realization, as I use it, means *making real*. In other words, it is a direct, immediate immersion into things as they absolutely are: no preconceptions, no interpretations, no judgment. It is oneself becoming true. Like the transformation itself, this kind of realization is not a matter of personal initiative or accomplishment; it simply comes as part of the gift.

Confidence and humility are unified in the realization of one's rightful, natural being within and responsiveness to a situation exactly as it is, irrevocably interconnected and interdependent. True confidence arises only in this atmosphere of interdependence, where nothing is isolated or cut apart. Pride and arrogance come from a separated sense of self, which is set over and against something or someone else. Humility comes from the realization that one's own being is rooted—as is everything else—in all being. "Humility" comes from the Latin *humus,* "earth." In one sense it connotes lowliness, but in another it means groundedness, being rooted in the earth. For some people, this kind of humility comes gently and gracefully. For others, it may involve considerable feelings of humiliation; arrogance must be defeated by learning that one cannot handle things on one's own. In whatever way it comes, humility arises with confidence— and also with *humor,* another word with a similar root.

I do not know how to explain the sense of humor that grows with realization. It seems to be a kind of buoyancy, an irrepressible lightness that survives all suffering and loss. Perhaps in part it expresses the relief that comes with learning that not only can one not handle things on one's own, but one does not have to. Perhaps it comes from a growing appreciation of divine play, the endless exuberance of creation. Maybe it comes from the sheer experience of freedom. And it probably includes recognizing how silly we all become in trying to understand ourselves and control our destinies. It is likely a combination of all these things with something far more profound: a wisdom perspective that eludes understanding and words.

There is no doubt, however, that humor grows along with confidence and humility. I have seen it too often to doubt it. I have found it in the writings of all the mystics I have quoted here. I have seen it in hospices and cancer wards, and in the rooms of recovery where people laugh so hard at their own tragic stories that they cannot continue to speak. I saw it in an old Bosnian grandmother who, after crying over the loss of her entire family, suddenly winked and announced she was in the market for a new husband. I saw it in a Tibetan Lama who, when asked what it was like to have his country occupied and its people dispersed, smiled and winked and said, "Sparkles." Whatever the humor is, wherever it comes from, it is inevitable. And I am deeply grateful for it.

Vulnerability and Innocence

Normally we use a multitude of devices to defend ourselves against pain and insult. It is as if we walk through our lives wearing armor, shielded as much as possible from any assault. We let our guard down only in particular settings where we can feel trusting and safe—and even then most of us maintain a certain vigilance for danger. This defensiveness results from repeated experiences of being psychologically and physically hurt; we learn where the threats lie and adapt ourselves to avoid them. One could say, as did Sigmund and Anna Freud, that a major task of early childhood is to develop effective defense mechanisms that allow us to function without being damaged.

It would be an exaggeration to maintain that this childhood quest is directed solely toward achieving invulnerability. Because human beings require openness and availability to others, the developmental process is delicate and complex: too much defensiveness and one becomes isolated and unable to connect, too little and one's sense of self is undermined by victimization. Thus "normal" childhood development seeks a functional balance of defense and vulnerability. Through years of psychological effort most of us have achieved such a balance, and we naturally seek to maintain it. Viewed from this vantage point, the prospect of transformation can seem very threatening. Openness to things just as they are is a clear invitation to radical vulnerability.

To be vulnerable literally means "able to be wounded." Much as we might want to avoid it, this is precisely what true transformation calls for. The call has been repeated through millennia in one spiritual tradition after another. We can ignore it, but the meaning is undeniable. It is the clear intent of Jesus' admonitions and examples of turning the other cheek, loving one's enemies, and taking up one's cross. It is exactly what the fourteenth-century Tibetan Vow of Mahamudra expresses: "For the boundless suffering of all sentient beings, may I be filled with great unbearable compassion." Mohandas Gandhi stated it precisely in describing *ahimsa,* his path of nonviolence: "Ahimsa means infinite love, which again means infinite capacity for suffering."

It is not surprising that human beings have always been intimidated by such challenges, nor that we would try our best to reinterpret them in less threatening, more domesticated ways. Still, the invitation is clear: to enter into this life just as it is we must become vulnerable. A saving grace—paradoxically remaining hidden until the experience of transformation itself—lies in realizing we are not separate and that the self-images we struggle so

hard to establish and protect are just that: images. Grace lies in the indescribable joys of freedom and love that Teresa so aptly called *gustos*.

There is also a saving grace when we remain centered in the present.
We normally conceive of a situation in terms of what has gone before it
and what it may lead to. For example, if I am to visit a dying person who
is suffering an agonizing illness, I may be besieged not only by the person's immediate pain but also by the suffering, fear, and desolation they
have experienced in the past and the specter of the dying soon to come.
When I add to all this my own personal fears, doubts, and hopeless desires
to make things better, it may indeed seem too much to bear. I have to gear
myself up to go at all, and I am likely to be tense and tight in the meeting.

But if by some miracle I am given the capacity to simply be in the present moment with the person just as they are, the burden is suddenly
lightened—not only made less heavy but also somehow filled with light.
In that light, freed from causes, consequences, and self-concerns I can
truly meet the person, join a precious moment with them. There may be
sadness there, to be sure, and I will be open to sharing something of their
pain. But who knows? Perhaps there will be surprises of joy and laughter
as well, and maybe even hope.

In that kind of moment, empowered by grace, one finds oneself not only
vulnerable but innocent. *Innocent* comes from the Latin *in-nocere*, meaning "not yet harmed." When one enters a situation fresh, just as it is, vulnerability and innocence are synonymous; one is able to be wounded, but
not yet wounded. This pristine state only lasts for an instant, of course,
but then the next moment comes, and the next. And in each moment
innocence is immediately reborn. Perhaps, where it counts, one truly does
become like a little child.[10]

The inner experience of transformation, then, consists of an irregular
but growing realization of the fundamental falsehood of our separateness.
To put it another way, when we do not feel or see ourselves as separate,
we realize unity. The precise feelings in such times are largely determined
by the situation, but even very painful feelings are likely to be accompanied by an indescribable sense of freedom and availability, an openness to
everything around us and a lightness that frequently becomes filled with
joy and humor. Confidence, humility, vulnerability, and innocence also
characterize this experience, but they are not generally sensed as separate
feelings. Instead, they simply become manifest in our responses. All this
happens in a general absence of understanding and comprehension—what
the mystics call "unknowing." Yet somehow a deep wisdom emerges that
allows for incisive and wholly accurate responsiveness to the situation.

The ground of that responsiveness is compassion, and it becomes manifest in moments of liberation from attachment, the primary root of cruelty.

What Actually Changes?

All major spiritual traditions in some way address the possibility of liberation from attachment. It may be called salvation, conversion, metanoia, enlightenment, realization, any of a variety of other names. Regardless of the names and the different theologies that lie behind them, there is a consistent sense of a new way of being; one that is more loving and less cruel. I believe modern science has come to a place where we can begin to appreciate how this new, more loving way of being might be expressed physically.

I have made a case that the human capacity for cruelty is innate, "hardwired" into our brains. I also propose that our capacities for compassion, tenderness, and justice are just as innate, just as organic as are our violent capacities. In his superbly integrative work *Zen and the Brain,* neurologist James Austin cites a number of research studies that support this idea. Such studies demonstrate, for example, that newborn babies cry when they hear another infant crying, that actual behavioral responses to assist others are evident by the second year of life, and that most children demonstrate a sense of justice and sharing by the time they enter elementary school.[11]

Austin concludes, as does Zen master D. T. Suzuki, that compassion is a "native virtue." Austin says that the "primitive, biological roots" of compassion may go back to "highly instinctual interpersonal behavior: the way small fellow creatures huddle together, finding warmth while sharing it." He goes on to speak of the "young seedlings" of compassion that are naturally rooted in human beings and, given the chance, "ready to grow taller."[12]

Austin's metaphor of the seedlings of virtue is strikingly similar to one used four centuries earlier by Teresa of Avila. Asked to describe her experience of prayer, she likened the human soul to a garden. God dwells in the center of this garden, she said, so it is natural for us to want it to be as beautiful and bountiful as possible. She proposed that the flowers in this soul-garden are the virtues, and that it is our role to tend the garden. But she quickly asserts that it is not our job to till the soil, or to plant the seeds, or even to pull the weeds, for God has already done all that. Our role is only to see to the watering of the garden, and the water is nothing other than prayer.

Just as our capacity for cruelty is part of our nature, so is our capacity for lovingkindness. True transformation, then, consists not in the repression or layering-over of vicious impulses, but in the actual decrease of such impulses and the consequent emergence of deep, wholly natural impulses of tenderness and love.

Neuropsychological studies as well as the experience of countless spiritual authorities indicate that neurological patterns that function like streambeds to conduct strands of our behavior exist within us for vice and virtue, for cruelty and kindness. It seems to me that only two possibilities exist for positive transformation of these patterns. The first involves actual structural change. Certain points in the streambeds of cruelty might actually be eradicated, thus preventing the flow of activity through them. Austin uses the term "etching" to describe how this might happen, much as an acid might etch away precise points on a piece of metal. He also suggests that more global changes may take place in brain areas resulting in decreased destructiveness and increased openness to the flow of compassion.

The second possibility involves functional change, perhaps without any significant alteration of structure. My experience in working with chemical addictions indicates that although seemingly miraculous transformations can eradicate a specific addictive behavior completely, the patterns and pathways of the behavior often remain intact. This is why, for example, people in twelve-step programs speak of themselves as "recovering" rather than "recovered." It is why so many recovering alcoholics know that no matter how long they have been sober, a single drink can start the behavior all over again. It may also be why it is so easy to identify remnants of self-centeredness in the lives of even the most realized saints. And why the human journey toward compassion is nearly always one of fits and starts, steps forward and steps back. At least in terms of addiction, it seems to me that although the brain may change in both function and structure, it does not forget. To the extent that transformation of the brain might be structural, it is easy to understand how certain impulses toward cruelty might be wholly eradicated. Some or all of the cellular patterns comprising such impulses simply disappear. The streambed no longer exists.

If instead the changes are primarily functional, the old pathways remain, at least as a potential, but they have ceased their activity. The streambed remains, but it is dry. In either case, fresh, new, and spontaneously compassionate responses become possible. And in either case, what one first experiences can be a loving and accurate response to the real needs of the particular situation.

I am certain that functional transformation can occur; I have seen it happen. It is entirely possible that structural transformation may also occur. Either way though, I am convinced that the new way of functioning, the transformed way, bears little resemblance to the old. The expression of true compassion does not coalesce into residual cellular patterns. The flow of lovingkindness does not form a streambed. Instead, it is fresh and new in each moment, arising spontaneously. It is unexplainable and unpredictable. In contrast to all patterned manifestations of attachment, tribalism, and vengeance, true compassion has no pattern whatsoever. It is completely unconditioned.

The compassion, altruism, empathy, and love that emerge through transformation are radically different from what we normally mean by those words. We normally think of them in terms of ourselves: imagining what another is feeling, then extending ourselves for the sake of the other's well-being. But the transformed qualities are not based on ourselves; they arise with absolute spontaneity from the deep source of unity. No one can predict what form they will take.

Transformation comes as a gift and its manifestations are beyond references to ourselves and are outside our control. This raises a perennial question: What can I do, if anything, to help free myself from cruel behaviors? How can I grow in true compassion? Is there anything I can do to become more receptive to the gift?

What We Can Do

The different spiritual traditions tend to come together in recognizing a giftlike quality in the process of transformation, but they diverge markedly in their understandings of how one receives that gift. Most traditions emphasize practices and disciplines such as prayer, meditation, service, scripture study, participation in rituals and worship, moral behavior, and so on. A number also maintain that adherence to specific beliefs is necessary, for example, "No one comes to God without accepting Jesus," or "There is no God but Allah and Mohammed is his prophet."

At one extreme, it is assumed that such practices and beliefs will acquire merit and earn the gift as a reward for one's efforts. "Obey the commandments and you will gain eternal life. Disobey them and you will be eternally damned," or "Practice meditation with diligence and you will achieve enlightenment; otherwise you will remain trapped in illusion." At the other extreme, there is a sense that spiritual practices and disciplines bear no particular relationship to the giving or receiving of the gift; they are simply ways of prayer, of expressing one's concern and love. The gift is given when and how the Giver chooses, regardless of a person's intention and effort. Most commonly, there is an implicit middle-ground assumption that practices and beliefs somehow help prepare an individual to be more open and receptive to the gift when it is given, but do not necessarily make it happen.

In the Christian mystical tradition this "faith and works" question bears directly on the classical distinction between meditation and contemplation. Meditation is understood as the intentional effort one puts into disciplines of practice whereas contemplation comes as a sheer gift of grace beyond all effort and intention. The gift of contemplation is understood as synonymous with the gift of transformation as I have described it here, characterized by relative nonattachment and free loving responsiveness to the immediate needs of the situation at hand. As the gift of contemplation grows in a certain moment, the effort of meditation relaxes and finally, in moments of realized unity, ceases altogether.[13]

As I have indicated, the most common understanding is that meditation somehow prepares a person to receive the gift of contemplation. Perhaps the self-referencing patterns of the mind "learn" how to relax. Perhaps over time, as Austin postulates, meditation actually interferes with established pathways. Or maybe, as many of the mystics maintain, the self-knowledge gained through meditation leads a person to humility and surrender. Although all these explanations may bear some truth, I do not think one can conclude that there is any direct cause-and-effect relationship between meditation and contemplation.

I say this because I know of a number of people who frequently seem to manifest the compassion that comes from contemplative transformation without ever having meditated in any formal way and who do not hold to any formal religious tenets. Similarly, I have known and read of experienced meditators and fervent believers who do not seem to have grown in compassion and tenderness. An extreme example of the latter might be the traditional training of Japanese *Ninja,* originally established to prepare finely tuned assassins in the service of warlords. Ninja training included meditation practices very similar to those of Zen and belief systems similar to those of Taoism. It is clear that such practices resulted in many qualities associated with contemplation, such as present-centeredness, panoramic awareness, and immediate, incisive responsiveness. Yet the whole intent and effect was geared toward enhanced warfare. Similarly, I have encountered some people who have engaged in meditative practices and held traditional beliefs over time who, at least in my judgment, seem to be more self-centered and isolated than when they began.

My point here is that meditation practices, belief systems, and other spiritual disciplines—even those that are most contemplatively oriented—do not automatically and necessarily lead to a spiritual transformation characterized by true compassion. Christian and other theistic mystical traditions hold that what makes the difference is a loving God, who plants the desire for freedom and compassion in us and nourishes it toward fullness. A Buddhist interpretation might pose that the ground of everything, being compassion itself, has a similar effect.

Regardless of tradition, a person's deep desire and intent—the person's motivation for embarking upon a conscious spiritual journey in the first place—plays a very critical role. Somewhere, somehow, a person must *want* to love and be loved, must yearn for peace and justice. This desire may not be conscious at all in the beginning. As in Bernard of Clairvaux's stages, one often begins with what seem like completely self-serving motivations—more to be loved than to love. Yet the assumption is that somewhere beneath awareness, the person has willingly said "Yes" to all that love entails and requires. I can think of no better expression of this than the well-known words of Dag Hammarskjöld:

> I don't know Who—or what—put the question. I don't know when it was put. I don't even remember answering. But at some moment I did answer Yes to Someone—or Something—and from that hour I was certain that existence is meaningful and that, therefore, my life, in self-surrender, had a goal.[14]

Teresa of Avila and John of the Cross, whom I have quoted several times, say that God loves all persons with an "esteeming love," a love that is endlessly respectful of each person's unique personality, strengths, weaknesses, and desires. With many other Christian mystics, they affirm that God does not move actively within a person without first being welcomed. When loving transformation happens, then, it comes as an answer to a prayer—even when one may be unaware that one has asked for it.

Herein lies what, to me, is the greatest mystery of human transformation. How do I know if my heart has said yes? How can I know what true willingness is? I suppose it could be said that if one even cares about the question at all, one has already said yes, somehow and somewhere. I am old enough and have been through enough now to trust the yes in myself. Yet when I think of the population of this earth, I do not know how or why it seems that certain hearts say no. What might it have been, in the hearts of Hitler and the other notoriously destructive villains of history, or in the many ordinary people who grow crueler rather than kinder as they get older—what was it that turned them against the tender invitations of Being?

I have looked into psychology for an answer, and come up empty-handed. To be sure, it must be a deeply good thing for a child to grow up in a family where mercy and justice are both taught and modeled. And it must be helpful for spiritual practices to be undertaken within an authentic tradition and in a community of mutual support and accountability. But I have seen what—in my judgment—are screaming no's emerge from the best of such settings. Conversely, I have seen yes's come to life sweetly and victoriously in people who suffered terrible abuse as children and who themselves have repeatedly committed the most vicious crimes against others.

Many Christian contemplatives say it is all God and finally nothing other than God. God gives everyone the desire in the first place. As St. Paul said to the Greeks in Athens, "God created us to seek God" (Acts 17:27). And as St. Augustine echoed, "Thou hast made us for thyself, and our hearts are restless 'til they rest in thee." And the mystics go on to say that it is God who empowers our willingness, our yes. While I agree with it, this answer leaves me almost as unsatisfied as the answers I sought in psychology. It leaves something out. If God empowers us to say yes but does not *make* us do so, I am still left wondering where the no's come from. It is a question I must leave to better theologians than I am; it is a mystery I do not expect to solve.

The Seductiveness of Activism

Even though I do not know how or why people respond the way they do to the deepest spiritual invitations of life, I am convinced that yes's are happening all around us all the time—and that they far outnumber the no's. I am also convinced that the yes we say to compassion and justice must be nurtured inside of us. As I have said repeatedly, the primary prevention of human cruelty requires primary attention to the interior transformation of individuals.

To do so in this modern age is difficult. For one thing, we human beings are so accustomed to being motivated by attachment that we have trouble conceiving of being motivated by anything else. We all too often equate nonattachment with inaction. The popular understanding is that contemplation and action are different ways of being, sometimes in balance and sometimes in conflict. We have lost the great mystical promise that loving and effective action happens *within* contemplative living. Similarly, we continue to suffer reverberations from our European history that made people terrified of quietism, anything resembling not-doing. In this environment, any spiritual attention to the inner life other than for psychological self-improvement is viewed with suspicion. It has been called navel-gazing, self-absorption, New Age, a sign of the decadence of western self-determination. In my experience, much of this fear and suspicion arises from the concern that people will use their personal spirituality to opt out or "cop out" of their moral and ethical responsibilities. From this perspective "letting go and letting God" implies being a passive bystander in a wounded world that cries out for service and action.

I confess that I think this kind of fear is groundless. It is itself an aberration, a straw villain. In all my years of life, of practicing psychiatry and being a spiritual companion to others, I have seen my share of neurotic and psychotic distortions of spirituality. I have encountered spiritual rationalizations for psychological phenomena—and vice versa. And of course I have experienced the common use of religion as a tranquilizer or an outright escape: "It's all God's will," or "Let God sort them out." And I have met up with deep cruelty that is rationalized on the basis of religion. But in my experience, none of these distortions has been accompanied by serious attention to one's inner life. And for good reason: they are all defense mechanisms, and any real interior attentiveness would show them up for what they are.

In all this time I have yet to see one single person attending to the inner spiritual life who has been led to cop-out from life's responsibilities. What I have seen is the opposite; that people often feel so compelled to act, so immersed in doings that they neglect their interior life, leaving it impoverished. In many cases I am convinced that activity is used as a defense against interiority, a means of avoiding an encounter with what's really going on inside. It seems to me that the greater danger for our time is not escape into passivity and inaction but escape into the busyness of *activism*. I am convinced that monk and writer Thomas Merton was understating the truth when he said, "Absolute quietism is not exactly an ever-present danger in the world of our time."[15]

Sometimes I wonder if some of the world's great contemplative souls have not themselves been seduced by the temptations of activism. To be sure, inner realization always calls forth action in the world; this is precisely the way true compassion becomes manifest. But it is not always easy to discriminate between what is truly called forth and what is merely given into.

When I look at my beloved Mohandas Gandhi, for example, I see how he was a great spiritual teacher as well as a powerful activist. And I see that at many turnings he chose political activity over spiritual guidance. In the process, he and his influence liberated India from Britain's rule. To be sure, the whole of Gandhi's life, much like that of Jesus', was and is spiritual guidance for the world. But I look at India today, a nuclear power at the brink of war, filled with the very ethnic and economic inequities Gandhi so valiantly opposed. And I cannot help but wonder, might Gandhi have given more to the world, had a more lasting impact, if he had been able to give more of his life to teaching and guiding others spiritually?

In contrast I look at His Holiness the Dalai Lama, a man who has to attend to countless political issues and could so easily be wholly taken over by them. Yet he always seems to remain first and foremost a spiritual guide and teacher. There is no way I could ever make judgments about such things. I have far too much trouble discriminating between my own invitations and impulses to even begin to judge someone else's. As I say, it is just a wondering.

But I would pose the thought that in today's turbulent marriage of outer action and inner attentiveness, action is by far the more abusive partner. The contemplatives have forever been saying that there need be no conflict whatsoever. At best, they say, outer action and inner attentiveness do not constitute a marriage at all, but a perfect union. At best, action *is* contemplation and contemplation *is* action. But such a realization of unity can happen only through inner transformation—a transformation that, as the Dalai Lama says, is difficult but is the only way.

Is the World Ready?

One person, hearing the ideas presented here, responded simply: "The world is not ready for this." I agree. The world has never been ready; it isn't ready now, and without a God-given global dark night of the soul, it is unlikely that it ever will be ready. Throughout history only small and diverse pockets of people have found themselves on the inner path of liberated compassion. They have never for long constituted the mainstream life of any organization or religion, never developed a lasting program or project to change the world, never managed to stem the overall course of human cruelty.

The fact remains, though, that such individuals continue to appear in every generation, and there are perhaps more of them than one might think. Occasionally some are called into major public action and thus enter the spotlight of world attention. More often their outward actions are ordinary and nondramatic. From time to time they are drawn together in their shared desire for love and in their common hope for a transformed world. Alone or in small communities, they will probably always

pray and work for the liberation of humanity. They know, or soon discover, that the contemplative way of inner transformation can never be
turned into a project or program. It cannot be taught, learned, packaged,
evangelized, or institutionalized. Yet because they know it is the only way
they yearn for it themselves, and support and hold out hope not only for
all who are ready to listen, but also for those who cannot hear at all.

I began this essay with a short sentence that haunted me. I want to
close with a (very much longer) sentence that reassures me. Not long
before his death, Thomas Merton wrote in a letter:

> The contemplative has nothing to tell you except to reassure you and
> say that if you dare to penetrate your own silence and dare to advance
> without fear into the solitude of your own heart, and risk the sharing
> of that solitude with the lonely other who seeks God through you and
> with you, then you will truly recover the light and the capacity to
> understand what is beyond words and beyond explanations because
> it is too close to be explained: it is the intimate union in the depths of
> your own heart, of God's spirit and your own secret inmost self, so
> that you and God are in truth One Spirit.[16]

NOTES

1 His Holiness the Fourteenth Dalai Lama Tenzin Gyatso in Thich Nhat
   Hanh, *Peace Is Every Step* (New York: Bantam, 1991), p. vii. Here is the
   rest of the Dalai Lama's first paragraph: "Wherever I go, I express this, and
   I am encouraged that people from many different walks of life receive it
   well. Peace must first be developed within an individual. And I believe that
   love, compassion, and altruism are the fundamental basis for peace. Once
   these qualities are developed within an individual, he or she is then able
   to create an atmosphere of peace and harmony. This atmosphere can be
   expanded and extended from the individual to his family, from the family
   to the community and eventually to the whole world."

2 "Nature" comes from the same Latin root as "natal" and "nativity."
   In a literal sense, it means "close to our birth."

3 G. Hardin, "Population Skeletons in the Environmental Closet." *Bull.
   Atomic Scientist,* 1972, 28(6), 37ff.

4 R. P. Shaw and Y. Wong, *Genetic Seeds of Warfare: Evolution, Nationalism, and Patriotism* (London: Unwin Hyman, 1989).

5 For an excellent overview of this topic, see the article by J.M.G. van der
   Dennen of the Center for Peace and Conflict Studies, University of Groningen,

The Netherlands: "Ethnocentrism and In-Group/Out-Group Differentiation," in V. Reynolds, V. Falger, and I. Vine (eds.), *The Socio-biology of Ethnocentrism: Evolutionary Dimensions of Xenophobia, Discrimination, Racism and Nationalism* (London: Croom Helm, 1987), pp. 1–47. This article, from which I obtained a number of cited sources, is also available at http://rint.rechten.rug.nl/rth/dennen/ethnocen.htm.

6   A. Freud, "The Role of Bodily Illness in the Mental Life of Children." *Psychoanalytic Study of the Child,* 1952, 7, 69–81.

7   Spirit is archetypally associated with that most basic evidence of life: breath. For example, the same word is used for spirit and breath in Latin *(spiritus),* Greek *(pneuma),* Hebrew *(ruah),* and Sanskrit *(prajna),* among others.

8   Saint Augustine, *Confessions,* Book III, Chapter 6.

9   John of the Cross, *Commentary on the Living Flame of Love,* Stanza 3, Second Redaction.

10   I am indebted to my dear friend and colleague Fr. Richard Rohr, OFM, for sparking my thinking about vulnerability and innocence.

11   Cited in J. H. Austin, *Zen and the Brain* (Cambridge, Mass.: MIT Press, 1999), pp. 648–650; M. Hoffman, "Is Altruism Part of Human Nature?" *Journal of Personality and Social Psychology,* 1981, 40, 121–137; and M. Hunt, *The Compassionate Beast* (New York: Morrow, 1990), pp. 50, 204.

12   Austin takes the term *native virtue* from D. T. Suzuki, *Studies in the Lanka-vatara Sutra* (London: Routledge & Kegan Paul, 1930), p. 297: "Zen does not teach to destroy all the impulses, instincts and affective factors that make up the human heart; it only teaches to clear up our intellectual insight from erroneous discriminations and unjustifiable assertions, for when this is done, the heart knows by itself how to work out its native virtues."

13   There has been a long-lived confusion over the possibility that a certain form of contemplation can be achieved through practice. This has generally been called "acquired contemplation" as distinguished from "infused con-templation," which is the sheer gift. This entire notion is a distortion of the classical understanding, and stems primarily from an early misidentification of the writings of John of the Cross. For an excellent treatment of the sources and consequences of this misunderstanding, see J. Arraj, *From John of the Cross to Us: The Story of a 400 Year Long Misunderstanding and What It Means for the Future of Christian Mysticism* (Chiloquin, Ore.: Inner Growth Books and Videos, 1999).

14   D. Hammarskjöld, *Markings* (New York: Alfred A. Knopf, 1966), p. 205. Hammarskjöld wrote these words in 1961, a few months before he was killed.

15 T. Merton, *Contemplative Prayer* (New York: Doubleday, 1969), p. 91.

16 T. Merton, Letter written August 21, 1967. Quoted in H. Nouwen, *Thomas Merton: Contemplative Critic* (San Francisco: HarperSanFrancisco, 1972, 1981), p. 42.

SOURCES

Books

Austin, J. H. *Zen and the Brain.* Cambridge, Mass.: MIT Press, 1999.

Bailie, G. *Violence Unveiled: Humanity at the Crossroads.* New York: Crossroad, 1995.

Bernard of Clairvaux. *Treatise on the Love of God* or *On Loving God.* Bardstown, Ky.: Cistercian Publications, 1996.

Freud, A. *The Writings of Anna Freud.* Vol. 2: *The Ego and the Mechanisms of Defense.* New York: International Universities Press, 1936.

John of the Cross. *The Living Flame of Love.* Tempe: Arizona State University Medieval and Renaissance Texts and Studies, 1995.

May, G. *Addiction and Grace.* San Francisco: HarperSanFrancisco, 1988.

May, G. *Will and Spirit.* San Francisco, HarperSanFrancisco, 1982.

Merton, T. *Contemplative Prayer.* New York: Doubleday, 1969.

Namgyal, T. T. *Mahamudra: The Quintessence of Mind and Meditation.* Boston & London: Shambala, 1986.

Saint Augustine. *The Confessions.* New York: Alfred A. Knopf, 2001.

Teresa of Avila. *The Life of Teresa of Avila by Herself.* (J. M. Cohen, trans.) New York: Penguin, 1988.

Wink, W. *Engaging the Powers.* Minneapolis: Fortress, 1992.

Articles and Chapters in Books

Ayalon, A. "Children as Hostages." *Practitioner,* 1982, *226,* 1773–1781.

Byrnes, D. A., and Kiger, G. "The Effect of a Prejudice-Reduction Simulation on Attitude Change." *Journal of Applied Social Psychology,* 1990, *20*(4), 341–356.

Dorje, H. H. Rangjung (1284–1339), "Vow of Mahamudra." In Prabhu and Rao (eds.), *Mind of Mahatma Gandhi.* (3rd ed.) Ahmedabad, India: Navajivan, 1968.

Garbarino, J. "Children and Youth in Dangerous Environments: Coping with the Consequences." In F. E. Atkinson (ed.), *Treatment of Torture: Readings and References.* Ottawa: F. E. Atkinson, 1991, pp. 270–276.

Pynoos, R. L. and Eth, S. "Children Traumatized by Witnessing Acts of Personal Violence: Homicide, Rape, or Suicide Behavior." *Post-Traumatic Stress Disorder in Children*. Washington, D.C.: American Psychiatric Press, 1985, pp. 169–186.

Terr, L. C. "Forbidden Games." *Journal of the American Academy of Child Psychiatry*, 1981, 20, 741–760.

PART FOUR

PARTICIPATING IN THE WORLD'S SOUL

OPENING THE DREAM

BEYOND THE LIMITS OF OTHERNESS

Rev. Canon Charles Gibbs

A Citizen of the Earth

THE CONVERSATION really began when I asked where he was from. We were speeding down Broadway, deserted at 4:30 in the morning, on the way to John F. Kennedy International Airport. I was headed home and wondered where his home was originally. Through the opening in the barrier that separates passenger from driver in a yellow cab in New York City, he answered my question with a question: "Where do you think?"

Though I work with people from all over the world and have a good ear for accents (like recognizing the Iranian accent of the man who runs the Mexican restaurant just down from the Jewish Community Center in San Rafael), I offered a guess: "The Middle East?"

"Pakistan," he replied.

"I have many friends in Pakistan," I responded.

Soon I knew the broad contours of his life. He had recently lost the sales job he had held for several years. Driving a cab was a stopgap measure to help him survive until the economy turned around. It wasn't all bad, he realized. He could take a three-month vacation to be with his family—a wife, a daughter, and two sons—in Pakistan. Yes, he missed them, but he could find work here to support them. And it was easier for them as Muslims to live in Pakistan.

As I talked with him about my work of global interfaith cooperation, which often had me traveling and away from my family, he voiced his support of this effort to bring people of different faiths together to work for the well-being of all. Then he shared an insight. "Since I was a child," he offered, "I've felt that more than a Pakistani, I was ultimately a citizen of the earth. And more than a Muslim, I was ultimately a child of God."

As I listened to him, I knew that I had often said the same thing, replacing *Pakistani* with *American* and *Muslim* with *Christian*. I began to wonder why I saw life that way. Heard life that way. I began to wonder what the world would be like if more people saw and heard life that way. Not perfect, but better. Much better.

The Sacred Music of Humanity's Yearning

I can't sing. Or rather, when I sing, people want to leave the room. But I can hear, after my fashion, the extraordinary chorus of voices that fills each moment of life with the sacred music of humanity's yearning for peace, justice, and healing. Over the past seven years, as I have served as executive director of the United Religions Initiative, I have heard this chorus singing through the people of many faiths from over sixty countries with whom I have been privileged to work. I have come to believe that the voices of all faithful people committed to peace, justice, and healing, regardless of their religion or spirituality, are music to God's ears, are expressions of the Buddha nature that inheres in all life. I realize that this perspective may be heresy to some. To me, it simply reflects the truth of my experience—our lives are immeasurably enriched if we see the sacred diversity of life and life's diverse expressions of the sacred as a gift rather than as a threat. I believe that the positive future of life on earth depends on our willingness to experience this diversity and to be changed; that it requires us to appreciate, respect, and honor the diverse voices of the sacred and knit them together into a chorus that reflects a shared vocation for peace, justice, and healing.

Perhaps my openness to hearing music of the sacred in the richness of human diversity and to viewing that diversity as a gift rather than as a threat began in my early years in New Mexico when the music of the English my family spoke was enriched by the music of the Spanish spoken all around us and by the loving presence of a small brown woman whom many white folks would have dismissed as somehow of less worth with the single epithet "Mexican." But that was not my experience of her. Nana helped my mother take care of my sister, Ruthie, me, and my brothers, Eric and Peter. My memories of Nana are mostly sensory memories evoked by the music of spoken Spanish, which to this day touches a deep place in my soul and enfolds me in the womb of that undying, nurturing mystery—love.

How do you explain the journey from racially dismissing a person as being of less value to embracing that person with love as a sacred sister or brother and valuing that person's well-being as you value your own?

The only explanation I know is being open to experiencing the other person's full humanity and to seeing the light of sacred love shining through that person. Children, before they are polluted with prejudice and blind hatred, are able to make this journey in a heartbeat. The horrors of bloodshed, fueled by fear and hatred, that plague our planet and consume younger and younger boys and girls with each passing year is a tragic testament to how easily this fatal pollution can occur and how widespread it is.

I offer one specific memory of Nana. It is tied to a picture taken when I was sixteen and had returned to New Mexico, ten years after my family had moved to Oklahoma. In the picture, a tall, gangly young white man towers over a tiny, wrinkled brown woman. Bending down slightly, he has his arm around her. Though he doesn't know it and she is too wise to say it, the picture tells a truth. They are in love, a love that embraces human difference. It sings like the birds as the sun lingers in the treetops before diving below the horizon as the edge of night sweeps across the sky clearing the way for the stars.

I didn't begin to study Spanish until a few years after graduating from college. Though learning Spanish was often hard work, it was never a struggle. The language sang in my ears and my heart long before I could speak even a little. It felt as though the more I learned, the nearer I drew to a home I didn't know I had or had ever left. My love of Spanish drew me to the writing of Gabriel García Márquez, Pablo Neruda, and many other Latin American authors in whose words I discovered worlds I didn't know existed because I had never seen them and never would have if these writers hadn't opened my eyes, my mind, my heart to experience the gift of their worlds.

Over thirty years after I first read it in translation, the opening of García Márquez's masterful novel *Cien Años de Soledad (One Hundred Years of Solitude)* rings in my heart: "*Muchos años después, frente al pelotón de fusilamiento, el coronel Aureliano Buendía había de recordar aquella tarde remota en que su padre lo llevó a conocer el hielo.*"[1] ("Many years later, as he faced the firing squad, Coronel Aureliano Buendía was to remember that distant afternoon when his father took him to discover ice.")[2] The passage continues, describing the mythic founding of the village of Macondo in a time when the world was so new that many things lacked names and so to refer to them it was necessary to point with a finger.

The first time I read this passage, I was enchanted by the freshness of the language and the wonder of a world so new. It was incomprehensibly alluring to a young college student in New York City and eventually drew me to visit Central and South America, where I realized that these different worlds actually exist, with their own rhythm and logic. And they're different from my world, and yet the same. And sometimes language fails and it's necessary to indicate by pointing with a finger or by looking into the depth of someone's heart. Over time, I've come to see all our languages, all our theologies, all our science, all our literature as fingers pointing at what is real, as pointers to guide us into the heart of the amazing diversity and unity that is truth. Perhaps the Buddha, with his characteristic clarity, said it best: "The teaching is merely a vehicle to describe the truth. Don't mistake it for the truth itself. A finger pointing at the moon is not the moon. The finger is needed to know where to look for the moon, but if you mistake the finger for the moon itself, you will never know the real moon."[3]

Discovering a Deeper Humanity

Having the music and mystery of Spanish planted in my soul must have prepared me in some way to learn a different foreign language, the one that would have the greatest impact on my life. It was the language my brother, Eric, spoke. Since I was only sixteen months old when Eric was born, I was too young to remember his beginning. Too young to remember the extra thumb on his right hand or the clubbed feet that required him to be in casts for most of his first year—though this was probably when my father started to drift away from the family. I was too young to remember when the doctor diagnosed my brother as a "Mongoloid idiot" (the early clinical name for someone born with Down syndrome), informed my mother that Eric would never be anything but heartache to the family, and advised her to put him in an institution and forget about him.

The doctor was simply acting on the truth he knew. It was a medical truth. A scientific truth. He accepted the inability of modern medicine to make my brother "normal" or anything close to it. He *knew* that an abnormal life would never contribute anything of meaning to our family, our community, or the world. He also *knew* the incredible toll it would take on a family to try to raise a "Mongoloid idiot" at home. He was right about the inability of modern medicine (though that "truth" has changed dramatically in the fifty years since Eric was born) and about the toll that raising Eric at home would exact. But he was dead wrong about the rest. His scientific perspective blinded him to the deeper values that lie in the human soul.

Thank God my mother wasn't similarly blinded. Thank God she saw the value in my brother's soul and ignored the doctor's advice. If she hadn't, we might all have missed the closest thing to a miracle—along with the birth of a child and the unfathomable power of love—we were likely to experience in this life.

Eric was a study in difference. His slanted eyes gave him an Asian look, which led most strangers to believe that his heavily accented English was a foreign language. He was given to temper tantrums long past the age of "normal" children. It wasn't easy being Eric's brother, especially when he misbehaved in public, which was often. The combination of appearance, language, and behavior made Eric as distinct as a manatee in a herd of cattle—and to many, as laughable. Many of the people we encountered in Tulsa, Oklahoma, in the late fifties weren't accustomed to such obvious difference and would often point at Eric and stare. Little children would laugh, and so, sometimes, would their parents. Decades from the humiliation and anger that this sparked in me, I'm convinced that these children and their parents didn't mean to be cruel. They were simply unable to hear in Eric's voice and to see in his face and behavior anything but an object, a laughably incomprehensible "other" who didn't fit into any of the boxes they knew. Transforming this human tendency to turn those who are different into objects is a crucial piece of humanity's curriculum in the twenty-first century.

Though he did not live to see this century, Eric became a master teacher in this curriculum. As he grew and matured, his personality shone through more and more. Like many children with Down syndrome, he loved easily and indiscriminately. He was a passionate sports fan, especially dedicated to the Dallas Cowboys and the local minor league baseball team, the Tulsa Oilers. He became an accomplished Special Olympian, winning fistfuls of medals as a swimmer.

He also demonstrated a deep sensitivity to the holy. He loved church and God. At a certain age, he rebelled at not being allowed to receive communion like the rest of his family. In those days in the Episcopal church, you had to be confirmed to receive communion. To be confirmed, you had to possess an intellectually mature faith, demonstrated by mastering a body of material that included the catechism and two creeds—an impossibly high mountain to climb for someone with a mental age of four.

But somehow Eric's weekly Sunday scowls, as Father Daniels passed by his outstretched hands without offering him the bread and wine of communion, had their impact. Overturning conventional wisdom and his own understanding of a mature faith in God, Father Daniels created an alternative confirmation instruction for Eric, in the process making a profound statement about basic human worth. Father Daniels said, in essence, that Eric, who had been ridiculed as an inconsequential other, dismissed as a

"Mongoloid idiot," and deemed worthless by experts who *knew*, was, like everyone else, made in the image and likeness of God. Eric, like all God's children, was infinitely precious in God's eyes. And if in God's eyes, then how could he not be of great worth and precious in human eyes?

In the Gospel of Matthew (13:45), Jesus shares this teaching with his followers: "Again, the kingdom of heaven is like a merchant in search of fine pearls, who, on finding one pearl of great value, went and sold all that he had and bought it."

In Jesus' teaching, the pearl of great value represents not material wealth but the unfathomable beauty of the kingdom of heaven, that realm where the ultimate sovereignty of goodness and love, of peace and justice, is revealed. Where compassion reigns as the fallen are raised up and poverty is vanquished. Where all people see that they are sisters and brothers and together celebrate the preciousness of all life. And where all life is united in oneness with the Source of all life. But the pearl of great value is not only the kingdom of heaven; it is each priceless life. The challenge implicit in Jesus' teaching is to recognize the pearl of great value when we see it and then to give ourselves fully to gain it and to manifest its beauty in the world.

When he stepped back from a lifetime of training and shattered the rules that defined the path to faith in order to welcome Eric into full fellowship in the church, Father Daniels recognized the pearl of great value in a surprising way. Both the pearl itself and the path to acquire it were named Eric. To see that, though, it was necessary to accept that a human being's worth in God's eyes wasn't dependent on an arbitrary human standard of achievement, on a culturally conditioned understanding of accomplishment. It was necessary to accept that a person's ultimate worth came from being beloved by God and that the ultimate measure of that worth was not a person's level of education or job or income or gender or skin color or sexual orientation but how well a person manifested God's inclusive, abiding love. By that measure, Eric and his life were indeed a pearl of great value.

Though he died with heartbreaking suddenness when he was thirty, Eric lived a life of enviable richness. The evidence abounded at his funeral. The church, of which he was a founding member, was packed, including a large contingent of Eric's friends from Gatesway, the residential home for developmentally disabled adults where he lived. One measure of the impact of Eric's life was the warmth and affection that greeted his friends from Gatesway. The contrast with how Eric had been viewed by others years before could not have been more dramatic or more affirming of the human capacity to open to and be transformed by the experience of difference.

Another measure came after the service as people greeted Eric's family. One by one, they spoke of how knowing Eric had changed their lives. Simply put, his infectious joy, his evident and deep faith, and his enduring ability to reach out to others had gently demolished the wall of otherness they had built between themselves and Eric. With the wall down, they came to know Eric, and through that authentic knowing of another, they discovered a deeper humanity in themselves that led them to seek that deeper humanity in others. A Christian way to express this is to say that following Eric's example and inspiration, they became better at seeking and serving Christ in all people, loving their neighbors as themselves. They became better Christians. And to return to my conversation with the cab driver from Pakistan, they became better children of God.

What had transformed this life, a life that the experts were sure was of no value, into a pearl of great value? Into a life that was rich in itself and enriched the lives of others, who then enriched the lives of still others like the ripples flowing out from a pebble dropped in a lake? The grace of God, a loving family and community, and an indomitable human spirit that refused to be contained by the arbitrary limits of otherness.

By the time of his death, Eric's otherness had become commonplace for me. I was proud of my younger brother. Without knowing it, he taught me one of the most important lessons of my life. Through his practice of taking down the walls of otherness that separated him from others and reaching out to turn strangers into friends, Eric taught me that there are no "other" people. No matter how different we may seem, we share a common humanity that emanates from the Source of goodness and love that is the sovereign, creative center of all that is.

As Eric manifested so magnificently, I believe that the core human curriculum on this earth is to ground ourselves in the Source of life and to live in a way that develops our full humanity and serves to recognize and help realize the full humanity of all our sisters and brothers on this planet. I believe that our future, as Americans and as citizens of the earth, demands that we seek out experiences that will help us come to know others, to celebrate their uniqueness, to recognize our shared humanity, and to find common cause in working together for a better world.

Turning the Unfamiliar World into a Neighborhood

In this pursuit, I wish everyone could experience the education I have received over the past eight years through my work with the United Religions Initiative. I believe this education contains essential lessons for deepening the American dream in a way that honors not only the uniqueness and value of this country but also the uniqueness and value of the rest of the world. Like growing up with Eric, this education has opened my mind and heart, my eyes and ears, and it has caused me to ask fundamental and ongoing questions about how we determine what is of value and what isn't. What is significant accomplishment and what isn't. It has turned an enormous, largely unfamiliar world into a neighborhood and turned a world of strangers into members of one human family. I hope that what follows will give you a vivid and alluring sense of what that education was like and might help you to prize more your own experiences of heart-opening, life-changing education and to seek out new experiences.

First, I'd like to offer some background information about the United Religions Initiative (URI). The seed that has grown into the URI was planted in 1993 with a new recognition that the religions of the world were too often more part of the problem than part of the solution. Specifically, even though the nations of the world had been working together for global cooperation and peace for nearly fifty years through the United Nations, the religions of the world had all too often fanned the flames of division, mutual mistrust, hatred, and violence. They seemed neither to acknowledge nor to practice a common vocation for peace, justice, and healing. The founding vision of the URI was to knit together a global community of people of all faiths to develop and practice this common vocation.[4] In this community, the uniqueness of each tradition would be respected, all voices would be valued, and none would dominate.

Hired as the founding executive director in 1996, I was charged with sharing this vision with people around the world and inviting them to make it their own and to help it grow into a truly global reality. In this pursuit, I have traveled the world extensively and worked with people from more than sixty countries—from Argentina to India, from South Africa to South Korea, from Pakistan to Egypt, from the Philippines to Israel, from Brazil to England. I traveled bearing the passport of a United States citizen. I traveled as a Caucasian male. I traveled as an Episcopal priest, an ordained member of the worldwide Anglican Communion. But I also traveled as someone charged with carrying a global hope in a way that it would be inviting and accessible to anyone who wished to share in making that hope real. Here are some of the experiences that challenged me to learn—that compelled me to open my heart and mind; to see with new eyes and hear with new ears. They're lessons about what it means to be a citizen of the earth and a child of God. I believe they're also lessons that lead to a deepening of the American dream.

A Community That Belongs to Everyone
but Is Owned by No One

If we accept the insights of paleoanthropologists who cite fossil records placing the oldest known human ancestors in what are modern-day Ethiopia and Kenya 5.8 million years ago, we are one human family and Africa is our ancestral home. I felt this sense of returning to my ancestral homeland in a visceral way when I stood on the ground, first in South Africa in December 1996 and a year later in Kenya. In a way that I could feel but can't explain, the rich earth welcomed me. The spirit of the land embraced me as if I were a long-absent son returning to where I belonged. I was home.

Over the years, my trips to Africa and my experiences of African people have often reinforced that experience of a welcoming embrace. I cannot think about Africa without seeing beguiling smiles and a joy that flows effortlessly into song, dance, and laughter. I remember touring a community center in a Soweto church and hearing the most harmoniously joyful singing. I asked the pastor what the choir was rehearsing. He paused and started laughing. That isn't the choir, he informed me. That's a meeting of mail carriers.

I cannot think about Africa without remembering warm hospitality and a powerful sense of community, of the accountability of each individual for the well-being of the whole. I've seen a deep weariness at the struggle, but often in the context of an indomitable hope for a better tomorrow. I saw that hope reflected in the eyes of children kneeling to receive a blessing at the altar rail of another Soweto church where I was privileged to preach on a Sunday. The light in their eyes blessed me as I offered God's blessing to them. Each of these children was a pearl of great value, to be prized and nurtured by their community, by my community. As I looked into their eyes and they looked into mine, I knew we came from the same Source. I knew I was a part of their community as surely as I was part of the community of the church I attended or of the schools my children attended. As a good member of their community, I had a responsibility for the well-being of its members. My vision of the global community URI sought to create was deepened, challenged, and blessed by those children.

As much as I felt at home in Africa, I often felt that I was home in the midst of unimaginable difference that made me ache trying to take it in, let alone comprehend it. Eventually, this difference, like my experience of blessing at a Soweto altar rail, would give me glimpses of our shared humanity. But first I was merely different.

It is impossible to be human without at times feeling that you are different, that you're an outsider, that you don't belong. I often felt that way, myself, growing up, and I certainly experienced it through Eric. But I grew up a white, Christian male in a country dominated by white, Christian males (an extraordinarily diverse group at that). Though my family was not materially affluent, thanks to scholarships I had the privilege of an outstanding education at a private high school and private colleges. No one, other than I, placed any limits on what I could aspire to in my life. I may have felt countercultural, but I shared the privilege of being part of the dominant culture, with all its opportunity and diverse manifestations.

But in Africa, I was the *other*, and not necessarily an attractive other. Archbishop Desmond Tutu, Nobel Peace Laureate and hero of the struggle to overturn apartheid in South Africa, recounts that when white missionaries arrived in Africa, they had the Bible and black Africans had the land. The missionaries said, "Let us pray." The Africans closed their eyes to pray, and when they opened their eyes, they had the Bible and the missionaries had the land. Archbishop Tutu, a devout Anglican, goes on to say that even so, Africans got the better part of the transaction.

This story draws laughter when Tutu tells it, but underneath the laughter lurks a sense of profound deception and injustice that is central to the corrosive legacy of slavery and colonial domination. Since those early missionaries, Africa has been visited again and again by white people whose proclaimed altruism often masked an impulse toward exploitation and domination, and promised visions of a better world that failed to materialize and often led to a worse world for Africans.

Early on, I discovered that in the eyes of some people, I represented nothing more than the latest appearance of those early missionaries, peddling the promise of a better world that would ultimately make things worse for those it professed to help. From a few people, I experienced a thinly veiled hostility; from most others, a warm welcome that often masked a measure of skepticism.

My first, mostly gentle experience of this skepticism came in an all-day meeting with people from several East African countries to explore their interest in being part of the global effort to develop the URI vision and to give birth to a global organization that could make it real. People were intrigued but also cautious, willing to explore but with many questions and reservations. At the end of the meeting, Sister Laetitia Borg, a Franciscan nun from Malta who had lived and worked in Ethiopia for decades, came up to me. She had attended this meeting, she explained, because she was attracted by the URI vision of interfaith cooperation. But she had also come because she wanted to see if, as she expected, this was a large luxury liner pulling up and inviting people to climb on board and accompany its captain toward his destination. If this had been the case, she would have walked away. What I have experienced, instead, she said, is a small boat almost alone in a vast ocean looking for other small boats to join it on a journey to a new world they would create together. As she said this, she smiled and added, I want my boat to join. So did many, but not all, of the others.

I have had experiences like this again and again as people from diverse backgrounds from all different parts of the world came together seeking a new possibility for a better tomorrow. They came with a blend of hope and skepticism—the hope fueled by a deep yearning to make a positive difference; the skepticism because they knew how easily hope can be manipulated. They came yearning to be part of something global but not wanting the global aspect to destroy their uniqueness. They wanted to be proud of who they were and where they came from. They also wanted to be proud that they were part of a new global community connecting faithful people of hope, hopeful people of faith, with their sisters and brothers all over the world—a community that belonged to everyone but was owned by no one; a community where all were pearls of great value and each shared a responsibility for all. They wanted to be trusted and to trust, to be listened to and to listen. They wanted to have their own dreams, but they also wanted to be part of a shared dream that was much bigger and more magnificent than anyone could dream alone. And they wanted to believe that this dream could be real and that they could share it without losing it or losing themselves in it.

The Four Questions

A day after the Nairobi meeting, I encountered my most memorable and challenging skeptic, Reverend Jose Chipenda, who for two decades had led the All Africa Council of Churches in its work to address the issues of poverty and division that settled like a plague over this extraordinary continent. A man of practical spirituality, he welcomed me graciously on a Sunday afternoon, served me tea and cookies, and listened politely and carefully as I shared the United Religions Initiative vision. When I finished, he told me politely that he had heard many such visions over the previous twenty years. He had seen many cash-intensive efforts arrive from the North with great promises and little positive practical impact. He didn't see how the URI would be any different. In fact, in a world where organizations were failing right and left, he questioned the need for another organization that would likely fail. Creating the United Religions Initiative seemed to him to require a lot more energy than it was worth.

Reverend Chipenda was a tough, candid questioner who frequently punctuated the conversation with disarming laughter. His questions often had depth that I only sensed, as his life had been filled with experiences I could only inadequately imagine. He seemed to have a pessimistic view of the future, balanced by an enduring commitment to show up every day to do what he could to create a more positive future. Over the decades, he had experienced much defeat, but he worked tirelessly for victories that would address in practical ways the urgent African hunger for peace, for food, for education, for health care, for respect, and for the freedom to be joyously, proudly African. By the end of our time together, I'd had the workout of my URI life with someone whose depth of experience and wisdom gave him a deep skepticism about this Northern initiative but whose skepticism also walked hand-in-hand with a passionate commitment to serve God's kingdom.

In this spirit, he was open to the possibility that he might be wrong, that the URI effort might be different, might be of value. But as he listened, he was quite clear about how he would judge that value. Before he could support the URI, he would need to see what it would do for three groups of people he had come to recognize in his decades of work across Africa.

The first group, obscenely large given the level of affluence that existed in the world, was the people born to die. The poorest of the poor, they lacked the barest necessities to sustain the spark of life. They would die of malnutrition, of dysentery, of preventable diseases, of violence. Their time on this earth would be like the flare of a match that goes out without ever fully igniting. What, Reverend Chipenda wanted to know, would the URI offer these people who were born to die?

The second group, the overwhelming majority of humans, was the people born to survive. Though their match would ignite, they would spend their lives laboring merely to sustain a simple flame. What, Reverend Chipenda wanted to know, would the URI offer these people who were born to survive?

The third group, a tiny part of the overall population, was the people born to live. These were the candles lit with the matches of those born to survive. They were privileged to receive an education and have a path prepared for them so that they didn't have to struggle merely to survive. They would have the privilege of exploring what it meant truly to live. What, Reverend Chipenda wanted to know, would the URI offer to and ask of these people who were born to live?

I left my meeting with Reverend Chipenda grateful for the privilege of having stood for a brief time inside a world that was not my own, weathering difficult questions to challenge and guide my efforts. I had seen myself and the world I came from in a harsh new light. I wanted to say, "We're not like that. I'm not like that." But in my heart I knew that I *was* like that. I was part of that privileged minority who were born to live and who predominantly populated the northern hemisphere. I could climb on a plane, leave this world and its struggles behind, and return to the dominant culture of which I was, by accident of birth, a part. I could leave behind those children in Soweto and the struggles that would oppress their young lives.

But I could not leave behind Reverend Chipenda's questions, illuminated by the light from those children's eyes. The questions and the light will travel with me forever. They will always provide and illuminate a plumb line, like the one revealed to the Hebrew prophet Amos, with which I measure the success of my work.[5] In these days when so many people measure America's worth by military might and GDP, I would like us to take the measure of our worth by our ability to answer Reverend Chipenda's questions, adding to them a fourth: What will we do to respect and restore the web of all life on earth? In light of the pressing needs of the human family, it seems the American dream must send its roots deeper into the one earth from which it has risen in order to live with and give life to these questions.

The Deeper Water of Otherness

That day at dusk, I took a solitary walk from my hotel. Soon I was in a park with shirtless, barefoot men and boys playing soccer on dusty fields and families out for a Sunday stroll. In this living picture of community, I was alone. Even in the eyes of those who greeted me warmly, I saw that I was different. I realized that I was the only white person in sight. Suddenly, I felt that I was not home. I was a guest in other people's home. And for some of them, what they saw in me wasn't welcome. I felt a deep loneliness, a yearning to be among "my own kind." Inside, I couldn't have been any farther away from the blessing I had received in Soweto. I wanted to weep.

I would share this gift of momentary desolation some months later at a meeting at my son's high school where the students of color, who were a small minority, shared the searing difficulty of each day being the *other* in this open but majority-dominated community.

I think I understand your experience, I said, and recounted my experience of that evening in Nairobi. I think I understand your loneliness, but even in understanding, I know my experience that evening was different. Even as I felt so alone, I knew that I would get on a plane and return to my country, where my culture was dominant. I know you can't do that, I said to these young people. And I thought to myself that the URI's work, humanity's work, was to create a place where even minority cultures can feel at home, can feel that they belong, that their ways of being in the world and seeing the world are understood and respected. Because everybody is a minority somewhere.

For this to happen, we all need to move gently away from the safe shore of our belonging into the deeper water of otherness. If we do this intentionally and together, with the Spirit of Wisdom guiding our way, we just might discover that our little boat has been joined by many other little boats that we recognize as different and yet the same. We might sail into a new future that we create together—a new American dream that grows in humility and consciousness, including all voices, until it is a dream of the earth, cherished by all. Until it is a waking dream in which we've built bridges and taken down walls and are working together to answer Reverend Chipenda's questions so that all of the earth community might be born to live.

My experience of the anguish and experienced otherness of the ethnic minority students in a progressive private school that prided itself on its approach to diversity deepened the lesson I had learned in Africa. If we attempt to ground our common humanity on the foundational norms of a dominant culture, we will always be creating outsiders. Yes, everyone has to be from somewhere. Every one of us has a culture that is native to us, and those cultures, as they lead to a full experience of life that does not oppress and exploit others, deserve to thrive.

But if we are to live together as one community, whether in America or in the world, we have to experience, learn how to value, and be willing to have our vision of the world and our ways of doing things affected by our encounters with others. For people in the United States, this means opening ourselves more and more to the enrichment of cultural difference, within and outside the geographical boundaries of our country. It also means seeking out, in our country, the voices of minority cultures, which all too often have been repressed, to share in telling the story of the American people. For all the education I've had in my life, I find myself amazingly ignorant of these voices. When I travel to other countries, no matter how much I study in advance, I expect to be ignorant. But I shouldn't be ignorant in my own country. I should have heard the voices of minority cultures. I thank God that my work in the United Religions Initiative has taught me to seek them out.

Sojourner Truth

In this spirit, I'd like to share one such voice. In 1851, a women's rights convention convened in Akron, Ohio. Sojourner Truth, an escaped slave who had gained her freedom, attended, much to the concern of many of the white women there. They were afraid of having their cause derailed by having it lumped in with the abolitionist movement and were seemingly terrified at the prospect of having an *uneducated* black woman speak before an audience that contained highly educated men who were hostile to the rights of women, to say nothing of the rights of blacks.

On the second day of the convention, clergymen from various Christian denominations put forward a range of arguments against women's rights, including women's weaker intellect, the manhood of Christ, and the role of the first woman, Eve, in humanity's fall from grace. As it seemed that these arguments might win the day, Sojourner Truth stepped onto the stage and, though many of the women present objected, delivered the following speech, which was greeted with rising crescendos of applause, emboldening the assembled women and vanquishing the arguments of the objecting men:

> Well, children, where there is so much racket there must be something out of kilter. I think that 'twixt the negroes of the South and the women at the North, all talking about rights, the white men will be in a fix pretty soon. But what's all this here talking about?
>
> That man over there says that women need to be helped into carriages, and lifted over ditches, and to have the best place everywhere. Nobody ever helps me into carriages, or over mud-puddles, or gives me any best place! And ain't I a woman? Look at me! Look at my arm! I have ploughed and planted, and gathered into barns, and no man could head me! And ain't I a woman? I could work as much and eat as much as a man—when I could get it—and bear the lash as well! And ain't I a woman? I have borne thirteen children, and seen most all sold off to slavery, and when I cried out with my mother's grief, none but Jesus heard me! And ain't I a woman?
>
> Then they talk about this thing in the head; what's this they call it? [a member of audience whispers, "intellect"] That's it, honey. What's that got to do with women's rights or negroes' rights? If my cup won't hold but a pint, and yours holds a quart, wouldn't you be mean not to let me have my little half measure full?
>
> Then that little man in black there, he says women can't have as much rights as men, 'cause Christ wasn't a woman! Where did your

Christ come from? Where did your Christ come from? From God and a woman! Man had nothing to do with Him.

If the first woman God ever made was strong enough to turn the world upside down all alone, these women together ought to be able to turn it back, and get it right side up again! And now they is asking to do it, the men better let them.

Obliged to you for hearing me, and now old Sojourner ain't got nothing more to say.[6]

By the time Sojourner Truth had finished speaking, she had been transformed, in the eyes of the white women present, from an embarrassment to a hero. At least for a moment, these women had been drawn past obvious otherness onto the ground of common humanity. There they were united in the pursuit of basic human rights and justice, united in a struggle to claim as their birthright the history-shattering assertions of the Declaration of Independence: "We hold these Truths to be self-evident, that all Men are created equal, that they are endowed by their Creator with certain unalienable Rights, that among these are Life, Liberty and the Pursuit of Happiness."

Sojourner Truth's courageous eloquence, which was not refined by formal education but forged in the cruelly dehumanizing furnace of slavery, exposed lies that had been promulgated as divine truth—that women and people with dark skin were inherently, though differently, inferior. Following this belief, the dominant white male culture felt no need to extend America's fundamental human rights to women and people with dark skin. Instead, while claiming to champion these basic rights, those in power could violate them with seeming impunity. They cast a long and destructive shadow, which to this day blocks out the sun of equal opportunity in many of this country's inner cities and populates our prisons disproportionately with people of color.

As I have learned through my travels in Africa, we all, wittingly or unwittingly, cast a shadow as we seek to protect and preserve our rights and privileges at the expense of the basic rights of others. Thank God we also carry within us the seeds of righteousness and justice that have animated every movement for human freedom and justice in history. We need to develop a keen awareness of the shadow we cast, and we need to nurture the seeds of righteousness and justice that motivate us "to form a more perfect union." In this pursuit, we must ask who are the Sojourner Truths of our time whose messages we may be reluctant to hear though they have the potential to draw us, as Sojourner Truth and my brother, Eric, drew us, past an experience of obvious otherness onto the ground of our common humanity, allowing us to see otherness as an enriching and essential gift in the human journey toward peace, justice, and healing.

The Shadow We Cast

Scientists speculate that up to 225 million years ago, the earth was home to one supercontinent, called Pangaea, surrounded by one enormous ocean, called Panthalassa. Then everything started to move. By 200 million years ago, Pangaea had broken into two continents—a northern one, Laurasia, and a southern one, Gondwanaland. By 65 million years ago, today's continents and oceans existed, though they have been drifting for all these years to reach the locations they are in today. And they're still drifting. Who knows where they'll be in another 65 million years—or if there will still be life on earth?

Recent fossil discoveries place the oldest known *Homo sapiens* in Ethiopia about 160,000 years ago. Like the continents, our human ancestors didn't stay put. They too started moving. Scientists speculate that the first *Homo sapiens* to migrate from Africa to the Americas, the ancestors of today's Native Americans, arrived in the Americas at least 30,000 years ago. The first Europeans set foot in the Americas a little over 500 years ago and soon had a profound impact on the people who had been living here for thousands of years. Here is one face of that impact:

1562
Fray Diego de Landa throws into the flames, one after the other, the books of the Mayas.

The inquisitor curses Satan, and the fire crackles and devours. Around the incinerator, heretics howl with their heads down. Hung by the feet, flayed with whips, Indians are doused with boiling wax as the fire flares up and the books snap, as if complaining.

Tonight, eight centuries of Mayan literature turn to ashes. On these long sheets of bark paper, signs and images spoke: They told of work done and days spent, of the dreams and the wars of a people born before Christ. With hog-bristle brushes, the knowers of things had painted these illuminated, illuminating books so that the grandchildren's grandchildren should not be blind, should know how to see themselves and see the history of their folk, so they should know the movements of the stars, the frequency of eclipses and the prophecies of the gods and so they could call for rains and good corn harvests.

In the center, the inquisitor burns the books. Around the huge bonfire, he chastises the readers.[7]

As I have discovered in my work with the United Religions Initiative, that impact continues up and down the Americas to this day. In May 1997, I was in Buenos Aires, Argentina, for a URI conference. Returning from a break on the first day, I saw a group of indigenous men and women huddled together and by themselves. Wanting to be hospitable, I walked over and asked if I could join them. They welcomed me warmly. I asked their opinion of the conference. My question ignited a conversation that was carried on over the next three days as they shared their experience with me at increasingly deep levels.

Rosalia Gutierrez, a young Kolla woman, told me that she could barely speak her people's language. Missionaries had cut out her grandparents' tongues to keep them from teaching their *pagan* language to their children. This barbaric act, they assured me, was simply one example of how their people had suffered at the hands of the colonizers. Another of the group introduced himself as Santos Estrada but quickly added that his real name was Chiru Chiru, a name he was not allowed to use because it was a native name. Robbed of their languages and their names and forbidden to practice their rituals, they and their cultures had been pushed to the brink of extinction. And this was not simply an experience of the past. They were not welcomed in the present day by the dominant culture in Argentina. They were socially and economically marginalized. Their people were still preyed on by Christian missionaries who divided families and further weakened their tenuous hold on their heritage.

I returned home from Buenos Aires with a deep stirring in my soul and a commitment to help indigenous people find a place at the URI's table where they could speak from their own traditions with their own voices. The impact of my conversations in Buenos Aires and others with indigenous people in the coming years made it clear that the URI community would not be whole until indigenous people were full participants. This realization is reflected at the beginning of the URI charter: "We, people of diverse religions, spiritual expressions and indigenous traditions throughout the world, hereby establish the United Religions Initiative to promote enduring, daily interfaith cooperation, to end religiously motivated violence and to create cultures of peace, justice and healing for the Earth and all living beings."

The Wisdom of the Tribes

Over the years, I have received an extraordinary education at the hands of committed, patient indigenous people. I've learned new depths of gratitude and gained a deeper reverence for the earth and all life. I've learned anew the importance of sinking deep spiritual roots and listening carefully for the movement of the Spirit; I've learned the importance of seeing the sacred in each moment. I've experienced the power of a practice of community where each individual has a clear responsibility to serve the whole. I've been blessed with gracious hospitality. I've been challenged to see time as cyclical, not linear, to be experienced in the fullness of each moment rather than measured by an expensive watch or contained in a Palm Pilot. I've learned anew the value of deep deliberation in a world where there is such a rush to decision and decisive action.

This education was far different from the education I received in elementary school in Oklahoma when I was taught about the "five civilized tribes" of Oklahoma. As I learned it, the Cherokee, Chickasaw, Choctaw, Seminole, and Creek peoples were "civilized" because they adopted the ways of the white settlers. The education I was to receive from indigenous people around the world would force me to ask again and again what it meant to be civilized and what gave one people the right to determine that other people were not civilized.

I was taught about the "five civilized tribes," but I wasn't taught about the Iroquois Confederacy, perhaps the world's oldest participatory democracy, founded well before the arrival of Europeans in what is now the northeastern United States. In the late fourteenth or early fifteenth century, leaders of five nations—Mohawk (People Possessors of the Flint), Onondaga (People on the Hills), Seneca (Great Hill People), Oneida (Granite People), and Cayuga (People at the Mucky Land)—created the confederacy to ensure peace among their peoples. In the eighteenth century, they were joined by the Tuscarora (Shirt-Wearing People). For centuries before the American Revolution, the founding wisdom of the Iroquois Confederacy, which would have a profound impact on the drafters of the United States Constitution, was passed down orally from generation to generation. This wisdom invoked the guidance of the Creator and reflected a deep reverence for the whole earth community:

> Whenever the Confederate Lords shall assemble for the purpose of holding a council, the Onondaga Lords shall open it by expressing their gratitude to their cousin Lords and greeting them, and they shall make an address and offer thanks to the earth where men dwell, to the streams of water, the pools, the springs and the lakes, to the maize and the fruits, to the medicinal herbs and trees, to the forest trees for their usefulness, to the animals that serve as food and give their pelts for clothing, to the great winds and the lesser winds, to the Thunderers, to the Sun, the mighty warrior, to the moon, to the messengers of the

Creator who reveal his wishes and to the Great Creator who dwells in the heavens above, who gives all the things useful to men, and who is the source and the ruler of health and life. Then shall the Onondaga Lords declare the council open.[8]

It created a democratic government that honored the leadership of women as well as men:

If at any time it shall be manifest that a Confederate Lord has not in mind the welfare of the people or disobeys the rules of this Great Law, the men or women of the Confederacy, or both jointly, shall come to the Council and upbraid the erring Lord through his War Chief. If the complaint of the people through the War Chief is not heeded the first time it shall be uttered again and then if no attention is given a third complaint and warning shall be given. If the Lord is contumacious the matter shall go to the council of War Chiefs. The War Chiefs shall then divest the erring Lord of his title by order of the women in whom the titleship is vested. When the Lord is deposed the women shall notify the Confederate Lords through their War Chief, and the Confederate Lords shall sanction the act. The women will then select another of their sons as a candidate and the Lords shall elect him.[9]

It created a high vision of enlightened leadership founded in deep, spiritual values:

The Lords of the Confederacy of the Five Nations shall be mentors of the people for all time. The thickness of their skin shall be seven spans—which is to say that they shall be proof against anger, offensive actions and criticism. Their hearts shall be full of peace and good will and their minds filled with a yearning for the welfare of the people of the Confederacy. With endless patience they shall carry out their duty and their firmness shall be tempered with a tenderness for their people. Neither anger nor fury shall find lodgement in their minds and all their words and actions shall be marked by calm deliberation.[10]

Though I was taught about the "five civilized tribes," I wasn't taught about this extraordinary example of the "civilization" of Native Americans enriching the understanding of democracy that informed the founding of the United States. I learned nothing of the deep spiritual values that shaped their reverence for the earth and all life, their recognition of women's vital leadership role, and their understanding of the essential qualities of leadership.

Looking at this nation's numerous environmentally ravaged Superfund sites, I wonder what might have been different if our founding fathers had adopted more of the environmental ethic of the Iroquois Confederacy and other indigenous peoples. Seeing how greatly our nation has been enriched by the increasing presence of women in leadership roles in every walk of life, I wonder how our history might have been different if our founding fathers had, like the members of the Iroquois Confederacy, seen the necessity of women's leadership for a healthy society. And perhaps most important, I wonder how the history of this nation might have been altered if the people of European ancestry who came to and developed this country had been more open to seeing, learning from, and living with the different civilizations that had existed here for centuries before the first European settler set foot on this land. Today, I yearn for the wisdom of this ancestry to reinvigorate and deepen the American dream.

"Civilizing" the Other

My formal education in American history also avoided the Indian boarding schools that were developed to "civilize" Native American children, beginning in the late eighteenth century. During this time, the government removed Indian children from their homes and placed them in boarding schools where they were forced to learn the *civilized* ways of the dominant Christian culture. At the Native American Prayer Vigil for the earth in September 2000, held next to the Washington Monument, I received a present-day perspective on these schools from Clyde Bellecourt, an Ojibway and one of the founders of the American Indian Movement. The prayer vigil is an annual event that makes a powerful, if largely invisible, contribution to the future of this country by bringing people of all faiths together under the leadership of Native Americans to pray for the earth and for peace, understanding, and justice. From sunrise Saturday until midafternoon Sunday, people gather around a sacred fire for prayer, meditation, teaching, music, dance, and the celebration of life.

During one teaching, Clyde Bellecourt spoke movingly of his mother's experience at a boarding school. He explained that she had hidden this part of her life from him until he nearly died from a gunshot wound at the Indian occupation of Wounded Knee, North Dakota, for seventy-one days in 1973. Moved by her son's struggle to regain his culture, she finally told him of the hardships she had endured when she was forcibly removed from her home and placed in a boarding school. There the children were forbidden to speak any language other than English and to say any prayers other than Christian prayers. If she was caught speaking her native language or praying in a native way, Clyde's mother told him, she was forced to clean floors on her knees with a toothbrush. When this punishment wasn't enough to keep her from speaking and praying in her native way, she was forced to clean the floors wearing kneepads with marbles in them. She had hidden this from her children because she hadn't wanted them to grow up plagued by bitterness.

"We hold these Truths to be self-evident, that all Men are created equal, that they are endowed by their Creator with certain unalienable Rights, that among these are Life, Liberty and the Pursuit of Happiness." Though I often studied these words from the Declaration of Independence in school, I was never taught about boarding schools for Indian children, and I imagine that to this day, most Americans don't know they existed. It is difficult to see what these boarding schools had to do with Indian peoples' inalienable right to life, liberty, and the pursuit of happiness. If the words of the Declaration of Independence are to have real meaning, our society needs to hear the voices of Indian people, to hear their grievances and their wisdom. These voices have been and remain indispensable to deepening the American dream. This story calls all of us to be accountable for the injustices of the past. That it is told in the context of an interfaith prayer vigil led by Native Americans affirms that out of the seeds of bitterness and hatred can grow the fruit of reconciliation and hope.

Sharing the Dance

In 1999, the URI held a visioning conference for 120 Brazilians from thirty-five religious and spiritual traditions. We met in Itatiaia, a national park in the middle of the rain forest halfway between São Paulo and Rio de Janeiro. Our main meeting room had windows on all sides and seemed suspended above the rain forest canopy, giving us the feeling that we were floating in midair above this lush, tropical beauty. Early in the conference, people were asked, in small groups, to collectively envision the positive future they wished to inhabit. Then they were asked to find a creative way to present their vision to the whole group.

One group's presentation captured and enhanced the spirit of the gathering perfectly. To begin, members of the group circulated throughout the room, distributing different-colored pieces of card stock, each about eight inches long, the size of an envelope, with a diamond-shaped hole in the center. Once the pieces were distributed, the group began singing a familiar Brazilian song with a refrain that, loosely translated, went, "There are times when we ask ourselves why don't we gather everything together into one!" As everyone joined in the song, one member of the group, an indigenous man in ceremonial dress, circulated around the room and collected the brightly colored cards on an arrow. Then the arrow, with the cards adorning it like a rainbow of feathers from rain forest birds, was hung from the ceiling, where it remained for the rest of the conference as a symbol of unity in diversity.

The symbol sprang to life that evening as the indigenous people, whose leadership had been especially invited, led the whole group in a ceremony of peace and reconciliation. We gathered in a clearing in the rain forest, in a large circle around a bonfire, under a full moon. In turn, representatives from each of four different Indian nations, dressed in ceremonial clothing, performed a sacred dance around the fire. Then all four nations danced together. We later learned they had never danced together before.

The previous night, it had grown later and later as they struggled to create the ritual for this evening. Finally, one member of the community wondered if the reason they were having so much difficulty was that historically, their peoples had been more enemies than friends. All agreed that there was wisdom in his observation. They realized that they needed to perform a ritual of peace and reconciliation among themselves before they could lead the rest of the group in such a ritual. Dancing together was their expression of an intention to work for peace and reconciliation among themselves.

Once they had finished their shared dance, they stepped back into the larger circle and led the whole group in a sacred circle dance. Holding hands in the circle were Buddhist monks, Dominican priests, Hindu swamis, Sufi sheikhs, a rabbi, Candomble elders, and many others. Every size, shape, and color, men and women, young and old. Holding hands and dancing in a circle of peace and healing around a bonfire under a full moon in the middle of the Brazilian rain forest—a living, sacred symbol of the unity that is possible in the extraordinary diversity of humanity. Or to put it in the words of a Lakota prayer that acknowledges the sacred interconnectedness of all life, *mitakuye oyasin,* which means "all my relations" or "we are all related."

Our dance that night did not solve the world's problems. It didn't even solve all the problems that arose from all the diverse views presented at the conference. But it did transform us all for an evening that would reverberate over the years with a living experience of *mitakuye oyasin.*

The Risk to Shed Otherness

My experience working with the United Religions Initiative is that again and again, people's initial experiences of otherness turn into experiences of *mitakuye oyasin*. This happens because we take great care to build relationships among people in ways that turn differences into points of connection. For instance, in many places around the world, people of different faiths barely know each other and often regard each other with suspicion, if not open hostility. I encountered that vividly in the conference that grew out of the 1997 meeting in Nairobi, Kenya, I mentioned earlier. The conference brought together people from nine different countries in East Africa. Two days into the conference, people came up to me, saying, "I'm a Muslim, and I was afraid to come to this conference because I was afraid I was going to have to sit down and talk with a Christian"; or "I'm a Christian, and I was afraid to come to this conference because I was afraid I was going to have to sit down and talk with a Muslim."

Beneath these fears was an almost paralyzing perception of otherness—otherness of belief, otherness of culture—and sometimes a history of conflict between local Christian and Muslim communities. But it was also true, more often than not, that the individuals who felt this otherness had never really taken the time or found the opportunity to sit down and get to know the other in a way that made them both fully human, in a way that was grounded not on what separated two groups of people but on the powerful points of connection that might give them an experience of their common humanity.

In the URI, we have always attempted to provide such experiences, beginning with one-on-one conversations that invited people from different backgrounds to come to know each other in an appreciative way. For instance, Christians and Muslims who came to the conference in Nairobi paired up and took turns answering questions such as these:

○ I'd like to get to know you better so we can work together in this conference. Please think about your life. You've probably experienced ups and downs, peaks and valleys. I would like you to think about a peak—a time when you were involved in something meaningful and felt truly alive, proud, creative, effective, engaged. Please share the story of this experience. What made it a peak experience? What felt truly special? Are there lessons that might be brought to this work?

○ To help me know more about your religion, would you please share with me the most precious gift you have received from your faith? It might be a teaching, a value or a practice, or a passage from a sacred text or a particular leader. Would you please share this with me as though I am child in school and you're giving me your most precious gift?

○ Without being too humble, what is it that you value most about yourself that you would like to contribute to the work of interfaith cooperation? What are your best qualities, skills, experiences?

○ We all have visions of a better world, often inspired by our faith. Imagine that our communities have been working together for thirty years and have succeeded in creating a better world for everyone. Please share with me your vision of what life is like in that better world.

After sharing such questions with someone you've never met before, someone whom you have viewed only as an other, a transformation takes place. First, in answering the questions, you are put in touch with deep personal experiences and beliefs that represent the best of who you are, and this best of who you are is experienced and appreciated by this strange other. At the same time, that person is put in touch with the best of who he or she is, and as you listen appreciatively, you see that person through new eyes. Otherness is transformed into *mitakuye oyasin*. This doesn't mean that the differences have disappeared. It doesn't mean that there will be no disagreements, tensions, or conflicts. But it does mean that those disagreements, tensions, and conflicts will be worked through on a foundation of mutual respect rather than on a foundation of suspicion.

And so it was, in Nairobi, that when Christians and Muslims shared that they had been afraid to come to the conference because they would have to talk with the other, each of them went on to say that they had overcome their fear and were grateful they had come. In place of a misunderstood, untrustworthy other, they now had a new colleague. Yes, differences still existed. They didn't agree on everything, but they had discovered common experiences and shared yearnings that led to a shared commitment to work together to make their visions of a better world real.

Together, they had experienced a deeper identity than Christian and Muslim. They had come to see each other and themselves as children of God. Together, they had experienced a deeper identity than Rwandan and Ugandan. They had come to see each other and themselves as sisters and brothers of Africa and of the earth. This transformation in vision was not the end of a journey but the beginning of one, a journey to build bridges across the chasms that divided them so that they might work together for the common good. This experience of transformation, like the manna from heaven that sustained the Hebrew people during their forty years in the wilderness, was a gift that made new life possible but must be renewed every day.

And it has been. Inspired by that conference, thousands of people of different faiths all over Africa have come together as part of the URI. Each day they cooperate to help stop the spread of HIV/AIDS and to care for those suffering from the ravages of this disease. They conduct trainings in peace-building skills and work to resolve violent conflicts. They do economic development work. They visit the sick and care for the needy. They do interfaith education. And much more. It is a small part of all that needs to be done, but the people involved are filled with purpose, hope, and a sense of accomplishment. They have taken a small step toward answering Reverend Chipenda's questions.

We Are Still One

In all my work with the United Religions Initiative, my most extreme experience of otherness came on a 1996 trip to Cairo. The journey had begun with a flight to Buenos Aires on Thanksgiving Day, followed by a flight from there to Johannesburg four days later. After eight days in South Africa, I flew up the length of Africa and landed in Cairo as the sun was rising. As I climbed down the stairs to the tarmac, I looked across a vast, sandy emptiness and saw a thin crescent moon and the morning star sitting just above the horizon in the pink of early dawn. I was so disoriented from this trip—it had taken me southward down the spine of the Americas, from the northern hemisphere to the southern hemisphere, then eastward across the Atlantic Ocean from the western hemisphere to the eastern hemisphere, then northward up the length of Africa from the southern hemisphere back to the northern hemisphere—that I had an unshakable sense that the sun was rising in the west. My disorientation was only beginning.

After I had navigated my way through immigration, claimed my baggage, and cleared customs, I found a cab to take me to the Royal Crown Hotel. Once we were under way, I realized that all the signs were in Arabic. Only occasionally was a sign in English, and that was likely to be for McDonald's or KFC or Baskin-Robbins, which reinforced the disorientation I felt because they seemed so out of place. While I marveled at the beautifully flowing Arabic script, I could not begin to decipher what it said. During the six days I spent in Cairo, I quickly learned to have someone write my destination out in Arabic so that I could show it to a cab driver. That helped the cab driver, which was essential, but it wasn't much help to me. Even when I had my destination written out, I could not match what was written on the paper with what was written on the signs all around me. Even when I knew where I was going, I had no way of knowing when I had arrived.

Growing up in Tulsa, Oklahoma, from the late fifties through the sixties, religious diversity was largely an abstract concept. The community was overwhelmingly "religious" and in that context overwhelmingly Christian, being part of the buckle of the Bible Belt. Public schools observed Good Friday as an official holiday. For me, being religious meant attending an Episcopal church, and that's what I knew. My experience of religious diversity was hearing stories about Roman Catholics and how they had lists of books they couldn't read and movies they couldn't see or seeing the evangelists who regularly popped up on the television. I was aware of Judaism mainly because we Christians had appropriated the Hebrew scriptures as our own. I did go to school with a few Jewish children, and I knew that Jews (and blacks and probably Indians as well) were denied membership at most country clubs. If there were Muslims in Tulsa at that time, I never heard them mentioned and certainly have no recollection of ever meeting anyone who was identified as a Muslim.

It's interesting to note that in the months after September 11, 2001, Muslims around the United States held "open mosques" in an attempt to get to know their neighbors better and have their neighbors get to know them better. In their way, they were attempting to do what the URI did in that conference in Nairobi and has done all over the world—bring people who don't know each other and may have negative stereotypes of each other together in an appreciative way, to build a new and more broadly inclusive community. To my surprise and delight, a mosque in Tulsa held an open house. My mother, who still lives in Tulsa, attended and came away with a new appreciation for her Muslim neighbors.

It was a long journey from this Tulsa experience (or lack of experience) to Egypt, where Muslims are the overwhelming majority and Christians a tiny minority. As you drive through the streets of Cairo, which are generally impassable, mosques are everywhere. Five times a day, the Muslim call to prayer is broadcast in Arabic from towering minarets that make mosques the most conspicuous structures around. Friday is the sacred center of the week, the day all shops close and people spend their time worshiping God and being with their families. On Fridays, the streets are nearly deserted. In Cairo, Sunday is just another day.

I felt profoundly *other* in Cairo as I rode in a taxi through the barely moving traffic—no familiar sights, no road signs I could read, feeling conspicuous in my whiteness and in the assumed affluence that led most people to treat me as if I were a walking dollar sign. Then I met Dr. Mohammed Shaalan, a Muslim psychotherapist who was interested in interfaith work.

He welcomed me to his apartment, offered me tea, and immediately asked me a question about the United Religions Initiative. Let's say we have a spectrum, he proposed. Aldous Huxley's perennial philosophy, which makes all religion into one religion, is on one end, and the present condition of extreme division is on the other. Where does this Initiative fit in? I responded by saying that the URI did not seek to make one religion but to bring people of different faiths together in mutual respect to work for the well-being of all. He nodded his head and asked what motivated me, a Christian, to be involved in interfaith work.

In response, I shared with him a story from the twenty-fifth chapter of the Gospel of Matthew: At the end of time, the Son of Humanity comes in great glory surrounded by his angels. After calling the nations to him, he separates the righteous from the unrighteous as a shepherd separates the sheep from the goats. Then he turns to the righteous and invites them to enter the paradise that was prepared for them at the foundation of the world, because he was hungry and they fed him, thirsty and they gave him something to drink, a stranger and they welcomed him, naked and they clothed him, sick and in prison and they visited him. The righteous are startled and ask the Lord when they have done these things for him. He responds that whenever they have done these things for the most unfortunate, they have done them for him.

As I finished this story, Dr. Shaalan looked at me, smiling, and said, "You have just recited for me the Koran."

His response could not have been more unexpected—or more welcome. The feeling of otherness that had taken hold of me the moment I landed in Cairo melted. Coming from different religions, different nations, and different cultures, we had found the common ground of our dedication to lives of service. Yes, he was a Muslim and I a Christian. Yes, he was an Egyptian and I an American. But in that moment, we were humans together. We were children of God together. And we saw a common vocation: to bridge the chasms and take down the walls that divide and to work together for the well-being of all.

Thousands of experiences like the ones I have recounted here have gone into the birth of the global community that is the United Religions Initiative, an organization that belongs to everyone and is owned by no one—like the earth. It is a tiny beginning, but one that holds hope for a positive future, one that leads away from terror toward community, one that lights a path toward a deeper American dream that joins a common dream for all people on earth.

Scientists speculate that up to 225 million years ago, the earth was home to one supercontinent, called Pangaea, surrounded by one enormous ocean, called Panthalassa, Then everything started to move. My experience growing up and my work with the United Religions Initiative have taught me that we are still moving and yet we are still one. The future of America cannot be separated from the future of the rest of the world. There are no longer chasms deep enough or walls high enough to protect us from others or to protect others from us. So what do we do? We might begin by seeing ourselves as citizens of the earth and children of the abiding Mystery at the heart of all that is. Then, with open hearts and appreciative, inquiring minds, set out on a journey to encounter the other and find ourselves. It might be as simple as hailing a cab on the deserted early-morning streets of Manhattan or as disorienting as stepping out of an airplane at sunrise into the different world that is Cairo. I've begun such a journey with tens of thousands of other people. It's a sacred journey toward our shared human vocation for peace, justice, and healing. I commend it to you. It has changed my life. It has changed many lives. I believe it will change the world—not make it perfect, but make it better. Much better.

NOTES

1   Gabriel García Márquez, *Cien Años de Soledad* (Madrid: Colección Austral, 1967), p. 1.

2   Gabriel García Márquez, *One Hundred Years of Solitude,* trans. Gregory Rabassa (New York: HarperCollins, 1991), p. 1.

3   Thich Nhat Hanh, *Old Path, White Clouds* (Berkeley: Parallax Press, 1991), p. 384.

4   See Charles Gibbs and Sally Mahé, *Birth of a Global Community* (Cleveland, Ohio: Lakeshore Publications, 2004).

5   Amos, a shepherd in the small Judaean village of Tekoa, was called around 760 B.C.E. to prophesy a message of justice and righteousness to a nation that placed its faith in military might while it committed grave injustices.

He is perhaps best known for the stirring challenge to "let justice roll down like waters, and righteousness like an ever-flowing stream" (Amos 5:24). In one of his visions, God shows him how a plumb line is used to make sure the wall of a building is true and then says that he, God, is setting a plumb line of justice and righteousness in the midst of his people to ensure that they are true (Amos 7:7–9).

6   This text is from the Internet Modern History Sourcebook, http://www. fordham.edu/halsall/mod/sojtruth-woman.html; the background to it is explained at http://www.fordham.edu/halsall/mod/sojtruth2.html. Electronic version copyright © 1997 Paul Halsall (halsall@murray.fordham.edu).

7   Eduardo Galeano, *Memory of Fire: I. Genesis,* trans. Cedric Belfrage (New York: Norton, 1985), p. 137.

8   "Constitution of the Iroquois Nations: The Great Binding Law, Gayanashagowa," art. 7. Prepared by Gerald Murphy; distributed by the Cybercasting Services Division of the National Public Telecomputing Network. Obtained from the Internet Modern History Sourcebook, http://www.fordham.edu/halsall/mod/iroquois.html.

9   Ibid., art. 19.

10 Ibid., art. 27.

THE POLITICS OF THE BROKENHEARTED

ON HOLDING THE TENSIONS OF DEMOCRACY

Parker J. Palmer

"The human heart is the first home of democracy."
—Terry Tempest Williams[1]

I WRITE AT A HEARTBREAKING moment in American history. This "one nation, indivisible" is deeply divided along political, economic, racial, and religious lines. And despite our historic dream of being "a light unto the nations," the gaps between us and our global neighbors continue to grow more deadly. The conflicts and contradictions of twenty-first-century life are breaking the American heart and threatening to compromise our democratic values.

We think of heartbreak as a personal, not a political, condition. But I believe that heartbreak offers a powerful lens through which to examine the well-being of the body politic. I want to use that lens to examine the way we hold tensions in politics as well as private life—a critical connection in a democracy that rises or falls on our individual and collective capacity to respond to conflict in a life-giving, not death-dealing way.

The image of a broken heart may seem too sentimental for politics, yet diagnosing, addressing, and sometimes manipulating heartbreak has long been implicit in realpolitik. The "values vote" that helped swing the 2004 presidential election seemed to take the media by surprise. But politicians have long understood that advocacy related to the issues that break people's hearts—such as abortion, marriage and the family, patriotism, religion in public life, and fear of many sorts, not least of terrorism—always elicits votes. Indeed, railing against the sources of heartbreak, real or imaginary, keeps winning elections even when the rhetoric consistently outstrips legislative results. The word *heartbreak* may be infrequent in the literature of political science, but the human reality it points to is an engine of political life.

There are at least two ways to picture a broken heart, using *heart* in its original meaning not merely as the seat of the emotions but as the core of our sense of self. The conventional image, of course, is that of a heart broken by unbearable tension into a thousand shards—shards that sometimes become shrapnel aimed at the source of our pain. Every day, untold numbers of people try to "pick up the pieces," some of them taking grim satisfaction in the way the heart's explosion has injured their enemies. Here the broken heart is an unresolved wound that we too often inflict on others.

But there is another way to visualize what a broken heart might mean. Imagine that small, clenched fist of a heart "broken open" into largeness of life, into greater capacity to hold one's own and the world's pain and joy. This, too, happens every day. Who among us has not seen evidence, in our own or other people's lives, that compassion and grace can be the fruits of great suffering? Here heartbreak becomes a source of healing, enlarging our empathy and extending our ability to reach out.

Broken-open hearts are in short supply these days, at least in politics. Formed—or deformed—by an impatient and control-obsessed culture, many of us do not hold social and political tensions in ways that open us to the world. Instead, we shut our hearts down, either withdrawing into fearful isolation or angrily lashing out at the alien "other": the alien at home becomes unpatriotic, the alien abroad, an enemy. Heartbroken and heavily armed, we act in ways that diminish democracy and make the world an even more dangerous place.

The capacity to hold tensions creatively is the key to much that matters—from a life lived in love to a democracy worthy of the name to even the most modest movement toward peace between nations. So those of us who care about such things must work to root out the seeds of violence in our culture, including its impatience and its incessant drive toward control. And since culture is a human creation, whose deformations begin not "out there" but in our inner lives, we can transform our culture only as we are inwardly transformed.

As long as we are mortal creatures who love other mortals, heartbreak will be a staple of our lives. And all heartbreak, personal and political, will confront us with the same choice. Will we hold our hearts open and keep trying to love, even as love makes us more vulnerable to the losses that break our hearts? Or will we shut down or lash out, refusing to risk love again and seeking refuge in withdrawal or hostility?

In personal life and politics, one thing is clear: when the heart breaks in ways that lead us to retreat or attack, we always give death dominion.

Habits of the Heart

The image of a heart "broken open" into largeness of life by contradiction and tension is not merely my private poetic fancy. It is a central strand of three wisdom traditions that are deep-woven into the fabric of American life: Judaism, Christianity, and secular humanism.

For Jews, learning to live openheartedly in the face of immense and devastating heartbreak is a historical and spiritual imperative. So it is no surprise that Jewish teaching includes frequent reminders of the importance of a broken-open heart.

Take, for example, this remarkable Hasidic tale. A disciple asks the rebbe, "Why does Torah tell us to 'place these words *upon* your hearts'? Why does it not tell us to place these holy words *in* our hearts?"

The rebbe answers, "It is because as we are, our hearts are closed, and we cannot place the holy words in our hearts. So we place them on top of our hearts. And there they stay until, one day, the heart breaks and the words fall in."[2]

In Christian tradition, the broken-open heart is virtually indistinguishable from the image of the cross. It was on the cross that God's heart was broken for the sake of humankind, broken open into a love that Christ's followers are called to emulate. In fact, the cross as a symbolic form embodies the notion that tension—"excruciating" tension—can pull the heart open. The arms of the cross stretch out four ways, pulling against each other left and right, up and down. But those arms converge in a center, a heart, that is pulled open by the tension of opposition so we can pass through it into the fullness of life.

Secular humanism does not speak explicitly of the broken-open heart, but the essence of the idea is laced through that ancient and honorable tradition. Humanism advocates that scholars and citizens alike develop a "habit of the heart" (to use de Tocqueville's famous phrase) that allows them to hold the tension of opposites without falling apart. So a "liberal" education—that is, the education befitting a free person—emphasizes the ability to comprehend all sides of an issue, to be comfortable with complexity and ambiguity, to honor paradox in thought, speech, and action. Liberally educated people know how to let the tension of opposites open them to new insight, or so the theory goes.

Given the power of these three traditions in shaping the American dream, it is no wonder that division, conflict, and tension, far from being the enemies of democracy, are among its primary reasons for being. Democracy at its best is both a celebration and a demonstration of the benefits of creative conflict; democratic institutions are designed as looms strong enough to hold the political tensions that accompany our efforts to weave the fabric of a common life. The differences that emerge whenever two or three are gathered are the very stuff of our political system, in which the freedom to express diverse values and viewpoints is valued, encouraged, and protected. Only in a totalitarian state, where the "dangerous other" is silenced or driven underground, are differences regarded as intolerable.

But the litmus test for a democracy is not merely whether it allows our differences to be on display: we must be willing to engage each other around those differences. Democracy depends on the unwavering trust of its citizens and leaders that the free play of conflicting views will open us to a larger and truer view of the world—its needs, its resources, and its potentials—eventually issuing in political decisions that serve the common good.

When we hold that trust and act on it by participating in the democratic process with commitment and goodwill, we not only live up to our own ideals but also model hope to the rest of the world. Today, too many American citizens, and some of our leaders, seem to have lost that trust—and with it our democratic capacity to debate real issues and envision new possibilities with tenacity, intelligence, and hope.

Later I will explore the national and global consequences of our failure to hold tension creatively. But because the concept of "tension holding" is elusive and "the nation" and "the world" are near-impossible abstractions, I want first to offer some small-scale examples from organizational life, personal relationships, and solitude. In the recognizable detail of everyday experience, I hope to show that the way we hold tension matters, drawing insights from our private lives that can illuminate our public life.

On Holding Tension

We need not wander far from home to examine the real-life consequences of different ways of holding tension. Talk, for example, with the mother or father of a teenager!

Parents often experience a tension between their hopes for a child and what is happening in that child's life. When they fail to hold the tension between those poles, they are tugged one way or the other, either clinging to an idealized fantasy of who "their baby" is or rejecting this "thorn in their side" with bitter cynicism. Both ways of responding reflect a fractured heart, and both are death-dealing for parent and child alike.

But many parents will testify that when they hold that tension in a way that opens their hearts, they serve their children well—and more: they themselves become adults who are more open, more knowing, and more compassionate. The child who grows up in the force field that lies between the paradoxical poles of hopeful vision and hard reality has a chance to thrive, and the parent who holds the paradox thrives along with the child.

E. F. Schumacher found words to describe this force field when he wrote about the "divergent problems" that are familiar to all who care for the young:

> Through all our lives we are faced with the task of reconciling opposites which, in logical thought, cannot be reconciled. . . . How can one reconcile the demands of freedom and discipline in education? Countless mothers and teachers, in fact, do it, but no one can write down a solution. They do it by bringing into the situation a force that belongs to a higher level where opposites are transcended—the power of love. . . . Divergent problems, as it were, force us to strain ourselves to a level above ourselves; they demand, and thus provoke the supply of forces from a higher level, thus bringing love, beauty, goodness and truth into our lives.[3]

That the way we hold tension matters can be seen not only in one-on-one relationships but in the dynamics of groups and organizations as well. Take, for example, the process by which we make collective decisions.

We are at a meeting where a choice must be made between alternative paths of action, and it soon becomes clear that we cannot agree on what to do. As we listen to viewpoints that seem irreconcilable, we get fidgety and frustrated. Uncomfortable with holding the tension and wanting to "get on with it," we "call the question" and take a vote, letting raw numbers decide what course the group should take.

What I have just described is, of course, majority-rule decision making. The process appears to be straightforward, clean, and efficient, all of which appeals to an impatient, control-obsessed culture. But making decisions this way allows and even encourages us to resolve tensions prematurely, before they have had a chance to open us to something new, to possibilities that are excluded by or hidden within the positions of the contending parties.

This might not be the case if we were willing to let the debate "drag on"—the telling image we use for any disagreement that persists for more than five or ten minutes! But in our culture, time is always deemed scarce, and debate itself can make time feel even scarcer, especially when things get acrimonious. The soon-to-be-losers, feeling wounded, look around for a quick escape, while the winners are eager to secure their victory as swiftly as they can. Unable or unwilling to hold the tension, we "resolve" it with a vote.

Majority-rule decision making may appear to be straightforward, clean, and efficient, but appearances can be deceptive. We persistently ignore the radical inefficiency of creating an alienated minority of losers who sometimes leave the meeting determined to conduct a long-term guerrilla war to undermine the decision we thought we had made. Majority rule may not resolve the tension but merely drive it underground.

The democratic alternative to majority rule is consensus, a process often misunderstood even by people who claim to use it.[4] Consensus does not mean that we can make a decision only when everyone involved is equally enthusiastic about a course of action; if it did, very few decisions would have been made this way! Consensus means that we can make a decision only when no one in the group feels a deep need to oppose it, usually on the grounds of conscience.

Of course, that definition does not reassure the skeptics! Their minds immediately turn to the many times they have suffered the professional naysayers, people who seem to object to the group's direction no matter what it is. "How in heaven's name can consensus work," ask the critics, "when it is a virtual law of group life that someone will insist on saying no?"

My answer comes from decades of watching consensus at work: naysayers are, for the most part, made and not born that way. (I make an exception for the handful of people who have been sent here by Beelzebub to destroy Western civilization as we know and love it. And we all know who they are . . .) Typically, naysayers are people who have been deformed by a lifetime of "being on the wrong side" in situations where the majority always has its way. As members of a disempowered minority, they have learned to seize the only power they possess, the power of being a hair shirt.

But give the naysayers legitimate power, as they have in consensual decision making, and—not instantly, but soon enough—they are likely to become more open in their listening and in their speaking. The simple fact that now they cannot be overpowered but have the power to stop the group in its tracks creates a new consciousness in them about the right uses of power.

The most important difference between consensual decision making and majority rule lies in the different "habits of the heart" the two processes engender in us, habits of listening and speaking that reflect different ways of dealing with tension.

When we make decisions by majority rule, I listen to you first to determine whether we are on the same side. If I sense that we are not, I start listening for everything that is misguided, weak, or incorrect in what you have to say. Then I rise to call attention to your wrongheadedness while proposing my "superior" solution. Majority rule often makes us into adversarial listeners and speakers, thus ratcheting up the tension and making it less bearable.

But in consensual decision making, we cannot proceed as long as anyone in the room feels a deep need to object. Now I listen more openly to what you have to say—listen for what I can make common cause with and for what I might learn from our differences—because I know there is no way forward unless we move together. Now, when I rise to speak, I am much more likely to seek shared understanding that might bridge our positions than to try to strike your viewpoint down. Consensus teaches us to be collaborative listeners and speakers who hold tension in a generative way.

When we make decisions by consensus, we are not allowed to "resolve" the tension of conflicting viewpoints prematurely. Instead, we are required to hold it until it has a chance to break us open to a synthesis that embraces the thesis and antithesis. Doing so requires patience, of course, but the rewards of patience are considerable. Not only are we more likely to be drawn toward a resolution superior to anything anyone had envisioned at the outset, but in the process we have deepened our sense of community instead of breaking into the warring fragments that majority rule can breed.

Of course, results come more slowly when we are compelled to hold the tension, and the critics of consensus often claim that there are issues of such practical or moral urgency that holding the tension before we act is not only inefficient but irresponsible. That may be true on occasion, but not always.

Consider the story of John Woolman (1720–1772), a Quaker who lived in colonial New Jersey. His story is of special interest because Quakers—who believe that majority rule is a form of violence—have always made decisions by consensus, and the decision at stake in Woolman's story was one of immense moral urgency.[5]

A tailor by trade, Woolman lived among Quaker farmers and merchants whose religious beliefs held all human beings equal in the eyes of

God but whose affluence depended heavily on slave labor. Woolman received "a revelation from God" that slavery was a moral abomination and that Quakers should set their slaves free. For twenty years, at great personal cost, Woolman devoted himself to sharing this revelation with members of his religious community, "walking his talk" with every step. When he visited a remote farmhouse to speak of his conviction, he would fast rather than eat a meal prepared or served by slaves. When he discovered that he had inadvertently benefited from a slave's labor, he would insist on paying that person.

Woolman's message was not always well received by his fellow Quakers, who were, and are, as adept as anyone at contradicting their own beliefs. In the words of a self-satirizing Quaker quip, "We came to this country to do good and ended up doing well." Woolman's message, if embraced, would require the comfortable Quaker gentry to make a considerable financial sacrifice.

John Woolman held a terrible tension as he traveled from town to town, farm to farm, meeting to meeting, speaking his truth and standing in the gap between the Quaker vision of "that of God in every person" and the reality of Quaker slaveholding. But hold the tension he did, for two decades, until the Quaker community reached consensus that it was called to free all of its slaves.

On one level, this is the story of a Christian community that embraced evil and clung to it far too long. Yet the Quakers were the first religious community in this country to free their slaves, fully eighty years before the Civil War. In 1783, the Quaker community petitioned the Congress of the United States to correct the "complicated evils" and "unrighteous commerce" created by the enslavement of human beings. And from 1827 onward, Quakers played a key role in developing the Underground Railroad.

Quakers took a stand against slavery early in American history partly because one man, John Woolman, was willing and able to hold the tension between belief and practice. But it is important to note that the entire Quaker community was willing and able to hold that tension until its members were opened to a way of life congruent with their deepest convictions. They refused to resolve the tension prematurely either by throwing Woolman out or by taking a vote and allowing the slavery-approving majority to have its way. Instead, they allowed the tension between vision and reality to break their individual and collective hearts open to justice, truth, and love.

I recognize the irony of praising consensus as a path of creative tension holding in this meditation on democratic politics. All democracies decide critical questions by majority rule, and I entertain no fantasy that we could, for example, choose a president by consensus, as desirable as that might be!

But irony can yield to insight in at least two ways. First, if more of us had experience with consensual decision making in small-scale organizations where the process is practicable—in the places that Edmund Burke called the "little platoons" that ready us for a life-giving relationship to the larger society—more of us would have the habit of the heart necessary to hold tensions creatively in the public sphere.

Second, majority-rule decision making would move toward consensus if we took the idea of *deliberative* democracy more seriously and cultivated the patience required for an ongoing and authentic public debate about our real problems. When voting in a democracy is preceded by extended and intelligent public discourse, we approximate the tension-holding virtues of consensus.

Surely Abraham Lincoln had these virtues in mind when he delivered his first inaugural address in 1861, saying, in reference to the pending issues of slavery and secession, "My countrymen, . . . think calmly and well upon this whole subject. Nothing valuable can be lost by taking time. If there be an object to hurry any of you, in hot haste, to a step which you would never take deliberately, that object will be frustrated by taking time; but no good object can be frustrated by it."[6]

America's Heartbreak

On September 11, 2001, America received a huge blow to its collective heart. I do not mean the heart of our economy, as symbolized by the World Trade Center towers. I do not mean the heart of our military might, as symbolized by the Pentagon. I mean the heart of our heart, the core of our national identity, our deepest sensibilities about who we are and who we aspire to be as a nation among others.

Because heartbreak knows no national boundaries—and because many nations know heartbreak more intimately than we do—there were days and weeks after September 11 when much of the rest of the world responded to us not as a "nation at war" but as friends and neighbors of a family that had suffered a great loss. People in far-off lands, most of them poorer than we and some of them victims of American greed, revealed their deep empathy by offering the equivalent of flowers or food or a friendly visit, all those small but meaningful acts of kindness that can help a grieving family make it through.

As the brokenness of the American heart cracked open our facade of wealth and power and brought down our often arrogant, unfeeling, and self-serving way of standing like a Colossus above the world's pain, many of us were deeply touched to hear people around the world saying, "Today, I too am an American." It was a moment of national vulnerability that offered a historic opportunity to keep the heart open, to ask how to return the gifts of love we had received, even as we explored ways to bring our attackers to justice.

Had we held the tension of our heartbreak longer, we might have begun to understand that the terror Americans felt on September 11, 2001, is the daily fare of many people in many places, including some here at home. That insight might have deepened our capacity for global empathy, empathy for the alien "other." That empathy, in turn, might have helped us become a more compassionate member of the international community, altering some American policies and practices that contribute to the terror felt daily by people in distant lands. And those actions might have made the world a safer place for everyone, including us.

Had we held the tension longer, we might have been opened to the kinds of actions proposed by William Sloane Coffin, whose proposal does not ignore the evil of September 11 but recognizes that the way we respond to evil helps determine how far evil will spread. It is a proposal that holds the tension between love and justice in a life-giving way:

> We will respond, but not in kind. We will not seek to avenge the death of innocent Americans by the death of innocent victims elsewhere, lest we become what we abhor. We refuse to ratchet up the cycle of violence that brings only ever more death, destruction and deprivation. What we will do is build coalitions with other nations. We will share intelligence, freeze assets, and engage in forceful extradition of terrorists if internationally sanctioned. [We will] do all in [our] power to see justice done, but by the force of law only, never the law of force.[7]

But as a people and as a nation-state, we were unable to hold the tensions of September 11 for long. Instead of being opened to the possibilities Coffin names, the American heart soon closed down like a fist and struck back. We succumbed to that ancient animal instinct called "fight or flight," unable to let the tension created by the September 11 attacks open us to a more life-giving response. And our historic opportunity was lost.

Driven by biological and political "imperatives," we did what nation-states always do when their hearts are broken: we declared war on those who injured us—or, more precisely, on whoever could be made to represent them. And we did so unilaterally, rejecting the international voices that were saying, "Let us take counsel together and find the most life-giving response." We shut down and lashed out, with predictable results: our fears have deepened, and the dangers we face have multiplied.

The shrapnel of the broken American heart has done great damage around the world, a world where one no longer hears people saying, "Today, I too am an American." Now more than ever in my lifetime, the world's view of America is one of unfettered greed, cruelty, and the arrogance of power, fueled by a studied ignorance of other people's realities, to say nothing of our own. Now more than ever in my lifetime, some of our key democratic values are threatened. Our actions since September 11 have, arguably, increased the pool of potential terrorists ready to bring their barbarism to our shores and strengthened the climate of support abroad for such heinous acts.

Could we have chosen differently? Could we have held the tension created by September 11 in a way that might have broken the American heart open to greater capacity rather than creating such widespread devastation? If you buy the notion that biological and political imperatives are irresistible and immutable, the answer is no: we did what nation-states always do and always will do, given the power to do it. But if you cannot abandon the possibility that human beings, who created cultures and nation-states, are moral agents and spiritual beings who have freedom and the power of choice, then the answer has to be yes.

I believe that we could have held the tensions of a post–September 11 world more creatively, not ignoring the crimes committed against us but responding to them in a more life-giving way. If we are willing and able to understand the dynamics of the broken-open heart, we might yet learn to be in the world that way.

But the heart does not break into receptivity merely because one wishes it would. It opens only as we do the inner work necessary to learn how to hold life's tensions—in trust that the heart can be broken open into largeness—holding our tensions honestly, gently, patiently, and persistently, seeking always to give and receive the kind of love that alone makes this kind of "heartbreak" possible.

Learning to hold tensions in a life-giving way is a cultural, not a political, project; only a totalitarian state attempts to dictate people's inner lives, an attempt that always fails. The inner work we need to do is properly the purview of individuals, families, religious communities, voluntary associations, and educational institutions—and the best of them are constantly at work teaching openheartedness.

But this does not mean that the nation has no role. As Jacob Needleman has written, "One of the great purposes of the American nation is to shelter and guard the rights of all men and women to seek the conditions and the companions necessary for the inner search."[8] In the spirit of that observation, I want to keep weaving together the personal and political meanings of the broken-open heart.

Practices to Open the Heart

Rainer Maria Rilke has a poem that does more justice to the mystery of the heart broken open than any brief assemblage of words I know. Remarkably, it even suggests a path that can take us from destructive to creative heartbreak. I want to explore the first and the last of its four stanzas:

> As once the wingèd energy of delight
> carried you over childhood's dark abysses,
> now beyond your own life build the great
> arch of unimagined bridges.
>
> . . .
>
> Take your practiced powers and stretch them out
> until they span the chasm between two
> contradictions. . . . For the god
> wants to know himself in you.[9]

Rilke begins in childhood, reminding us of our inborn capacity to hold tensions creatively. Look carefully at the very young, and you find evidence that human beings arrive on earth with great elasticity of heart. Young children often demonstrate astonishing resilience in the face of hardship, even horror, refusing to let those "dark abysses" frighten them away from life but persisting in living and loving. As children, we are so large with heart that we can deal with heartbreak without being destroyed, carried across life's tragic gaps by "the wingèd energy of delight," the energy of love itself.

But as we move toward adulthood, we start losing the child's capacity for transcendence. As the adult heart becomes tighter, more muscular, more fearful and self-defended, the experiences that break our hearts are more likely to damage us and may turn us into people who damage others. So Rilke, who begins by describing the child's gift of an open heart, turns to his adult readers with a challenging exhortation: "now beyond your own life build the great / arch of unimagined bridges. . . . Take your practiced powers and stretch them out / until they span the chasm between two / contradictions."

How better to describe a heart broken open, not apart, than to say that it spans "the chasm between two contradictions"—the contradiction, for example, between loving things that are mortal all the while knowing that we will lose the things we love? And how better to describe the result of doing so than to say that such love reaches "beyond your own life" to build "unimagined bridges" to the world? Here is Rilke's affirmation that when we are willing and able to hold tension in a heart-opening way, we will have a great contribution to make to the common good.

Poems are not meant to serve as how-to-do-it manuals. And yet this poem includes a compelling clue about what is required of us if our hearts are to be broken open, not apart: "Take your practiced powers and stretch them out." Here Rilke speaks, I think, of what all of the wisdom traditions call spiritual "disciplines," a word that means discipling ourselves to the deepest truths of the human heart.

In fact, the wisdom traditions advocate spiritual disciplines for the same reason Rilke does: "For the god wants to know himself in you." If we want to bring the sacred within us into the world, allowing an even larger sacredness to flow through us, we cannot do it by becoming disciples of the ego, the intellect, the emotions, or the will. The holiest thing we have to offer the world is a broken-open heart, emptied of fear and vengeance, filled with forgiveness and a willingness to take the risks of love. And we can offer our hearts only by becoming disciples of the heart's own imperatives.

What are the spiritual disciplines? Unfortunately, I am not someone who could credibly write a handbook of spiritual practices! My own spiritual path has been less about intentional practices than about falling down, getting up, and then doing it all over again. But along the way, I have learned three things about what it takes to get up again and perhaps about falling down a little less often. I offer them here as one person's version of the "practiced powers" that Rilke exhorts us to call on.

First, when my heart breaks and I am filled with self-pity and hopeless longing that things might somehow be different, I must look at myself in the clearest possible mirror, *trying to penetrate the illusions about myself and the world that have taken me into this pain.* Those illusions, however comforting they once were, have now become death-dealing. As long as I cling to them or try to revive them, my heartbreak will not give me, or anyone else, life.

While writing this essay, I have been dealing with some personal heartbreak. The details are commonplace, familiar to anyone who draws breath, especially to those of a certain age: the deaths of people I love, the transitory nature of the work to which I have devoted myself for forty years, and the impossibility of realizing some of my dreams for my life.

As I try to penetrate the illusions that lie behind my heartbreak, one has become clear: I have allowed myself to hold the unconscious conviction

that the people I love, the work I care about, and I myself will not die and
that I can therefore have life as I want it, on my own terms. Of course, I
know this is not true, since it defies all the laws of nature and their spiritual equivalents. So my deeper illusion must be that God and nature will
make an exception to their laws for me!

It is very hard to admit illusions; they are so embarrassing in the light
of day. I have published many words about "penetrating illusions and
touching reality," and people have told me that they find my words helpful.
But I have been counseling others away from a trap that I was in without
knowing it. Perhaps this is an example of the work of the "wounded
healer," the kind of counsel that comes from someone who understands
a wound well because he or she has it. As much as I appreciate that possibility, I still find my illusions embarrassing. And yet only by moving into
and through them can I find life on the other side.

National illusions are also embarrassing. We deploy our military might
in an effort to liberate a distant land from a dictator who committed un-
speakable atrocities against his people. But our effort, as it turns out, was
guided by a long list of illusions: that the dictator possessed weapons that
he would unleash against us; that the people under his control would welcome us as liberators and collaborate fully in the rebuilding of their
nation; that the best model for that rebuilding is democracy, American-
style; that we are always good and our enemies are always bad, as defined,
for example, by the fact that we would never torture or humiliate prisoners the way the dictator did.

Then we commit war crimes against some of the people we jail in the
course of our occupation. This is so embarrassing that we try to justify it
as the actions of a few "bad apples," ignoring the fact that their actions
were supported not only by the worship of violence inherent in the spirit
of war but also by specific directives (or indirectives) that originated in
high places. Our national heartbreak will start turning from destructive
to creative only as we are able to face into our illusions about ourselves
and the world, as painful as that will be, rejecting the political strategy
that tars those who do so as "unpatriotic."

There is a second "practiced power" that we, or at least I, need to keep
working on. When I touch the painful truth behind my illusions, I must
abandon all my clever ways of trying to ignore, flee from, or numb myself
against my suffering. *Instead, I must allow myself to go to the center of
my pain and stay there until I have felt it as fully as I can.* In personal life,
this might mean letting myself cry and cry again—a "practiced power"
well known to people who have lost a spouse or a lover or a friend whose
presence defined their lives.

Not long ago, my own heartbreak took me into a time when the tears came in great washes. When I felt the grief rising, I tried to go with it, resisting the temptation to seek out distractions. One night, the floodgates opened again, and the rush of grief seemed greater than the sum of what had gone before. As it began to subside, I was exhausted and went to bed. When I awoke the next morning, I felt a peace that surpasses all understanding. Somehow, I had turned a corner toward healing, toward a place where my heartbreak was more likely to serve life. What happened in and through my tears cannot be put into words, at least not by me. Tears are a language of their own: we need to let them speak.

There are many tears to be shed in America today, for reasons ranging from loved ones lost to war and terrorism to dark forebodings about the future facing our children. Many tears have been shed in private, and some have been shed in public, but many more are being suppressed, or so it seems to me.

The public equivalent of private grieving is a challenge for American leaders, who tend to be past masters of the "power of positive thinking"— partly because the public demands that they be forever strong and partly because they need to keep trying to convince themselves that they are. But American history is not without exemplars of public grief expressed in ways that serve national unity as well as personal therapy: elected officials could do worse than reread Lincoln's second inaugural address every few weeks.

If the leadership rhetoric around our national heartbreak is all "cheer-leading" and "rallying the troops," we will continue fill a great aquifer of hidden lamentation that will sooner or later overflow and threaten to drown us. Have we not learned in the last few years that our national grief over Vietnam never really disappeared but was driven underground? We need leaders who can let us know that they are capable of "weeping over the city" (Luke 19:41), that they understand the capacity to grieve as a sign not of weakness but of strength.

There is a third "practiced power" that I am learning more and more about, perhaps because it is one of the gifts of age. If our hearts are to be broken open rather than apart, we must claim periods of what Taoists call *wu-wei*—literally "purposeless wandering," or creative nonaction, *making space within and around ourselves so that conflict and confusion can settle and a deeper wisdom emerge*.[10]

Wu-wei is hard enough for born and bred Taoists, I am sure, but for Americans it is difficult in the extreme. Our can-do culture and our eager-to-impress egos want to show the world that we are in charge. We cannot abide the thought that when challenged, we might respond in a way that makes us look like witless, weightless wimps. So we do not wait; we act, even if our action simply triggers the next step in an endless and predictable chain reaction that ultimately brings more calamity down on us as well as others.

But deep down, we know that when we step back, breathe, allow our agitation to settle, and simply start paying attention, we often see new possibilities in situations that once seemed intractable. The wisdom traditions, religious and secular, have always claimed that only in this contemplative state are we able to touch the truth, whether truth be understood as the fruit of mental acuity or of mystical experience.

When we stifle our knee-jerk reaction to conflict, we are simply bathed in pain or fear or anger for a while—and that is exactly what we must allow ourselves to be. Our challenge is to absorb these terrible feelings so that they can be transformed in the alchemy of the heart rather than allowing them to bind us reactively to the logic of violence. On the other side of pain, fear, and anger, there is almost always a love that feels threatened; when we give ourselves space and time to follow our suffering to its source, we also give ourselves a chance to rediscover and reassert that love.

Are there public counterparts to the private practice of *wu-wei*? In our fast-paced, high-tech age, they will be hard to find. But because holding conflict creatively is essential to a democracy, we need to invest energy in creating trustworthy "containers," private and public, where the tension engendered by conflict can reveal its creative potentials before "fight or flight" sets in.

In our private lives, we need safe relationships in which we can explore our inner turmoil, small-scale communities where we can get help from others in naming our illusions and absorbing and transforming our suffering. In such relationships, we must learn to resist the gravitational force of conventional culture, to resist especially the constant temptation to "fix" or "save" the other person. Instead, we must learn to listen deeply and ask honest, open questions, cultivating the trust that meaningful responses to suffering can come only from within the one who suffers.[11]

In our public lives, we need to reclaim or reinvent the fast-disappearing public spaces of our increasingly privatized world. In settings such as cafés, museums, city parks, markets, festivals, and fairs—settings that Ray Oldenburg has called the "great good places" of any society—strangers gather naturally in the course of their daily lives.[12] We come to these places with *private* agendas, but as we relax and sip coffee or just enjoy the sights, we find ourselves becoming part of a *public*, experiencing the heart-opening potentials of pluralism. And as our public experience grows, we find the differences among us turning from a frightening and explosive brew into a renewing and resilient ecological diversity.

In these great good places, we do not interact directly with strangers but spend time in each other's company in a way that reduces fear and enhances our sense of community: we start feeling at home with one another. Public spaces that are well designed (and well protected against other, more lucrative kinds of development) allow the heart to be slowly opened into greater capacity by the gift that more than any other can take us toward larger truth—the gift of "otherness" that has become, sadly, a source of fear for many Americans these days.[13]

The Fundamentalist as "Other"

In the texts of my own religious tradition, there are frequent reminders that encounters with "otherness" are neither accidents nor misfortunes but instead play a vital role in determining whether the faith journey will take us closer to or farther from God.

In biblical tales ranging from the Genesis account of Abraham and Sarah encountering God's angels in the desert (Genesis 18) to Luke's story of the disciples encountering the risen Christ on the road to Emmaus (Luke 24), the message is simple: if we fail to offer hospitality to the stranger, we will never have a chance to learn God's surprising, unsettling, and liberating truth, a truth that can never be domesticated. If we fail to offer hospitality to the stranger, these stories tell us, our spiritual journey will come to a sudden halt.

But hospitality to the stranger, which is a political as well as a spiritual virtue, is in short supply these days. And the "otherness" that most deeply challenges democracy today is neither racial nor economic but religious. Fundamentalists—who spent much of the twentieth century feeling marginal to, and marginalized by, contemporary culture—are now at the center of the action. Fueled by deeply held religious convictions, Islamic fundamentalists around the world have mounted far-flung campaigns of violence against groups they perceive as their enemies. And Christian fundamentalists in the United States have had remarkable success in shaping our government's domestic and foreign policy, which some citizens, myself included, fault for its reliance on economic and military violence.

Fundamentalists, like all religious believers, embrace what Rudolf Otto called "the idea of the holy," a sacred center of creation in which life originates, on which life depends, and to which life returns, a center that lies beyond the vagaries of personal viewpoint and social construction.[14] But they differ from other believers within their own traditions in the conviction that *their* idea of the holy can be equated with the holy itself. As Bruce Lawrence has written, fundamentalism is "the affirmation of [a particular] religious authority as holistic and absolute, admitting of neither criticism nor reduction."[15]

In a "postmodernist" culture where truth itself is a discredited concept, fundamentalists have frequently found their hearts broken as the convictions at the core of their identities are denied or denigrated. At the same time, such a culture makes fundamentalisms of many sorts—intellectual and political as well as religious—more appealing for the way they promise to rectify life. In the words of Jeffery Hadden and Anson Shupe, fundamentalism is "a proclamation of reclaimed authority over a sacred tradition which is to be reinstated as an antidote for a society that has strayed from its cultural moorings."[16]

Assuming that people like me have much to learn from the otherness of fundamentalism—or that at very least we must learn to coexist with it—how can we who are not fundamentalists hold a creative tension with a view that is "holistic and absolute"? How do we allow our hearts to be broken open instead of apart by people who have closed their hearts against anyone not in their fold? I have three responses to that question, none of them easy, all of them deeply challenging to me and my way of being in the world.

First, as fundamentalism continues its cultural ascendancy, we who are liberals have a chance to understand what it feels like to be marginalized, an exercise in empathy that can help break the heart open. I have experienced this cultural sea change in the course of my own seven decades on earth, and rehearsing it from time to time gives me some much needed perspective.

During the 1960s, liberal Christianity was in a renaissance, and its representatives—people like myself who relished our place in the catbird seat and were often guilty of arrogance—had some success at working the political process on issues ranging from poverty to race to war. Fundamentalist leaders decried this involvement in "Caesar's realm," arguing that religion's rightful place was in private life, while we liberals berated them for preaching an "irrelevant" and "irresponsible" religion and urged them to get involved. And so they did, with a vengeance! Today, fundamentalists are in the catbird seat, and liberals have been driven to the margins.

It is an exercise in humility simply to acknowledge that historic reversal, and humility is one of the virtues required for the heart to be broken open rather than apart. But more important still, we brokenhearted liberals now have a chance to identify with the experience of brokenheartedness that still characterizes critical segments of the fundamentalist community.

Arrogance may have replaced brokenheartedness among the triumphal leaders of Christian fundamentalism in this country—the same arrogance of power that liberals fell prey to forty years ago. But anyone who doubts that the violence practiced by some Islamic fundamentalists is fueled by broken hearts lacks a capacity for empathizing with those who feel marginal, devalued, and disempowered. Marginalization is in itself a form of violence against the human heart—a reality that liberal Christians should now be in a position to understand.

How do we allow our hearts to be broken open instead of apart by people who have closed their hearts against anyone not in their fold? My second answer is that we need to become discerning and doubtful about stereotypes. As I take in the news of the day and hear Muslim fundamentalists characterized as evil murderers, my mind turns to the caricatures of the Japanese that were commonplace during World War II. Posters and media portrayals in that era portrayed the Japanese as rats and worse, hammering home the message that "Japs" were evil, subhuman creatures who have only one goal on earth: to kill Americans.

Today, with our image of the Japanese as a creative, intelligent, and industrious people, it is hard to remember that we once believed otherwise. But remembering is a moral imperative, because our image of the Japanese as evil—fueled by the memory of December 7, 1941—helped lead America, not Islamic fundamentalists, to create the first "Ground Zero," dropping "weapons of mass destruction" on Hiroshima and Nagasaki and killing at least a quarter of a million civilians.

I do not doubt the presence on earth of people who have lost their hearts, people who are so full of anger and so numb to the suffering of others that they will gladly take innocent lives on behalf of a belief system. But such people can be found in the United States as well as elsewhere in the world, and they are always in a very small minority. Refusing to accept gross stereotypes of "the enemy" and recognizing our own shadow, the enemy within, is a second way to open the heart. And that, of course, applies as much to the way people like me stereotype Christian fundamentalists as it does to the way the media stereotype Muslim fundamentalists.

How, I ask again, do we allow our hearts to be broken open instead of apart by people who have closed their hearts against anyone not in their fold? A third answer is to consider the possibility that fundamentalists can be correct in their critique of contemporary culture even when people like me find their proposed remedy unacceptable. For example, when fundamentalists protest the crudeness of the mass media, I find it hard to argue with them—if I pause long enough to get past my knee-jerk reaction to their protest. Then candor compels me to ask how I became so desensitized that I barely notice the blatant sexuality and pornography of violence that are the media's stock in trade?

I know at least one answer to that question: I tend to screen such things out because I do not want to be allied with the fundamentalists, even when they are right. Since I cannot assent to their remedy—"that specific creedal and ethical dictates derived from scripture be publicly recognized and legally enforced"—I do not want to assent to their critique.[17] Here is a true closure of my heart, taken to the extreme of closing against my own sense of what is true. When I have the wit to recognize that my reaction to extremism is itself extreme, I need to hold that tension long enough to allow it to open my heart.

Of course, if it turns out that we share some of fundamentalism's concerns about contemporary culture, it may also turn out that we have an obligation to work for cultural change. We must be clear, of course, that the work we need to do is cultural, not political; we will respond to the crudeness of the mass media, for example, not through legislation that restricts free speech but in the marketplaces of commerce and ideas. The latter seems especially important to me: we need more and more "public intellectuals" who are willing to engage in risk-taking forms of advocacy that do not polarize people but make common cause with even the strangest bedfellows.

Those of us who embrace nonfundamentalist religious beliefs have, ostensibly, one advantage that fundamentalists lack in the context of the postmodern world: we do not equate our idea of the holy with the holy itself. We hold our religious concepts as tentative and penultimate, believing that our ideas can never grasp the mystery of the numinous but can only point in the general direction of a truth that will always elude capture by concepts or creeds.

In theory, this conviction should allow us to be openhearted in all kinds of relationships, to engage in dialogue with many forms of otherness, and to grow from what we learn. So it would be a great irony if it turned out—as it too often does—that the one form of otherness we refuse to be in dialogue with is fundamentalism. And the charge that "we cannot be in dialogue with them because they refuse to be in dialogue with us" cannot be taken seriously until we have made steady and earnest efforts to transcend our own biases and reach out to the alien other. Until then, our closure of the heart is a self-fulfilling prophecy that fails to serve the ends of community, democracy, and peace.

The Third Way

Though I have not yet used the word, I have been making a case for nonviolence from the opening lines of this essay. It is a case not easily made in America, in part because our culture contains a strong stream of violence and in part because our concept of nonviolence is diminished and distorted: we reduce it to a single-focus protest against war or twist it into an irresponsible passivity in the face of evil. But nonviolence, rightly understood, is a mode of deep engagement with every aspect of everyday life—and it rises or falls on our ability to hold tension in a way that opens the heart.

We misunderstand nonviolence because we misunderstand violence, which goes well beyond the physical savagery that gets all the press. More common by far are those assaults on the human spirit so endemic to our time that we may not recognize them for the violent acts that they are. Violence is done when parents demean children; when teachers humiliate students; when supervisors treat employees as disposable means to economic ends; when physicians treat patients as objects; when people denounce homosexuality "in the name of God"; when racists regard people of a different skin color as less than human; and when religious believers of any stripe condemn those outside the fold. These forms of violence, like their physical counterparts, result from holding tension in ways that cause our hearts to explode.

By violence I mean *any way we have of violating the identity and integrity of the other.* I find that definition helpful because it reveals the critical connection between violent acts small and large, from humiliating a child in a classroom to dropping bombs on civilians halfway around the world.

Most of us live out our lives in the home, the neighborhood, the classroom, the workplace; we do not make decisions of global consequence. And yet for better or for worse, the choices we make in the small arenas of our lives contribute to what happens in the world at large. If we do no more than acquiesce to daily minidoses of violence, we become desensitized to it. By embracing the popular madness that violence is "only normal" and assenting to its dominance in human affairs, we exacerbate its evils.

But as we learn to hold tension in ways that open our hearts, we begin to see how abnormal violence is. Now—as openheartedness looses what Lincoln called "the better angels of our nature"—we experience our innate capacity to honor, not violate, the identity and integrity of others. We witness the remarkable things that can happen within us, between us, and beyond us when we relate to one another in a nonviolent way. We learn a "third way" to respond to the violence that is always around us and within us, so called because it offers an alternative to the "fight or flight" response.

To fight is to meet violence with violence, generating more of the same. To flee is to yield to violence, putting private sanctuary ahead of the common good. The third way is nonviolence, by which I mean *a commitment to act in every situation in ways that honor the soul*. Defined this way, nonviolence is not a path of high heroism reserved for the likes of Gandhi and King. It is a path that can, and must, be walked by mortals like you and me.

In fact, walking the third way is much like literal walking: it involves taking simple steps, one at a time, doing the best we can to make sure that each step honors the soul. Here are three brief examples of what I mean, important because they involve small actions that any individual or organization could take. They come from the workplace, one of those micro-arenas of our lives where people too often find their souls violated.

- I know people who practice nonviolence by finding a new way to participate in organizational decision making. Where once they were quick to create tension by opposing any hint of "wrong-headedness" among their colleagues, now they are more likely to ask honest, open questions about things their colleagues say, questions that invite dialogue, generate insight, and sometimes reveal more unity than people thought they had.

- I know supervisors of work groups who practice nonviolence by starting some of their meetings with a few minutes of personal storytelling, posing a low-stakes question that allows people to learn a little about one another's lives and helps them feel less like replaceable parts—for example, "What was the best vacation you ever took?" or "How did you earn your first dollar outside the home?"

- I know about a large health care system whose CEO practices nonviolence by creating safe spaces within her organization where employees can tell the truth without penalty. The organization eventually won a coveted quality award in part because of this blame-free zone where doctors and nurses can report their mistakes. "Half the reported incidents lead directly to system improvements," says the CEO, herself a former nurse who "once failed to report her own error in medicating a patient."[18]

If we want to walk the third way, it is important to see how simple such steps can be—and it is equally important to see that they are not as simple as they may look! It is daunting to ask honest, open questions in a corporate culture that values speed above thoughtfulness or to evoke personal stories in a workplace where people are cautious and self-protective or to invite truth telling in a field where people habitually dissemble to protect themselves and their colleagues.

A person who walks the third way in such settings will likely meet with suspicion, resistance, scorn, or worse, reminding us of how pervasive nonphysical violence is. So people who wish to serve as agents of nonviolent change need at least four resources in order to survive and persist: a sound rationale for what they are doing, a sensible strategy for doing it, a continuing community of support, and inner ground on which to stand.

The core rationale for nonviolence is simple and self-sustaining: we act in ways that honor the soul because the soul is worthy of honor. When we act from that motivation, we may or may not change the world. But we will always change ourselves for the better by practicing reverence and respect. And yet agents of nonviolent change do not lack practical motivation: they know that honoring the soul as an end in itself can strengthen our capacity to do the world's work well.

People who ask honest, open questions in meetings know that when we think together, instead of in isolation or in combat, we are more likely to make good decisions. Supervisors who provide opportunities for team members to learn more about one another's lives know that colleagues with personal connections are more productive in general and more resilient in a crisis. CEOs who create blame-free truth-telling zones know that no organization can improve until people feel free to acknowledge and correct their mistakes.

The second resource needed by agents of nonviolent change is a sensible strategy. When people decide to participate in decision making by asking questions instead of arguing, their "strategy" is simply to play this new role with competence and an open heart, modeling new possibilities without attempting to manipulate the outcome. Done this way, a movement toward collaborative decision making may proceed without resistance, because no one notices what is happening! And if the organization starts making better decisions in support of its mission, the practice may multiply.

When supervisors decide that some storytelling could strengthen a work group, they do not drop it on people out of the blue. They share their rationale in advance, and if they obtain enough consent to proceed, they introduce the practice gradually, gaining advocates as they go. Done carefully and respectfully, with honorable "outs" for those who are uncomfortable with it, a "bizarre" practice such as getting to know one another better can become the new normalcy, making people feel more visible and more valued.

When CEOs decide to invite risky truth telling in order to strengthen the corporate mission, they know that the process must begin with some risky truth telling of their own. It is no accident that the story of that award-winning health care system includes a CEO who publicly acknowledged her own failure to admit a critical mistake when she was working as a nurse. Her strategy was simple: truth telling by a leader can legitimate truth telling at every level.

The third resource vital to agents of nonviolent change is an ongoing community of support, which might mean something as simple as two or three trusted friends with whom one gathers regularly. With such people, we can find support for our forays into the world, sharing our failures and successes, our hopes and fears, and finding the courage to take a next step on the third way. With such people, we can get help keeping our hearts open when the world threatens to shut them down.[19]

Finally, agents of nonviolence need inner ground on which to stand. We cannot walk the third way and survive in a "fight or flight" world without knowing how to find our way toward a place of inner peace, which is why we need something like the three spiritual practices I explored earlier. But that inner sanctuary is not for our survival alone: it is the soulful ground of nonviolent actions that serve others well.

Asking honest, open questions, inviting people to tell their stories, and encouraging organizational truth telling cannot be mere techniques of management or methods of social engineering. Done from a desire to manipulate and control and from the fear behind that desire, they are fraudulent and destructive acts. But done vulnerably and with goodwill, done from a heart of hope, such acts can evoke the goodwill and vulnerability of others. We can be peacemakers in our small part of the world only when we have peace within ourselves.

Standing in the Tragic Gap

Finding inner peace requires us to hold perhaps the most subtle and yet most difficult tension of all: the tension between reality and possibility. I have come to think of this as "standing in the tragic gap," the gap between our knowledge of what is and our knowledge of what might be. If we find ourselves unable to stand in that place, we will be pulled to one side or the other, toward the paralyzing cynicism that too much "reality" can breed or toward the wistful and irrelevant idealism that is bred by too much "possibility."

The gap between what is and what might be is "tragic" not simply because it is sad. It is tragic because in the classic sense of the word, it is the inevitable outcome of the flawed nature of human life. There will always be a gap between reality and possibility, and the moment that gap is closed in one situation, another gap opens up as new and vital visions call us forward.

We live, for example, in a society laced with racism. Over the past fifty years, we have made progress in outlawing the most egregious institutional forms of this cancer. But institutions are endlessly inventive in finding their way around the law, and no law can eliminate the racism we harbor within. So those of us committed to eliminating racism will never achieve success. We will forever find ourselves standing in a tragic gap, reaching for what is right, and if we fail to hold that tension, we will render ourselves irrelevant to the ongoing struggle for a just and humane society.

People who collapse into "reality" untempered by possibility often become cynics, embracing a realpolitik that targets and tries to exploit the worst human impulses as a way of gaining power. They tell us that life is a jungle and then proceed to make it more so by becoming social, economic, or political predators.

People who collapse into "possibility" untempered by reality often become dreamy-eyed idealists, embracing a utopianism that can be as dangerous as cynicism. They float above the political fray, leaving the ongoing struggle for power untouched by the values they claim to represent. In the words of Edmund Burke, "The only thing necessary for the triumph of evil is for good [people] to do nothing."[20]

Democracy depends on our capacity to stand in the tragic gap with hearts of hope—which means hearts that can hold the pain to which hope exposes us—refusing to abdicate our citizenship by collapsing into either resigned cynicism or irrelevant utopianism.

Name anyone famous for a devotion to justice and peace. I cannot think of a person fitting that description who has not spent long years in the tragic gap, holding the tension between what is and what could and should be. That, in brief, is the story of the Dalai Lama, Aung San Suu Kyi, Nelson Mandela, Dorothy Day, Martin Luther King Jr., Rosa Parks, Vaclav Havel, and Thich Nhat Hanh, as well as the millions of anonymous heroes who joined these icons in great movements for social change.

Such people came to trust, not resist, the journey of heartbreak described by the Sufi master Hazrat Inayat Kahn: "God breaks the heart again and again and again until it *stays* open."[21] Hearts like these have been broken open to a largeness that holds the promise of a better future for all, a "habit of the heart" without which democracy cannot survive, let alone flourish.

I began this essay with the words of Terry Tempest Williams: "The human heart is the first home of democracy." A few more words from Williams will help bring it to a close. The human heart, she says,

> is where we embrace our questions. Can we be equitable? Can we be generous? Can we listen with our whole beings, not just our minds, and offer our attention rather than our opinions? And do we have enough resolve in our hearts to act courageously, relentlessly, without giving up—ever—trusting our fellow citizens to join with us in our determined pursuit of a living democracy?
>
> The heart is the house of empathy whose door opens when we receive the pain of others. This is where bravery lives, where we find our mettle to give and receive, to love and be loved, to stand in the center of uncertainty with strength, not fear, understanding this is all there is. The heart is the path to wisdom because it dares to be vulnerable in the presence of power.[22]

And history teaches that when the heart dares to be vulnerable in the presence of power, it can become a source of countervailing power, keeping our best hopes alive in the hardest of places and times.

NOTES

1 Terry Tempest Williams, "Engagement," *Orion,* July-Aug. 2004, p. 4.

2 I heard this Hasidic tale from the philosopher and writer Jacob Needleman, who kindly put it in writing for me so that I could recount it correctly.

3 E. F. Schumacher, *Small Is Beautiful: Economics as If People Mattered* (New York: HarperCollins, 1973), pp. 97–98.

4 The best book I know on consensus is Michael J. Sheerhan, *Beyond Majority Rule: Voteless Decisions in the Religious Society of Friends* (Philadelphia: Religious Society of Friends, 1983).

5 Go to www.geocities.com/CollegePark/Union/3417/quaker.htm.

6 Lincoln's first inaugural address, as posted at www.bartleby.com/124/pres31.html, paragraph 33.

7 William Sloane Coffin, "Despair Is Not an Option," *Nation,* Jan. 12, 2004.

8 Jacob Needleman, *Two Dreams of America* (Kalamazoo, Mich.: Fetzer Institute, 2003), p. 3.

9 Rainer Maria Rilke, "As Once the Wingèd Energy of Delight," in Stephen Mitchell, ed., *The Selected Poetry of Rainer Maria Rilke* (New York: Vintage Books, 1984), p. 261.

10 Definitions of *wu-wei* are from www.jadedragon.com/archives/june98/tao.html.

11 I examine this form of community in greater detail in *A Hidden Wholeness.*

12 Ray Oldenburg, *The Great Good Place: Cafés, Coffee Shops, Bookstores, Bars, Hair Salons, and Other Hangouts at the Heart of a Community* (New York: Marlowe, 1999).

13 I explore these ideas more fully in *The Company of Strangers: Christians and the Renewal of America's Public Life* (New York: Crossroad, 1981).

14 Rudolf Otto, *The Idea of the Holy* (New York: Oxford University Press, 1958).

15 Bruce B. Lawrence, *Defenders of God: The Fundamentalist Revolt Against the Modern Age* (San Francisco: HarperSanFrancisco, 1992). See also the discussion at religiousmovements.lib.virginia.edu/nrms/fund.html.

16 Jeffrey K. Hadden and Anson Shupe, *Secularization and Fundamentalism Reconsidered* (New York: Paragon House, 1989). See also the discussion at religiousmovements.lib.virginia.edu/nrms/fund.html.

17 Lawrence, *Defenders of God.*

18 David S. Broder, "Promising Health Care Reform Passes Almost Unnoticed," *Washington Post,* Apr. 9, 2003.

19 For further exploration of relationships that help keep the heart open, see *A Hidden Wholeness.*

20 Edmund Burke, quoted at www.bartleby.com/66/18/9118.html.

21 Hazrat Inayat Kahn, quoted in Mark Nepo, *The Exquisite Risk* (New York: Harmony Books, 2005), p. 50.

22 Williams, "Engagement," p. 4.

The Editor

MARK NEPO is a poet and philosopher who has taught in the fields of poetry and spirituality for over thirty years. Nominated for the Lenore Marshall Poetry Prize, he has written several books, most recently *The Exquisite Risk: Daring to Live an Authentic Life* (Harmony, 2005), which *Spirituality and Health Magazine* cited as "one of the best books we've ever read on what it takes to live an authentic life." Other titles include *The Book of Awakening* (Conari, 2000), *Acre of Light* (Greenfield, 1994; also available as an audiotape from Parabola under the title *Inside the Miracle), Fire Without Witness* (British American, 1988), and *God, the Maker of the Bed, and the Painter* (Greenfield, 1988). He has also contributed to numerous anthologies. *The Book of Awakening* was also a finalist for the 2000 Books for a Better Life Award and was cited by *Spirituality and Health* magazine as one of the Best Spiritual Books of 2000. His most recent books of poetry are *Suite for the Living* (2004) and *Inhabiting Wonder* (2004), both available from Bread for the Journey (www.breadforthejourney.org).

A cancer survivor, Nepo remains committed to the usefulness of daily inner life. Through his writing and his teaching, he devotes himself to the life of inner transformation and relationship, exploring the expressive journey of healing where the paths of art and spirit meet. For eighteen years, he taught at the State University of New York at Albany. He now serves as a program officer for the Fetzer Institute in Kalamazoo, Michigan. He continues to give readings, lectures, and retreats.

The Contributors

DAVID M. ABSHIRE is president of the Center for the Study of the Presidency and also heads the Richard Lounsbery Foundation of New York. He helped found the Center for Strategic and International Studies in 1962, which he then headed for many years. In government, he has served as assistant secretary of state, chairman of the U.S. Board for International Broadcasting, U.S. ambassador to NATO, and special counselor to President Reagan in 1987.

Dr. Abshire graduated from the United States Military Academy and received his doctorate in American history from Georgetown University, where he was an adjunct professor for many years. He is the author of *Preventing World War III* (HarperCollins, 1988), among other works, and the editor of *Triumphs and Tragedies of the Modern Presidency: Seventy-Six Case Studies on Presidential Leadership* (Praeger, 2001).

ROBERT N. BELLAH is Elliott Professor of Sociology Emeritus at the University of California at Berkeley. He was educated at Harvard University, receiving the B.A. in 1950 and the Ph.D. in 1955. He began teaching at Harvard in 1957 and left there as professor of sociology in 1967 when he moved to Berkeley to become Ford Professor of Sociology. His publications include *Tokugawa Religion, Beyond Belief, The Broken Covenant, The New Religious Consciousness,* and *Varieties of Civil Religion.* In 1985 he published *Habits of the Heart: Individualism and Commitment in American Life,* written in collaboration with Richard Madsen, William Sullivan, Ann Swidler, and Steven Tipton, and in 1991, with the same collaborators, *The Good Society.* In 2003 the University of California Press published *Imagining Japan: The Japanese Tradition and Its Modern Interpretation.* In 2000 Bellah was awarded the National Humanities Medal.

CAROLYN T. BROWN leads the Collections and Services directorate of the Library of Congress, where she manages collections development, collections management, reference services, and public programming for the Library's general and special collections. Before assuming this position, she directed the international collections for the non-Anglo-American world. At the Library of Congress she has held several prior positions overseeing cultural programs, including exhibitions, publications, scholarly and poetry programs, special events, visitor and educational programs, and public affairs. She designed the visitors center and the volunteer program that staffs it and initiated the Library's Islamic Studies Program. Prior to joining the Library she served on the faculty and in the administration of Howard University.

Dr. Brown holds a B.A. in Asian Studies and an M.A. in Chinese Literature from Cornell University, and a Ph.D. in Literature from the American University. Her professional writing examines the interrrelationship of literature, culture, and psychology, with a special focus on modern Chinese literature. She is a founding board member of the Center for Contemplative Mind in Society and serves on the Board of Trustees of the Fetzer Institute.

Dr. Brown has two grown sons and lives with her husband in Silver Spring, Maryland.

Since 1996, **REV. CANON CHARLES GIBBS** has served as the founding executive director of the United Religions Initiative. URI's membership includes 270 Cooperation Circles whose work in sixty countries involves one million people annually and includes peacebuilding, interfaith education, HIV/AIDS prevention, environmental awareness, human rights advocacy, and community building. More information about the URI is available at www.uri.org.

In his work for the URI, Charles has traveled extensively, working with religious, spiritual, and other leaders in Europe, Africa, the Middle East, North and South America, and Asia. He has been a featured speaker at many international gatherings, including the Parliament of the World's Religions and the Annual Symposium of the International Association of Sufism. He coauthored, with Sally Mahé, *Birth of a Global Community,* chronicling the birth of the United Religions Initiative. He contributed a chapter to *Interfaith Dialogue and Peacebuilding* and coauthored, with Barbara Hartford, a chapter in *Positive Approaches to Peacebuilding.* In addition, he has published many articles on interfaith work and Christian spirituality.

Charles is an Episcopal priest, who brings to his ministry a strong commitment to spiritual transformation and work for peace, justice, and healing. He has an abiding belief in the sacredness of all life.

REV. THEODORE M. HESBURGH, C.S.C., priest, educator, and public servant, is internationally recognized as one of the most influential leaders of the American Catholic Church because of his commitment to Catholic education and his passion for ensuring the protection and preservation of human rights everywhere. President emeritus of Notre Dame, he has played an active and influential role in national and international affairs over the past half century, holding sixteen presidential appointments that involved him in civil rights, peaceful uses of atomic energy, campus unrest, treatment of Vietnam offenders, and Third World development and immigration reform. He was appointed a charter member of the U.S. Commission on Civil Rights in 1957 and chaired it from 1969 to 1972. Father Hesburgh is the recipient of 150 honorary degrees, the most ever awarded to one person. He received the Congressional Gold Medal, the highest honor presented by the U.S. Congress, in 2000, and was honored in 1964 with the Medal of Freedom, the nation's highest civilian honor.

ROBERT INCHAUSTI is a professor of English at Cal Poly State University, San Luis Obispo, and the author of four books: *Subversive Orthodoxy, Thomas Merton's American Prophecy, Spitwad Sutras,* and *The Ignorant Perfection of Ordinary People.* He also edited a collection from the work of Thomas Merton titled *Seeds.*

GERALD G. MAY was born on June 12, 1940, in Hillsdale, Michigan. He graduated from Ohio Wesleyan University and Wayne State University College of Medicine. He completed his internship and residency in the United States Air Force and served a tour of duty as a psychiatrist in Vietnam.

Following his military discharge, he accepted the position of director of the drug abuse center in Lancaster, Pennsylvania. He moved his family (wife Betty and four children) to Columbia, Maryland, in 1973 and joined the psychiatric staff of the Patuxent Institute in Jessup and the Spring Grove Hospital Center in Catonsville. He remained a practicing psychiatrist until 1988. In 1973 he joined the Shalem Institute for Spiritual Formation, ultimately serving as senior fellow in Contemplative Theology and Psychology. At Shalem he taught and mentored thousands of men and women seeking to deepen their spiritual lives.

Over a period of thirty-five years Dr. May wrote dozens of articles and nine books on spiritual growth and enlightenment, including *Addiction and Grace, The Awakened Heart,* and most recently *The Dark Night of the Soul.*

Dr. May passed away on April 8, 2005, after a lengthy battle against cancer and a heart condition.

JACOB NEEDLEMAN is professor of philosophy at San Francisco State University and former director of the Center for the Study of New Religions at the Graduate Theological Union in Berkeley, California. He was educated in philosophy at Harvard, Yale, and the University of Freiburg, Germany. He has also served as research associate at the Rockefeller Institute for Medical Research, as a research fellow at Union Theological Seminary, as adjunct professor of medical ethics at the University of California medical school, and as guest professor of religious studies at the Sorbonne, Paris (1992).

Needleman is the author of *The New Religions; A Little Book on Love, Money and the Meaning of Life; A Sense of the Cosmos; Lost Christianity; The Heart of Philosophy; The Way of the Physician; Time and the Soul;* and *Sorcerers,* a novel. In addition to his teaching and writing, he serves as a consultant in the fields of business, psychology, education, medical ethics, and philanthropy. He has also been featured on Bill Moyers's acclaimed PBS series, "A World of Ideas." His most recent book *The American Soul: Rediscovering the Wisdom of the Founders,* was published by Tarcher/Putnam in February of 2002. His Web site is www.jacobneedleman.com.

ELAINE H. PAGELS joined the Princeton faculty in 1982, shortly after receiving a MacArthur Fellowship. Perhaps best known as the author of *The Gnostic Gospels; The Origin of Satan;* and *Adam, Eve and the Serpent,* she has published widely on Gnosticism and early Christianity, and continues to pursue research interests in late antiquity. Her most recent book, published in May 2003, *Beyond Belief: The Secret Gospel of Thomas,* was on the *New York Times* best-seller list for nineteen weeks and was nominated for a Pulitzer Prize.

PARKER J. PALMER is a writer, speaker, and activist on issues in education, community, leadership, spirituality, and social change. Widely regarded as a master teacher, he serves as senior associate of the American Association of Higher Education, senior adviser to the Fetzer Institute, and founder and senior adviser to the Center for Teacher Formation. He received his Ph.D. from the University of California at Berkeley.

Dr. Palmer's books include *A Hidden Wholeness, Let Your Life Speak, The Courage to Teach, The Active Life, To Know as We Are Known, The Company of Strangers,* and *The Promise of Paradox.* His work has been recognized with eight honorary doctorates, two Distinguished Achievement Awards from the National Educational Press Association, an Award of Excellence from the Associated Church Press, and major grants from the Danforth Foundation, the Lilly Endowment, and the Fetzer Institute.

In 1998, the Leadership Project, a national survey of ten thousand administrators and faculty, named Dr. Palmer as one of the thirty "most influential senior leaders" in higher education and one of the ten key "agenda-setters" of the past decade. In 2005, *Living the Questions: Essays Inspired by the Work and Life of Parker J. Palmer,* was published by Jossey-Bass/John Wiley.

The Fetzer Institute

THE FETZER INSTITUTE is a private operating foundation whose mission is to foster awareness of the power of love and forgiveness in the emerging global community. This mission rests on the conviction that efforts to address the critical issues facing the world must go beyond political, social, and economic strategies to the psychological and spiritual roots of these issues.

Inspired by the vision of John E. Fetzer, the Institute's guiding purpose is to awaken into and serve Spirit for the transformation of self and society, based on the principles of wholeness of reality, freedom of spirit, and unconditional love. The Institute believes that the critical issues in the world can best be served by integrating the inner life of mind and spirit with the outer life of action and service in the world. This is the "common work," through which the Fetzer Institute contributes to the emerging global culture. Please visit our website at www.fetzer.org.

Index